JEWISH ENCOUNTERS

Jonathan Rosen, General Editor

Jewish Encounters is a collaboration between Schocken and Nextbook, a project devoted to the promotion of Jewish literature, culture, and ideas.

>nextbook

FORTHCOMING

Yehuda Halevi

HILLEL HALKIN

YEHUDA HALEVI

NEXTBOOK · SCHOCKEN · NEW YORK

Schocken Books and colophon are registered trademarks of
Random House, Inc.

Library of Congress Cataloging-in-Publication Data
Halkin, Hillel, [date]
    Yehuda Halevi / Hillel Halkin.
        p. cm.
    ISBN 978-0-8052-4206-5
    1. Judah, ha-Levi, 12th cent.   I. Title.
PJ5050.J8Z694 2010
892.4'12—dc22   2009023651

www.schocken.com
Printed in the United States of America
First Edition
2 4 6 8 9 7 5 3

CONTENTS

Yehuda Halevi

1

It may be the only time on record when a young man in a tavern has insisted, not that he was old enough to drink, but that he was not old enough to stop drinking.

It happened in Andalusia, in the Muslim-ruled south of Spain. We can't say exactly where. It could have been in Córdoba, or in Granada, or in Seville, or in any of the other towns that the young man passed through and lived in after leaving the Christian north as an adolescent. We can't say exactly when it happened, either. Since the young man was born sometime between 1070 and 1075, we know only that it was toward the end of the eleventh century. This was a time—a thousand years after the destruction of the Second Temple, eight hundred years after the redaction of the Mishnah, and five hundred years after the compilation of the Babylonian Talmud—in which 90 percent of the world's Jews lived in a Muslim expanse that stretched from the Atlantic coasts of Spain and Morocco to the Indian subcontinent, and from Yemen to the Aral Sea. Andalusia was in the far northwestern corner of this vast territory, pressing against and pressed back on by Christian Europe. It had been a part of the Islamic realm ever since Arab and Berber warriors from North Africa stormed the Straits of Gibraltar in 711 and conquered most of Spain.

If the night was warm and rainless, as most Andalusian nights are, the young man was probably sitting at a table out-of-doors, in an interior courtyard of the sort still found everywhere in the south of Spain. (What tourist to the region has not seen, on a street of seemingly plain houses, a door swing open and shut on a gardened patio like the tantalizing flash of a secret existence?) Perhaps, if it was springtime, a blossoming orange or lemon tree gave off its sweet-and-sour scent. The young man was unlikely to have been drinking alone, since he was too popular to be left by himself for long. From a neighboring table, an admirer sent a jug of wine. The young man thanked him with a poem. It may have been written afterwards and delivered by a messenger. Yet judging by the young man's gifts and the art of poetic improvisation in Muslim Spain, it was most probably composed on the spot and carried back by the waiter who had brought the wine. It went, in a free English translation:

> I shall sing your praise all my days
> For the nectar you sent for my lips.
> Brother Jug joins in my lays,
> And from him I won't cease my sips
>
> Even though all my friends say, "Come, come!
> How much longer will you play the rake?"
> "What?" I'll reply. "I have Gilead's balm
> And shan't drink to cure every ache?"
>
> I'm too young to put down the cup
> I've only begun to pick up. To and for
> What end should I stop
> When my years are not yet two and four?

In Hebrew, the language in which this poem was written, the young man's punning avowal that he was under twenty-four (which need not mean he was twenty-three; he could just as well have been sixteen or seventeen) works differently from my English rendition. Traditionally, each of the Hebrew consonants has a numerical value, and the word *kad*, "jug," is composed of the letters *kaf*, which stands for twenty, and *dalet*, which stands for four. Literally, then, the poem's last two lines read:

> And how can I give up the *kad* [jug]
> When my years have not yet reached *kad* [twenty-
> four]?

Its pun aside, the young man's poem obeyed complex rules, since not only was the Hebrew verse of his day required to have meter and rhyme, its standards for both were more stringent than those of formal English poetry. Regardless of its length, a poem in the classical style was allowed only a single mono-rhyme, with which each of its lines had to end. When it came to meter, on the other hand, a poet had to choose among a dozen possible patterns, each consisting of a rigidly adhered-to alteration of "long" and "short" syllables. For this particular poem, the young man chose the meter, known as the *marnin* or "allegro," *short-long-long-long*, *short-long-long-long*, *short-long-long*, a single sequence of which made up the half-lines or hemistiches into which each of the poem's full lines was divided.

Dashing off, amid the hubbub of a tavern, a poem so demanding yet wittily accomplished would have been an impressive feat. It would not have ranked, however, as a singular one. Talented poets in Andalusia were expected to do such things. It is told of Shmuel Hanagid (993–1056), the first of the great Hispano-Hebrew poets, that he once had quoted to him a couplet on the subject of biting into an apple. Not to be outdone, he proceeded to compose, one after another, fifteen short but perfectly constructed poems on the same theme before running out of time, breath, or inspiration.

Indeed, if calling an age "poetic" refers, not to some supposed collective sublimity or imaginativeness of mind, but, more mundanely, to the widespread use of poetry in ordinary life as a medium of communication and social exchange, the young man was born in one of the most historically poetic of ages. When, for instance, the same Shmuel Hanagid decided one spring day in Granada to throw a party for his friends, the invitations he sent out were in the form of a poem telling them to "Take note, make haste, and do not fail / To gather in my garden." But this would have been only the beginning. Hanagid's invitees might have informed him of their acceptance by sending him a poem in return; some might have turned up at his door with poems as gifts; if there were toasts or speeches, these would have been in poetic form, too; any party games played would have included competitions in which the guests were asked to write a poem on the same theme or having the same formal properties; and a good time having been had, poems would be sent as thank-you notes. It was a world in which, in cultivated circles, no solemn occasion and no occurence of note went without a poem to commemorate it; in which friends wrote each other letters in poetry or, if they were in a hurry, in a more easily composed rhymed prose; in which the ability to pen a creditable poem was considered as indispensable a part of an education as filling out a job application is in our own age. A poet who was more than merely creditable was a sought-after figure, often supported by wealthy patrons for whom he wrote verse to order.

In the Arabic-speaking Jewish society in which our young man lived, the language of these poems was always Hebrew. Yet the central role accorded to poetry did not stem originally from a Jewish impulse. Its history went back to the pre-literate life of the Arabian desert, whose Bedouin tribes had poured out of it following the founding of Islam in the early seventh century and rapidly overrun much of the world under the new religion's martial banner. Among these desert nomads, the ability to extemporize verse had always been valued greatly. Poems were an everyday vehicle for the expression of emotion; for the sending of messages and requests; for the carrying of news from one encampment to another; for the recording and remembering of unusual events; for the wooing of the opposite sex; for the enhancement of celebrations; for the flattering of authority; for the vaunting of one's exploits; for the praising of one's friends and the derogation of one's enemies, and the like. The popular poetry tournaments held at the commercial fairs of pre-Islamic times testified to the regard in which gifted poetic improvisers were held—and when, at moments of high drama or strong feeling, characters in medieval Arabic prose narratives like *One Thousand and One Nights* break into poetic speech, they are harking back to the traditions of the desert.

The cosmopolitan culture of the great Islamic cities of the East, such as Baghdad, Damascus, and Cairo, with their class of professional poets supported by the patronage of royalty and wealth, was far removed from Bedouin life. Yet the special place of poetry persisted in Arab society and spread from the East to Andalusia. The annals of Muslim Spain are replete with stories that illustrate how readily men and women were moved to, and swayed by, poetic diction. The eleventh-century poet-king of Seville, Ala'llahi Al-Mu'tamid, we are told, owed his marriage to this propensity. Once, as a young prince, he was sailing on the Guadalquivir River with a friend when, struck by the ripples on it, he spontaneously exclaimed, *Sana'a 'r-rihu min el-mai zarad*, "The wind has spun a coat-of-mail from the water," and challenged his companion to add a second line. Some slave girls were doing their laundry on the riverbank, and while the friend racked his brain, one of them, a stunning beauty who had overheard the prince's challenge, called back across the water, *Eyyu dir'in li-qitalin low qamad*, "What armor for battle if it stiffened!" Al-Mu'tamid was so taken by her cleverness and looks that he bought her from her master and married her. She was to be the love of his life.

Jewish Andalusia was not an exact replica of its Muslim surroundings. But while Jews in the Muslim world lived, on the whole, within a social framework of their own, they were more heavily influenced by their host culture than any previous rabbinically regulated Jewish society in the Diaspora. This was why Hebrew poetry, which was modeled on its Arabic counterpart in form and content, was so important to them, and why our young man had left home in his teens to seek his literary fortune in Spain's south, where the art of poetry was more advanced.

In the Christian north in which he was born and raised, he had received a solid Jewish education. In those days, this meant amassing a far greater fund of knowledge than a Jewish day-school or yeshiva student would be expected to acquire in our own age, one that included a thorough mastery of Hebrew and its grammar, a comprehensive familiarity with the Bible, a rigorous training in the Talmud and rabbinic texts, and a detailed acquaintance with Jewish religious law. In fact, it is likely that, by the time he set out for Andalusia, our young man had acquired the title of "rabbi" that was frequently prefixed to his name in later life. This did not mean that he ever was considered, or acted as, a religious authority. A rabbinic ordination was routinely granted to anyone who had progressed far enough in his studies, and signified little more than a college degree does today.

The young man had begun to write Hebrew poetry in his school years, and in setting out for the Muslim south, where he hoped to find a friendlier and more stimulating environment for his talents, he was acting in the same spirit of adventure that, centuries later, brought a Balzac and a Stendhal to Paris from the French provinces and a Hart Crane and a Thomas Wolfe to New York from rural America. Andalusia had a rich Hebrew literary life that did not exist in Castile. Its greatest luminary at the time was the wealthy Granadan poet Moshe ibn Ezra (1055–1135), to whom the young man now sent a rhymed prose letter, angling for an invitation to meet him. "Though a humble youth from Castile," he wrote, "it is my hope that I still may bask in the suns of the South's greatest sons. The thought of meeting them sets my heart beating."

Disappointingly, Ibn Ezra failed to respond. For a while, the young man led an itinerant existence, traveling from place to place in search of a position or patron to provide him with an income. At one point he probably lived a student's life in Lucena, whose yeshiva, Spain's foremost center of Jewish learning, was headed by the renowned Talmudist Yitzhak Alfasi. He need not have been either indigent or lonely. He may have brought money from home or found work tutoring pupils, and wherever he went, he would have run into aspiring young Hebrew poets like himself. He was with a group of them one night when an opportunity arose that he made the most of.

He was drinking again, this time with friends who were struggling with a poem. Or rather, with two poems. The first had been recently written by the great Ibn Ezra himself and sent to a younger colleague in Córdoba, Yosef ibn Tsaddik, at whose home the group may have met. Ibn Ezra's poem was in some ways an ordinary one. It belonged to a genre known in Hebrew as *shirey yedidut*, or "friendship poems," in which the poet customarily expressed his esteem and affection for the person he was writing to and—if the latter lived at a distance—his longing for him. The imagery of this particular friendship poem was conventional, too. In the intricate and allusive language that was typical of the Hebrew verse of the times, it began with the line "On this night of deep thought I sit up awake"; described the poet missing his friends so badly that he was unable to sleep; spoke of his consoling himself for their absence by repairing to the wine jug, his ailing heart's "physician"; and rejected the criticism of the "foolish scolds" who disapproved of drowning one's sorrows in drink. Thence it moved on to one friend in particular, Yosef ibn Tsaddik, praising him as a boon companion and paragon of virtue and concluding with the wish to see him soon.

All of this—the sleepless night, the missing friend, the fire of longing that wine alone could quench, the obnoxious carping of prudish moralists—was shopworn material, endlessly repeated and embellished by the poets of Ibn Ezra's age. The problem was the poem's formal structure, which departed from the classical rules that Ibn Tsaddik and his companions were used to. Ibn Ezra had written his poem as a *muwashah*, or "girdle song," to translate the Arabic term—a new, freer form of verse first developed in Andalusia in the late eleventh century, in which rhymes and meters were allowed to change within a pattern formed by two types of stanzas known as the "necklace" and the "girdle." Often sung to the musical accompaniment of lutes, guitars, and drums, the *muwashah* sometimes humorously mixed languages in a final stanza known as a *kharja*. On this occasion, Moshe ibn Ezra had ended with a *kharja* in Arabic inviting Yosef ibn Tsaddik to visit him in Granada. *B'Allah rasul*, / *Kul l'il khalil* / *Keif es-sabil* / *Wa-yabit 'andi*, it went: "By God, O messenger, / Tell my friend / The road to take / That he might lodge with me."

Ibn Tsaddik and his friends must have seen Hebrew girdle songs before and tried their hand at them. Yet now the challenge facing them was greater, for they had decided that night, as was often done with friendship poems, to reply to Ibn Ezra's tribute with an exact imitation. This wasn't easy. As was the practice when writing Hebrew, Ibn Ezra had penned his poem in a script consisting only of consonants, omitting the vowel points, which had to be supplied by the reader—a simple enough task had the language been ordinary, but not so when it was complex. Moreover, not only did the vocalization need to be correct for a poem to be fully understood, it also determined the alteration of short and long syllables that constituted the meter—and whereas a classical poem's strict regularity quickly revealed what this was, the meter of Ibn Ezra's girdle song kept shifting. How reproduce so tricky an original if one couldn't make out all its tricks?

In the end it was the newcomer, the young man from Castile, who came to the rescue. We know this from a jocular rhymed prose letter in which he later described the scene to an acquaintance. He was, he wrote, "making music on the wine cups" one night with some friends who were endeavoring to compose a girdle song. It was addressed to "their commander-in-chief—and to be brief, I made a good start on the poem's first part. But after continuing well, my companions soon fell into such a confusion that they cried in profusion, 'What you've started, please end!' I replied, 'God forefend! How can I add one more line with these poor skills of mine?'"

The poets' "commander-in-chief" was of course Moshe ibn Ezra, and in the end the young man, his "poor skills" notwithstanding, heeded his friends' pleas, successfully puzzled out Ibn Ezra's poem, and produced a perfect copy that was sent to the master. Indeed, not only did he impeccably mimic the formal structure of "On This Night of Deep Thought,"* he played repeatedly with its language,

---

* Hispano-Hebrew poems had no titles and were known by their first line or words.

echoing it, reflecting it, and sometimes surpassing it while following its every step like a consummate dance partner. First came his opening necklace. Using the same meter and rhyme as Ibn Ezra's, he began by high-spiritedly boasting of having parsed the text before him and banished the intrusive voice of propriety that its author had complained of:

> With the secrets [of Ibn Ezra's poem] revealed, what's
> > left to hide?
> See the cup in my hand, the friends at my side,
> And be gone, Mr. Snoop whom I can't abide!
> My abode is wherever you don't reside.

The young man continued to pursue this theme in his next stanza, the poem's first girdle. We can get a better idea of how he did it by transliterating both his and Ibn Ezra's Hebrew into Latin characters and providing each with a literal translation. A flat line above a syllable indicates that it is long, a dot that it is short; the short "uh" sound of the Hebrew *shva na* vowel is shown by an apostrophe; Ibn Ezra's girdle appears in ordinary typeface, the young man's in bold. (Readers lacking the patience for what follows are invited to skip a page while taking my word for it that the young man acquitted himself brilliantly and that they will not again be burdened in this book with so much technical detail.)

'Ash im k'sil, uvriv k'sil

The Hyades and Orion [above in the night sky] and a
> > scolding fool [below],

— — · — — — · —
Im at r'gil, simḥa v'-gil
If you [the scold] are snooping, joy and merriment,

— — · — — · — — —
Linvi f'sil ya'arokh negdi
As is to a prophet [i.e., a poet like myself] a false god,
   so he confronts me

— — · — — ·— — —
Eden v'-gil'ad r'eh negdi.
**[The garden of] Eden and [the balm of] Gilead, you'll
   see around me.**

— — · — —— · —
Otshi, y'val libi u-val
With my sadness. My heart languishes and is not

— — · — — — · —
Lo e'eval ka-yom aval
I will not mourn this day, but rather

— — · — — — ——
Nirpa, aval rof'i khadi.
Healed, but my physician is my wine jug.

— — · — — · — — —
Ba-tov eval kol y'mei ḥeldi.
Will live well all the days of my life.

In this girdle, as was permitted by the freer form of the *muwashah*, Ibn Ezra varied his meter in three lines out of four (his first and third lines are metrically identical); the young man matched him syllable for syllable, departing from his model only once, with an extra short vowel in line four. He was equally exacting when it came to the rhymes. His first line has an internal and final *-il* where Ibn Ezra's has the same; his second line, again like Ibn Ezra's, repeats the *-il* internally and ends with the word *negdi;* his third line follows Ibn Ezra's once more in changing the internal and end rhyme to *-al;* and his fourth line matches Ibn Ezra's with another internal *-al* while end-rhyming *negdi* with *ḥeldi* in place of Ibn Ezra's *khadi*. And yet though mirroring the master flawlessly, the young man opposed his own youthful joie de vivre to the older man's melancholy, his "balm of Gilead" a source of conviviality rather than a solitary solace.

It was a virtuoso performance, made all the more remarkable by its having had to be executed quickly while all around him the young man's friends joked, argued, gave advice, and refilled his and their glasses. Moreover, this girdle was only the poem's second stanza. Eight more stanzas came after it—and the young man tossed them off just as flawlessly, devoting half of them, as convention required, to praising Moshe ibn Ezra in even more laudatory terms than Ibn Ezra had praised Yosef ibn Tsaddik. This he did by comparing Ibn Ezra to his namesake, the Moses of the Bible, cleverly using scriptural language to make the point.

He must have had an exuberant feeling of achievement. It was of such moments that he wrote years later, in a book composed in middle age, that the true poet had nothing in common with those

> whose words, though they study verse and pay close attention to its structure, are like babble to the man who has such a natural sense of these things that he cannot sound a false note. They spend their lives trying to learn what is known to him intuitively, so that he cannot teach them what they think they can teach him. And yet were he to meet someone as gifted as himself, he could explain it all to him with the barest of hints.

As young as he was, he would not have been wrong to believe that the only other such gift in Andalusia belonged to Moshe ibn Ezra. Indeed, he was playing for higher stakes than his own satisfaction or the admiration of his fellows, for he could count on Ibn Ezra's soon finding out who had written the answer to his friendship poem. And so in finishing it, he allowed himself a sly hint. Taking from the Book of Proverbs the Hebrew phrase *tsir ne'eman*, "a faithful messenger," which rabbinic tradition applied to the biblical Moses, he ended his final necklace with the line *tsir ne'eman nishba leymor*, "The faithful messenger has sworn," and then, rather than compose his own *kharja*, quoted verbatim Moshe ibn Ezra's "Tell my friend the road to take that he might lodge with me," in effect transferring Ibn Ezra's invitation from Yosef ibn Tsaddik to himself.

Sent to the great poet, this girdle song accomplished its mission. Discovering its author's identity as the young man had surmised that he would, Ibn Ezra was sufficiently impressed this time to reply. He did so in a bit of light verse in which, still playing the role of the griever for absent friends, he opened with a military metaphor, comparing his heart to an army so decimated by "the sword of parting" that only a small sliver of it remained. The one bright note, he wrote, was the young man's poem that he had just received. It was wondrous how "One so young / And still unsung / Has shouldered all / Of wisdom's weight," so that "Come from the North, / His light shines forth / To everywhere / Illuminate." Appealing to whoever knew the young man's whereabouts and could deliver a message to him, the Granadan concluded:

> Have him make haste
> (No time to waste!)
> To the grounds
> Of my estate.
>
> There, where flowers
> Scent the bowers,
> He can rest
> And rusticate,
>
> And eat good things,
> Love's offerings,
> At no expense
> Till satiate,
>
> And live within
> My spacious inn,
> No matter who
> Else shuts his gate.

It was all the young man could have hoped for. Not only was he at last invited to meet the leading Hebrew poet of the age, he had been asked, in the most flattering terms, to be Ibn Ezra's houseguest. Although we have no concrete information about what he did next, it is safe to assume that he packed his bags and headed for Granada.

2

The young man, whose name was Yehuda ben Shmuel
Halevi, Judah the son of Samuel the Levite, was to
become one of the great Hebrew poets of all time. He was
also to write one of the most important works of religious
philosophy in the Jewish canon; to make, late in life, a personal decision that was to resound in Jewish history; to
then vanish mysteriously, leaving no record of whether this
decision was carried out in full; to be turned subsequently
into a legend, most of whose poetry was lost; to have, in
modern times, first, his lost verse miraculously recovered,
and then, his fate clarified with the help of an astonishing
archival discovery; and finally, to be implicated in our own
age, more than any other medieval Jewish figure, in the
great intellectual and political debates regarding Zionism
and the state of Israel. Such is the bare outline of our
story.

Halevi's poems were largely forgotten because, with the
passage of time, Jews ceased to take an interest in the genres
they belonged to and stopped copying and circulating them.
Apart from some of his religious verse, preserved in the
prayer books of various Jewish communities, little survived.
He remained known mainly for his philosophical defense of
Judaism *The Kuzari* until, in 1838, an antiquarian book dealer
discovered a *divan*, or medieval collection, of his poetry in
Tunis and purchased it for the Italian Jewish scholar Shmuel

David Luzzatto. Of the medieval compiler of this collection, one Yeshu'ah bar Eliahu Halevi, nothing is known, but his preface to it indicates that he worked from an earlier *divan* assembled by an editor whom Luzzatto identified as the twelfth-century Andalusian rabbinical judge Hiyya al-Da'udi.

In 1840, Luzzatto put out a scholarly edition of sixty-six of the *divan*'s poems under the title *B'tulat Bat Yehuda*, "The Maiden of Judah." In the following years, he gradually published the rest of its more than six hundred poems, of which fewer than eighty had been known previously. Most of our knowledge about Yehuda Halevi comes from them and from Yeshu'ah's annotations. They tell us a great deal about the man: how he perceived, what he thought, the things he felt. Yet since few can be dated accurately and the annotations are skimpy, it is often difficult to determine their biographical context or to make chronological order of the events and states of mind they refer to. There is thus no way of constructing a coherent account of Halevi's life without making educated guesses. On the whole, I have tried to let the reader know when I have made them.

Halevi, the original Hebrew form of a common Jewish name with many modern variants like Levy and Levine, is a title traditionally added in the synagogue to the first name and patronymic of all Levites called up to the Torah and so is of little value in tracing family connections. Apart from his referring to himself in a poem as *amun aley tola*, "raised in scarlet," a biblical idiom denoting a pampered childhood, nothing is known of Yehuda Halevi's origins. Not even his birthplace is certain; once thought to be Toledo in southern Castile, it is now generally believed to have been the more northern town of Tudela.* Both places were Muslim-ruled when Halevi was born, the first falling to Christian forces in 1085 and the second in 1115. Growing up in either would have given him, besides the Hebrew he learned in school, fluency both in Arabic, spoken at home, and in Spanish. From the outset he belonged to more than one language, though not to more than one people.

This distinction is important, since in speaking of the relative harmony—or *convivencia*, to use the Spanish term—in which Muslims, Christians, and Jews cohabited in Halevi's time, one encounters a common misconception. This is the belief that there was in medieval Spain a "culture of tolerance," as it has been called, that was akin to, or a forerunner of, the open societies of contemporary Western democracies like the United States.

Such an analogy is misleading. It is true that, in tenth- and eleventh-century Spain, relations among the three mono-theistic religions and their adherents were generally good and rarely tinged by religious extremism. The military and political balance of power between Muslims and Christians had forced each side to accept the other's permanent pres-ence on the Iberian Peninsula. By the early ninth century, the Ummayad caliphate based in Córdoba, which had broken away from the Abbasids in Damascus and Baghdad after their anti-Ummayad coup of the year 750, had reached its farthest extent, pushing Spain's Christian kingdoms back nearly to the Pyrenees, where their last bastions seemed about to fall. Yet by the time Yehuda Halevi was born, the

* For a fuller discussion of the time and place of Halevi's birth, see Appendix A.

Christian north had rallied and regained ground, especially after the collapse of centralized Ummayad rule in the eleventh century's early decades.

Thus, in Halevi's lifetime, Spain was divided into two roughly equal halves with a frontier that, though slowly shifting in the Christians' favor, swung frequently back and forth in accordance with local wars and battles. There were Muslim enclaves in Christian territory and Christian enclaves in Muslim territory; large Muslim and Christian populations governed by rulers of the opposite faith; Muslim rulers paying tribute to stronger Christian ones and vice versa; Muslim and Christian cities and states allied with each other against other Muslim and Christian cities and states; and Muslim troops fighting for Christian kings and Christian troops for Muslim kings as part of such alliances or as mercenaries. (A renowned example is Halevi's contemporary, the Christian warrior Rodrigo Díaz de Vivar. Known in medieval romances as "El Cid," he first fought for Christian Castile, then for Muslim Saragossa, and finally made himself the independent ruler of Valencia.) These campaigns had limited objectives—a city here, a swathe of land there. Neither side thought of eliminating the other. Whether conceived of as living in a state of war punctuated by interludes of peace, or in a state of peace interrupted by outbreaks of war, each was aware that whoever had the upper hand today could be on bottom tomorrow. Such conditions dictated prudence toward, and, as far as possible, normal relations with, one's intermittent enemies.

From this state of affairs, Jews tended to profit. The smallest of Spain's three religious groups, they were not directly involved in Christian-Muslim warfare, which made them more dependable in Christian and Muslim eyes than Christians and Muslims considered one another. Although Christian and Muslim rulers rarely appointed members of the other faith to political or administrative positions, they had no such qualms about Jews, who also acted as commercial and cultural intermediaries between the two sides. On the whole, therefore, the Jewish communities of both Muslim and Christian Spain were economically well off and safe from religious persecution.

But although they got along more often than not, Muslims, Christians, and Jews in medieval Spain, even in times and places free of war and religious tension, remained just that: Muslims, Christians, or Jews, with no blurring of the lines that divided them, which could be crossed only by religious conversion. Despite living side by side, maintaining good neighborly relations, and doing business together, the members of each group kept socially to themselves, never intermarried, were convinced of the superiority of their own faith, and shared no common identity except for a sometimes strong local attachment to a city or town. Certainly, they had no sense of being Spaniards in the way that WASPs, Jews, African Americans, Hispanics, Asians, and others feel American. If one is looking for a contemporary parallel, a better one might be the frequently troubled relations among Hindus, Muslims, Sikhs, and other communities in today's India—and even then, post-independence India is far more of a reality in the minds and lives of its different populations than was Spain in Yehuda Halevi's day.

Moreover, war and religious tension were never far away.

The city of Granada, where the young Halevi moved in the late 1080s when he was still in his teens, is a case in point. Barely twenty years earlier, in 1066, it had been the site of a frightful massacre in which some three thousand of its Jews were murdered by Muslims.

To be sure, anti-Jewish disturbances on such a scale never occurred again in Muslim Spain, and in Granada there had been special circumstances. In the decades preceding the massacre, Jews had wielded greater power in that city than they ever did before or afterwards in Spain—or, for that matter, almost anywhere in the history of the Diaspora. This happened under a dynasty of eleventh-century Berber kings who, after the fall of the Ummayad caliphate to Berber troops from North Africa originally enlisted in its defense, turned Granada into a powerful city-state that dominated eastern Andalusia. To help them govern, they appointed two Jews in succession as their chief ministers: the Hebrew poet, rabbinic scholar, and Jewish communal leader Shmuel Hanagid, already encountered by us, and his son Yehosef. (It was the latter who began the construction of the hilltop fortress overlooking the city that was later expanded into what came to be known—from the Arabic *ḥisn el-ḥamra*, "the red fort"—as the fabled Alhambra.) Second only to Granada's kings, the two men elevated other Jews to high positions and made no attempt to hide their Jewish allegiances. The events of 1066, in which Yehosef was killed by a mob, were triggered by rumors that he was planning to stage a palace coup, seize power, and turn Granada into a Jewish kingdom.

These rumors were undoubtedly false. Hanagid and his son could become what they did only because of the justified confidence in them that, as members of an ultimately powerless minority, they knew their wisest course was to remain loyal to those who promoted them. The case of Granada, rather, illustrates two things. The first is that, in the heyday of Spanish *convivencia*, before the "culture of tolerance" began to weaken, there was practically no limit to how high a Jew could rise. The second is that the higher Jews did rise, the more they aroused the anger and resentment of the Muslim or Christian majority, and the more vulnerable they became. The culture of tolerance stretched only so far.

Despite the massacre, the Jewish community of Granada was quickly reconstituted. When opportunities for advancement exist (and the slaughter of the city's Jews must have created many economic and administrative vacancies), the past is soon set aside. The Berber dynasty in whose ostensible defense the Muslim populace of Granada had risen was still in place and remained well disposed toward its Jewish subjects. And yet in thinking of the young Yehuda Halevi in Granada two decades later, one must also consider that, for a Jew, life in the city would have in a way resembled life in post–World War II Europe. On the surface, friendly relations between Muslims and Jews had been restored. No Jew, however, could walk Granada's streets in those years without wondering which of the Muslims he brushed against had recently taken part in murdering his kinsmen.

Nonetheless, Yehuda Halevi's stay in Granada must have been pleasant. The family of Moshe ibn Ezra was an old and honored one that had survived the 1066 disturbances unscathed. Apart from his literary and intellectual pursuits,

Moshe was a ranking government official, as apparently were his three brothers, Yitzhak, Yosef, and Yehuda, all of whom Halevi befriended. The Ibn Ezras belonged to the Jewish elite of Andalusia, and Moshe, who in later life was to write a history of Hispano-Hebrew verse, was in touch with nearly every important Jewish poet in Spain. A better patron would have been impossible to find.

The patronage of poetry in Andalusia took different forms. Among Muslims it was commonly extended by sovereigns, who maintained court poets at royal expense. As practiced by wealthy Jews, it ranged from the bestowing of minor gratuities to the providing of major assistance. In return for a poem, often written for a specific occasion, or simply in request of a donation, a patron might send a one-time remittance of money or even food. There is a poem by Yitzhak ibn Khalfun, an older contemporary of Shmuel Hanagid's, in which he humorously asks a man of means to make him the gift of some wine "as old as the hills, / Yet still virgin and had by no man," for which "You will be forever blessed and remembered, / And outlive the stars in the sky." Yet Ibn Khalfun, who had a weakness for drink, had his minimum wage. In another poem, he mocks a solicited donor ("I asked you, dear sir, in good spirits, / Pleading my cause at great length") for sending him a basket of cheese, and inquires: "What good is cheese to a man with a thirst?"

More serious patrons could be a source of substantial aid, providing financial support and even housing. Once, following a period of homelessness during which he wandered, as he put it, "without a place to set foot, day in and day out," the same Ibn Khalfun was taken in by Shmuel Hanagid's son Yehosef and given lodgings in his home. In a verse letter to Hanagid, Ibn Khalfun expressed his gratitude by writing:

> If the times had not left
> Your son Yehosef
> (Whose good deeds smell as sweet
> As a green tree in leaf)
> To flood me with kindness,
> And shelter and roof,
> I would surely have died
> Of sorrow and grief.

If, then, Yehuda Halevi's stay with Moshe ibn Ezra in Granada was more than just a brief sleepover, this would not have been unusual for a patron-poet relationship. Ibn Ezra had, as he boasted in his invitation to Halevi, a large enough home to accommodate him in comfort. It would have been built around a courtyard planted with a lush garden of the kind that Granadans still call a *carmen*, from the Arabic word for "vineyard," *karm*, in which would have grown grape vines, fruit trees, and aromatic shrubs and plants. Fountains and water channels would have irrigated them, fed by the streams running down from the snow-covered peaks of the Sierra Nevada that rose above the city. It is tempting to imagine the young Halevi sitting in the verdurous darkness of Moshe ibn Ezra's *karm* while composing a short poem that began:

> It's paradise with all these trees,
> The starlight on the myrtle berries.
> The blend of spices in the breeze
> Is God's and no apothecary's.

Tempting, too, to imagine him pleasing his host by reading these lines aloud in company. Probably also recited in public was more direct homage to Ibn Ezra, such as:

> Do I smell myrrh's fragrance?
> Taste sweet nectars?
> Hear wind in the bushes,
> See dew on the roses,
> Spy dewy-eyed youths?
> Is that a lute behind a lattice,
> Doves in the branches,
> The swift flight of swifts?
> Or has, with its eminence,
> The name of Moshe
> Filled my thoughts
> With all these
> To earth's ends?

There were other ways as well in which Halevi could have earned his keep. He might have acted as Moshe ibn Ezra's secretary, as an earlier Hispano-Hebrew poet, Menachem ben Saruk, had done in Córdoba for Hasdai ibn Shaprut (c. 915–c. 970), the personal physician of Caliph Abd-el-Rahman III. He also might have written poems for events in the Ibn Ezra household, or composed the rhymed riddles that served as entertainments at parties. A few of these have come down to us from his pen. One asks:

> What's flung on the ground, where it dies
> And is buried naked and bare,
> Then comes to life where it lies
> And has offspring with clothing to spare?

The answer, of course, is a seed.

Drinking parties, commonly held in a *karm*, were a common form of recreation in upper-class Andalusian society. Participated in only by men, who were attended by waiters and serenaded by musicians, they commonly lasted all night and involved the consumption of much wine, the Koran's prohibition of which was widely disregarded by the Muslims of Halevi's age. Whoever collapsed in the course of them, to judge by the literary evidence, lay where he fell until ready to resume drinking. Shmuel Hanagid has left us a poignant vignette of a homoerotic encounter that took place at such an affair as a crescent moon was fading in the first light of day:

> What would I not do for the youth
> Who awoke in the night to the sound of the skilled
> > flutes and lutes
> And, seeing me there cup in hand, said to me:
> "Here, drink the grape's blood from my lips."
> Oh, the moon was a comma writ small
> On the cloak of the dawn in a watery gold!

And from Moshe ibn Ezra comes the couplet:

> Drink, brother, and pour me more till I yield my grief
> > to the cup.
> And if I die before your eyes, tell the musicians to
> > play on and wake me up!

Whether Ibn Ezra was alluding to passing out from too much wine, or declaring that death itself could not prevent him from partying on, his second line is not fully translatable. This is because its Hebrew words *teḥayeni k'nagen ha-menagen*—literally, "Revive me as the musician makes music"—echo the biblical Book of Samuel's description of the young David playing his harp to soothe the troubled soul of King Saul. By means of this Scriptural allusion, Ibn Ezra, his light tone notwithstanding, was comparing himself, the brooding prince of Hispano-Hebrew poetry, to Saul, the melancholy king of Israel.

Known to modern Hebrew literary criticism as *shibbutz*, or "insetting," such placement in a poem of phrases or imagery taken from sacred sources, generally biblical ones, was widely practiced in Hispano-Hebrew verse. Like other techniques, it was borrowed from the Arabs, who made use of the Koran in the same way—and as with them, it could involve either a mere display of erudition or a genuinely apposite analogy. Ibn Ezra's *k'nagen ha-menagen* is as elegant an inset as could be wished for.

He and Halevi must have talked shop often. They may have been joined by other poets, such as Moshe ibn Ezra's brother Yitzhak, or their fellow Granadan Yehuda ibn Giyat. Unprecedented when it first appeared in Jewish life in the mid-tenth century, Hebrew poetry based on the rules of Arabic verse, and like it partial to intricate wordplay and encompassing a wide range of nonreligious subjects, had long ceased to be a novelty by Halevi's time. Andalusia was its main center, in large measure due to the influence of Hasdai ibn Shaprut. Besides being Abd-el-Rahman III's doctor, Hasdai was a financial minister and statesman at the caliph's court, the recognized political leader of Andalusian Jewry, and a generous patron of rabbinic scholarship; it was his support for the new poetry that first underwrote it and legitimized it. A flowery summation of his role in its dissemination was made long afterwards by the Hebrew rhymed prose author Yehuda Alharizi (c. 1170–1235). After declaring that, from time immemorial, "golden Poesy was the Arabs' legacy," so that "the boldest songs that ever lips have sung, have spilled from the Arabs' tongue," Alharizi went on:

> Now it came to pass in the year four-thousand-seven-hundred in the world's creation [940 C.E.] . . . there shone in Spain our lordly sun, Greatness' firmament, the prince, Heaven-sent, who held Dominion's rod, Rabbi Isaac ben Hasdai the Spaniard, may he rest in the shadow of Almighty God, whose viscounty show-ered petitioners with endless bounty. . . . Then swift did each resplendent scholar come, from East and West, from Araby and Christendom. He spread them the table of his loving care and set his Cloud of Glory hovering there. . . . Then did eyes open on Song's gold demesne; the heavens parted, and godly sights were seen; waking poet vied with dreamer, for here was Poesy's intimate and redeemer.*

The most "resplendent" of the scholar-poets brought by Hasdai to Córdoba was the Moroccan-born Dunash ben Labrat, who had studied in Babylonia with the renowned rabbinical authority Sa'adia Gaon. It was Dunash who first introduced the meters, and some of the themes, of Arabic poetry into Hebrew—and if these themes aroused surpris-ingly little public controversy, this was partly because the

---

* This translation is David Segal's, taken from his edition of Al-Harizi's *Book of Tahkemoni*.

more shocking of them, from the point of view of traditional Jewish religious sensibility, were initially smuggled in through the back door. A good example of this is Dunash's one and only wine poem, the earliest of its kind in Hispano-Hebrew literature. It is written in two voices, the first belonging to a friend who invites the poet to join him for a midnight drink in his *karm:*

> "Come, drink wine that is old
> Among myrrh and aloes
> And the scent of the rose,
> While soft water in rills
> Joins the lute in sweet trills
> Beneath grape vines and dates
> And tall pomegranates."

The second voice, however, the poet's own, indignantly rejects this invitation:

> "Say no more!" I did scold.
> "How can you make so bold
> When God's Temple lies seized
> By the uncircumcised?
> How dare you carouse,
> And uplift downcast brows,
> Who are nought but reviled
> And despised and exiled?"

It is this already familiar moralistic "scold" who has the last word in Dunash's poem. But is he the poem's true voice? Might not Dunash have been paying lip service to an opinion he didn't hold but felt obliged to express in order to keep from being attacked by the scolds himself? Or did he perhaps conflictedly identify with both points of view? All that can be stated with confidence is that when, several decades later, the young Shmuel Hanagid similarly urged a friend to quit his bed for some late-hour revelry, we find ourselves, not only on a different level of poetry, but in a different mental climate:

> Rise, friend! For every eye inquisitive
> And rude lies wine-bound in sleep's fumy pit,
> And I, in bravely bibbing company,
> Upon a bed of almond blossoms sit
> And watch the fair young cupbearer pour out
> The drink, and to and from the wine cask flit
> While a swain with inkless pen writes music
> On the lute, then dots and crosses it.
> Why, life is but a dance; the earth,
> A maiden laughing with her castanet;
> The sky, a tramping army camped by night,
> In front of each man's tent, a lantern lit.

Here, the conflict has ceased to exist. When life is a dance rather than the punishment of exile, a night on the town is no cause for guilt.

Something similar happened with another favorite theme of Arabic poetry, sexual passion and love, first encountered in Hebrew in the verse of Ibn Khalfun. There is a poem of his on the subject written in two voices like Dunash's, the difference being that conventional morality gets to speak first in it as well as last. The poem begins by lamenting a sexual relationship the poet has had with an "unbridled doe" who has seduced him with her "smooth talk"; flashes back to her practiced patter of "Come, my love, let us repair / To my roomy attic lair, / And there make love until the dawn /

Greets us with a joyous morn"; and concludes with the penitent admonition to the reader, urged to avoid being similarly entrapped, "Fear God, then, brother, mend your ways, / And turn to His that merit praise."

Another poem of Ibn Khalfun's, this time in a comic vein, is only four lines long:

Hot with desire, I dashed to the home of my love like
a stag—
And found there her father, her brother, and her
mother the nag.
Pretending not to know her, I took one look and ran,
More like a grieving woman than a man.

In this case, the breaking of the rabbinic taboo on such subject matter is justified by turning the male lover into an effeminate buffoon afraid of the vigilance of his beloved's family. Erotic attraction was allowed, as it were, to make its debut on the Hispano-Hebrew stage by being cast as a regretful naïf or a clown. Yet it was soon to graduate to more serious roles—and once again Hanagid is the pivotal figure. In one of his many love poems, he compares himself to a stag as Ibn Khalfun does. (Stags and does were common metaphors for male and female lovers in both the Arabic and Hebrew poetry of the age.) But this is all the two poems have in common, for Hanagid's goes:

Lady,
Will you not uncage the stag of love?
Send it, sweet-scented, word it is free,
You whose lips, so they say,
Are stained not with rouge,

But with the blood of young bucks.
Give love for love, for such are lovers' wages,
And take my soul and let that be the price.
My heart is cleft in two by your two eyes—
Unlock on yours the locket and revive it!

Hanagid's suavely resolute wooer is the very opposite of
Ibn Khalfun's timid suitor, and the woman pressed by him to
consent on her perfumed stationery to a liaison, though a
predatory femme fatale like Ibn Khalfun's, is being stalked
herself. The poem throbs with a swaggering and worldly
sexuality.

Clearly, new attitudes had come to prevail—and if they
did so with little protest in the rabbinical writings of the
age, this was due not only to the gradual manner of their
introduction or to the pervasive influence of Arabic models.
It was also because, by the time his poems were widely circulating, Hanagid had become the most powerful Jew of his
time, just as Hasdai ibn Shaprut was in the days of the Cordoban caliphate. Even religious conservatives outraged by a
poem like "Lady, Will You Not Uncage the Stag of Love?"
would have thought twice before challenging its author. It
was the new poetry's good fortune to have two such strong
shields in its formative years.

And so, during the first half of the eleventh century,
much of the conventional subject matter of Arabic verse—
the pleasures of drink; the love of women; male friendship;
the splendors of nature; the trials and vicissitudes of time;
travel, wandering, and separation; even the gore and glory of
war (Hanagid regularly accompanied Granada's armies onto
the battlefield and wrote about his experiences there)—

became domesticated in Hebrew literature. Never before in post-biblical times had Hebrew reached out to embrace the totality of human experience in this way. True, in many of the anecdotes related in the Talmud and the Midrash, we also find situations of all kinds, some involving a liking for alcohol (the Babylonian sage Rabbi Huna was said to have kept a wine cellar with four hundred casks in it) or (as in the story of Rabbi Akiva and his wife, Rachel) romantic love. Yet the point of view of these narratives is always that of rabbinic authority and values. In Hispano-Hebrew poetry, on the other hand, it moves elsewhere—to the poet-drinker or poet-lover, for example, who is indifferent to rabbinic attitudes though in most cases rabbinically ordained himself. Along with medieval Jewish philosophy, such poems were a wedge introducing into Jewish consciousness the possibility of a non-religious perspective, even if, in a pure form and without the counterweight of religion, this had to wait until modern times for its full development.

The new poetry thus marked a revolution in Jewish cultural life, although one uncommented on by those who lived through it. As though in a battle fought by proxy, the literary controversy that did break out concerned Hebrew's adoption, not of the content of Arabic verse, but of the form. This issue was hotly contested, and inasmuch as the circumstances surrounding it, dramatic in their own right, were to bear on Yehuda Halevi's later literary career, they are well worth a digression.

Hasdai ibn Shaprut, we have said, had a secretary, Menachem ben Saruk, a Hebrew poet and grammarian. Hasdai's wealthy father, Yitzhak ben Ezra ibn Shaprut, had been Menachem's patron, and when Yitzhak died around the year

950, Menachem wrote a series of poems in his memory and entered the service of Hasdai, then establishing himself at Abd-el-Rahman III's court. In this capacity, one of Menachem's duties was to compose verse for Hasdai as he had done for Yitzhak. Once, we are told, upon the death of Hasdai's widowed mother, Hasdai hurried to Menachem in the middle of the night to commission an elegy for the funeral only to discover his secretary already hard at work on it. Deeply moved by this show of devotion, he swore never to forget it.

This elegy has not survived. The one extant poem written for Hasdai by Menachem is of a different nature. It was attached to a Hebrew letter, no doubt composed by Menachem, too, that was addressed to the king of Khazaria, a Turkic domain between the Black and Caspian seas whose royal house had converted to Judaism in the eighth century. Long-circulating rumors about the Khazars connected them to the Ten Lost Tribes, and in the mid-950s, taking advantage of his official position, Hasdai attempted to contact their ruler with the help of two Jewish members of a Slavic diplomatic mission to Córdoba. The letter sent by him to the Khazar king started with an account of his interest in the latter's kingdom, which he first had heard about from Jewish travelers coming to pay their respects to him:

These emissaries, all bearing gifts, were always asked by me about our surviving Jewish brethren in the Exile, and whether they knew of any of our hard-pressed and weary remnants who lived a life of liberty. One day I was told by such a delegation, merchants from Khorasan [eastern Persia], of a Jewish kingdom called Al-Kozar. I could not believe what I heard, for I thought: They are only saying this to ingratiate themselves with me. My amazement continued until diplomats arrived from Constantinople with presents and a letter from their [the Khazars'] emperor to our caliph, and I asked them about the matter. They answered that it was so, and that the kingdom was called Al-Kozar, and that it lay a fifteen-day journey by sea from Constantinople, many other nations intervening on land, and that its ruler was a king named Joseph . . . and that it was most powerful, with divisions of soldiers going forth on campaigns. And upon hearing this I was overjoyed and greatly encouraged and filled with new hope, and I bowed down and prostrated myself before the Lord of the heavens.

Hasdai's letter continued with a description of the size, wealth, and power of the Ummayad caliphate and asked Joseph for similar information about his kingdom and its history. To it was prefaced a Hebrew poem celebrating Joseph's valor and military triumphs. Beginning "O breastplate, diadem, and dynast of a kingdom in far regions, / May God's peace and kindness be upon it and its men of law and legions," it was written in non-metrical mono-rhyme and bore the acrostic signature, formed from the initial letter of each line, "I Hasdai bar [son of] Yitzhak bar Ezra bar Shaprut Menachem ben Saruk."

Encoded signatures of this kind had for centuries been woven into their poems by composers of Hebrew liturgical verse. This one, however, was unusual, for it ran two names together as though they were one. Moreover, even if the Khazar king or his scribes understood that Hasdai and Menachem were not the same person, how was Menachem's name to be construed? As that of Hasdai's secretary? But what secretary cosigned a document written for his superior? As that of Hasdai's ghostwriter? Ghosts were then, as now, expected to remain invisible.

Hasdai, who knew Hebrew well, must have read Menachem's poem before approving its dispatch with the letter. Did he fail to react to the signature, as Menachem, unable to resist the temptation to vaunt his authorship of the poem, apparently hoped he would? There is reason to think otherwise, for the poem has come down to us in two different versions, in one of which some of the initial letters spelling "Menachem ben Saruk" have been changed. The most plausible explanation for these changes is that they were meant to erase the acrostic of Menachem's name—and if so, they must have been made by Hasdai or at his behest. Menachem, it seems, had not managed to get away with it.*

It is uncertain whether the Khazar king ever received the letter and poem or answered them, since a Hebrew text purporting to be his reply is of disputed authenticity. Nor is it known what passed between Hasdai and Menachem after Hasdai read the poem. Menachem, at any rate, left Córdoba and Hasdai's service soon afterwards. Although his reasons for doing so are not a matter of record, it would appear that Hasdai banished him in anger, for when he was summoned back to Córdoba a few years later with the commis-

* On the two versions of Menachem's poem, see Appendix B.

sion to write a Hebrew grammar, its terms were far from generous.

No formal grammar of the Hebrew language existed at this time. Hasdai wanted there to be one, modeled on such Arabic works as the eighth-century Sibawaih of Basra's *Al-Kitab*, and despite the incident of the letter to King Joseph, he deemed Menachem the best man for the job. And indeed when, around 960, Menachem published a grammar and lexicon of biblical Hebrew entitled *Sefer ha-Pitronot*, "The Book of Interpretations," it was immediately hailed as a major contribution to rabbinic scholarship.

Not everyone, though, thought so well of it. Among its critics was Dunash ben Labrat, then still a newcomer to Córdoba. Dunash had few rivals in his knowledge of Hebrew and saw at once that Menachem's grammar, which he enviously thought he should have been asked to compose himself, was riddled with errors. In a scathing attack, he listed some eighty mistakes detected by him and claimed to have found many more. Written in the Arabic-style Hebrew verse that he had pioneered, this "book review" consisted of 151 intricately phrased quatrains, the first 41 in praise of Hasdai, to whom it was dedicated, and the next 110 devoted to Menachem's alleged inaccuracies—which had, Dunash declared, "fractured the Holy Tongue."

From a strictly linguistic point of view, most if not all of Dunash's criticisms were valid. Either because he realized they were, or because he did not wish to dignify them with a response, Menachem declined to answer. Instead, he turned to three younger colleagues and asked them to reply on his behalf, which they did in a rebuttal written in imitation of Dunash's poem, including its opening panegyric to Hasdai.

As Dunash's arguments were hard to refute, however, they sought to discredit him by aiming at what they took to be his weak point, namely, his importation into Hebrew poetry of Arabic meters.

These meters represented a radical departure from Hebrew norms. Traditionally, both biblical and post-biblical Hebrew verse had counted only the stressed syllables in each line; the Arabic system, in which all syllables, divided into long and short, mattered equally, was unknown. Furthermore, nearly all Hebrew vowels were the same length, which forced Dunash to label some long and others short arbitrarily in order to adjust them to Arabic quantitative meter.* Although this enabled Hebrew to imitate Arabic poetry, it did so by imposing on it a foreign structure. For this, Menachem's defenders took Dunash to task—and to demonstrate that it was not a case of sour grapes and that they could master the new metrics as well as he could, they wrote in them, mocking him in jingly stanzas like:

> Dunash ben Labrat
> Is so certain that
> There is no point at
> Which he is wrong
>
> That he ruins and slants
> Hebrew's natural stance
> And commands it to dance
> To an alien song.

* Dunash's metrics are explained in Appendix C.

Under attack now himself, Dunash took a page from Menachem's book and asked a student of his, Yehuda Ben-Sheshet, to carry on the fight for him. Ben-Sheshet's riposte was nastily ad hominem and challenged the competence of Menachem's supporters to pass judgment on Dunash:

> Whom are you ill-naming,
> And cursing and blaming,
> And vilely defaming,
> You ignorant fools?
>
> Your thoughts are absurd,
> You garble each word,
> You stutter (that's third!),
> Your speech slobbers and drools.

No doubt followed by a keen audience, this exchange might have continued had not Hasdai put a summary end to it. One Sabbath morning he arrived at Menachem's home with a crew of goons armed with pickaxes and sledgehammers, made a shambles, and dragged Menachem off to jail, where he was left to languish with no formal charges filed against him. A letter that Menachem managed to send to Hasdai, asking to know what he was accused of, received the gnomic reply: "If you have done wrong, I have chastised you justly. And if you have done no wrong, I have delivered you to the World to Come."

Presumably, this was Hasdai's way of saying that if Menachem was blameless, he could plead his case in heaven when he died. Yet what new wrong had Menachem committed? Most probable is a theory first advanced by Luzzatto—

who, based on hints provided by Ben-Sheshet, suggested that Menachem was suspected by Hasdai of being a secret adherent of Karaism, the medieval Jewish heresy that denied the authority of rabbinic tradition and called for a return to a biblical literalism. If so, this might explain why Hasdai had Menachem's home vandalized on a Saturday, since such a seemingly sacrilegious act would have been considered fit punishment for a Karaite whose heterodox observance of the Sabbath laws made him unworthy of their protection. It is also possible that Hasdai, who had brought Dunash to Córdoba and was personally committed to the new style of poetry, took Menachem and his disciples' assault on it as a personal affront. Indeed, by insisting on a strict adherence to biblical rules of syllabic stress, Menachem was in effect taking a Karaitic position on Hebrew verse, too.

Upon receipt of Hasdai's answer, Menachem wrote him from prison, in defiantly unrhymed and unmetrical biblical cadences, a long poetic appeal demanding a chance to prove his innocence. Smarting at the injustice done him, he turned to Hasdai with the adjuration:

> I pray you, listen to me, my sire and lord!
> You consist of plain matter as I do.
> He who made me made you.
> Dust is our origin,
> Our days on earth are but a shadow,
> And in dust
> The mighty with all their power,
> And the lowly with all their pain,
> Will lie together.

Recounting his suffering, he called for a fair trial—if necessary, on the Day of Judgment to which Hasdai had consigned him:

> I bear the burden of my disgrace, I suffer my
> > tribulation,
> For I know that my Redeemer liveth!
> He will plead my cause and grant my day in court
> > though it linger.

Next, Menachem related the story of his arrest ("Why, before your eyes I was beaten, / My clothes were torn, / I was pulled by the hair on the holy day of rest!") and reminded Hasdai of how he had served his father faithfully, recounting the episode of Hasdai's mother's death:

> And after all this, sire, I pray you, remember the
> > bitter night
> On which my lady, she who bore you, passed
> > away,
> Her Maker have mercy on her!
> May God punish me and stoke your wrath
> If you did not come to me on foot that night
> To prepare the keening and lamentation.
> You found me at my desk,
> Foretold before you told me,
> And swore to Almighty God when you saw me:
> "Never will this be forgotten while you live!"

Yet not only, Menachem continued, had Hasdai betrayed his oath, he had done so even though he, Menachem, had spared no effort to enhance his patron's standing. Comparing the letters and poems written by him for Hasdai to mes-

sengers sent hurrying to their destinations, he complained
bitterly:

> And what is my reward,
> In what coin have I been paid—
> I, who dispatched the epistles of your exploits like
> charioteers,
> And the pages of your praise like mounted couriers,
> And the books of your renown like wheels of carriages
> Speeding from town to town?

Menachem did not refer in his poem to his unexplained
departure from Córdoba. Of his return, however, he gave a
full account:

> And after all this, sire, recall how I was summoned by
> you from afar,
> From a pleasant place of rest. . . .
> And I made haste and came to you at once.
> Summer's heat did not deter me,
> Winter's storms did not delay me,
> The bandit's dagger and the highwayman's sword
> could not hold me back.
> Nor was it fear of you that caused me to set out,
> Nor lure of recompense. . . .
> My friendship for Your Grace alone impelled me,
> And when I arrived,
> You charged me with a scholar's task of labor in the
> Holy Tongue,
> And I replied: "At your service, my lord!"

Having set to work on his commission, however, Menachem
was dismayed to discover that he was not being paid for it:

As God and my own soul are my witnesses,
I did as I was asked,
Anxious and hungry though I was,
Naked and penniless. . . .
But God hardened my lord's heart,
And drove all pity from it,
So that never did you think of my endeavors
Long enough to say: "This man, burdened by my
                                    bidding
And brought here from afar, all his business set
                                    aside,
Has nothing. His eyes are turned to me—
Wherefrom will he live and with what sustain his
                                    household?"

In the end, Menachem wrote, Hasdai had yielded to his pleas and granted him a small monthly allowance, "enough— and that, too, barely—for a bit of food and drink." "But now, sire," Menachem asked, unable to support his family from prison,

> To what saint shall I appeal,
> And to whom shall I flee for help,
> And to whom lift my eyes? How shall I live?

His poem nearing its end, he called on Hasdai to release him:

> You know, sire, that Job—put to deadly trial,
> Smitten with cruel afflictions and all human ills,
> The hand of the Lord laid upon him—
> Did not shrink from words.
> The harsher his illness,

The fiercer his quarrel with God. . . .
Yet after all this,
God restored to him what was lost,
And his latter days exceeded his former ones.
May you learn, sire, from God's ways!

It is unknown if this letter had any effect or if Menachem was ever released from prison. But the events themselves were not forgotten. Long afterwards, when Yehuda Halevi wrote his *Kuzari* in the form of a fictional dialogue, he made the Jewish king of Khazaria one of its two interlocutors. And having written Arabic-style poetry in Hebrew all his life, he expressed his opinion in the book that Menachem ben Saruk was right after all and Hebrew had been unnaturally shackled by Dunash ben Labrat and his followers.

Although unmetered and unrhymed verse continued to be written in Spain for liturgical use, Menachem ben Saruk's letter to Hasdai ibn Shaprut was its secular swan song. Henceforward, the new Arabic rules prevailed. Despite the eloquence of Menachem's lines from prison, it is easy to see why. When one compares them to the Hispano-Hebrew poetry that came after them, starting with Hanagid's, the latter's far greater sophistication is obvious. The musical precision of Arabic prosody helped raise the Hebrew poet to a higher plane of aesthetic self-consciousness. Perhaps, as Yehuda Halevi was to argue in *The Kuzari*, this could have happened equally well had Hebrew remained faithful to its own traditions and evolved them. But no such evolution took place. The bonds of an "alien song" were necessary to move Hebrew poetry onward.

Hasdai ibn Shaprut, it is safe to assume, read Menachem

ben Saruk's appeal. Yet even if moved enough by it to pardon him, he can be imagined putting it down with a connoisseur's sniff of disdain. Justly punished or not, Menachem was poetically passé.

It was, as we have said, a poetic age.

3

In 1090 Granada fell to a Berber army from North Africa. The invasion came at the request of the city-states of Andalusia, which—alarmed by the Castilian capture of Toledo in 1085—sought outside aid to stop the Christian expansion. Yet as had happened before in Andalusian history when the Ummayad caliphate was toppled, the relieving Berbers soon turned into conquerors. Known in Spanish as *los almoravides*, the Almoravids, a corruption of the Arabic *al-murabitun*, "people of the *ribat*" (a type of religious community established in Morocco by their founder, the Islamic reformer Abdullah ibn Yassin), the invaders reestablished Muslim control over all Andalusia and pushed the Christians back to Toledo's gates. In doing so, they also seized control of the Andalusian city-states. In Granada they deposed a dynasty, friendly toward its Jewish inhabitants, that had ruled for the better part of a century.

The Almoravids arrived in Spain as Islamic puritans suspicious of both Christians and Jews, especially of Jews in high places. Granada's Jewish elite, including Moshe ibn Ezra's three brothers, left or fled soon after the city fell. Moshe himself stayed behind for a while, apparently stripped of office and detained for political reasons (in a letter to an acquaintance, he complained, "I have remained like a stranger in the land"), then left for the Christian north, banished from Andalusia for life. For the second time in a generation, the city's Jewish community had been dealt a grievous blow. And for the first time in Andalusian history, religious intolerance was put into play as the policy, not of this or that local ruler, but of an entire ruling class. Although the Almoravids soon lost much of their original fervor, it was the beginning of the end for *convivencia* in southern Spain.

We have no knowledge of whether Yehuda Halevi was in Granada when the Almoravids entered it or had left in advance. In either case, he, too, abandoned it for good. Moshe ibn Ezra was no longer in a position to extend patronage, and the city had ceased to be a hospitable place for a young Hebrew poet. Yet Halevi's relations with Ibn Ezra were to continue and to develop into a deep friendship. Some time after the older man's relocation to the north, Halevi wrote to him:

> Where, now that you are gone, will I find rest?
> When you departed, with you went all hearts,
> And had they not believed you would return,
> The day you left them would have been their last.
> Be my witnesses, wild mountains that you crossed,
> That heaven's rains are scant when set against
> My wealth of tears. Beacon of the West,
> Be again our seal and coat-of-arms!
> What will you do, O peerless tongue, among the
> dumb,
> Like Hermon's dew on bare Gilboa cast?

Andalusia was commonly referred to as "the West" because of its geographical position in the Muslim world. To reach Christian territory, Ibn Ezra would have had to cross its high mountains to the Castilian plateau. Refigured by Halevi as Mount Hermon, the tallest peak in the Land of Israel, and lowly Mount Gilboa, cursed with barrenness by David for being the site of Saul and Jonathan's deaths in battle, these stand in the poem for the more cultivated Spanish south and the less lettered north.

Meanwhile Halevi had taken to wandering again himself. Although we cannot track his movements in the years after the fall of Granada, he apparently returned for a while to Lucena, where he had studied after leaving Castile. A nearly all-Jewish town described as far back as the ninth century as "a place of Israelites in which hardly a gentile lives," Lucena had been required to pay off the Almoravids' war debts in order to avoid the forced conversion of its population to Islam. Following the death of Yitzhak Alfasi in 1103, the headmastership of its yeshiva passed to his foremost pupil and Halevi's lifelong friend, Yosef ibn Megas.

Halevi also resided for a while in Seville, a wealthy port city on the Guadalquivir River in Andalusia's southwest, and Granada's traditional political rival. Its well-established Jewish community had fared better under the Almoravid takeover than Granada's, and he hoped to find a new patron there. This he eventually did in the person of Meir ibn Kamaniel, the young scion of a wealthy family who later became an Almoravid court physician in Morocco. Yet rebuffs came first, and Halevi's judgment of the Sevilleans was harsh. In a poem dedicated to Ibn Kamaniel, he attacked them for being stingy philistines, "donkeys too lazy to bear a saddle" and "beasts of burden all kneeling before the same wall." Too "sleepy-headed" to educate themselves, they worshiped money and recoiled from culture as though from "hot coals." He would have perished of poverty, he wrote, had not Ibn Kamaniel, whose "wisdom is as great as his years are few," providentially appeared.

Seville had a literary reputation for miserliness. After fleeing to it following the Christian conquest of Saragossa, the Arab poetry anthologist Abu-'l-Hassan ibn Bassam complained that interest in verse in the city was "scarcer than loyalty" and that although "the greater part of my soul was already gone" when he arrived there, he was forced to live on "what was left of it," since more material help was not forthcoming. But Halevi was also exaggerating the Sevilleans' faults in order to highlight Meir ibn Kamaniel's virtues, hailed in the poem's second half. Modeled on the classical Arabic verse form known as the *qasida*, in which a main subject follows one or more preliminary themes, such encomia to patrons saved their praise for last to create the illusion of being, not premeditated acts of homage, but spontaneous outbursts of gratitude triggered by an association in mid-poem.

A tribute of Halevi's to another patron, of whom no more is known than his name, Yitzhak ibn el-Yatom, follows this pattern. It begins with a brightly painted pastoral scene, a day in early spring when the rainy season is ending and the fields are a riot of color:

> The earth's an infant, sucking at the breast
> Of winter's showers, the clouds her wet nurse—
> Or better yet, a maiden, long kept indoors by cold,
> Who longed for love. Now, the warm days back,
> Her pining heart is healed. Coquettishly,
> She stepped outside today in a new dress,

White-trimmed with gold embroidery,
Long skirt spread wide. Yet every day
She wears a different pattern of wild flowers:
Now pink, now turquoise, now a pearly pale,
Now blushing red as though kissed by a lover.
So glorious a garland must have been
Stolen by her from the stars in heaven!

Into these rustic surroundings the poet proceeds to introduce a party of friends with a cooler of wine. Perhaps they have spent the night camping out in nature, or else they have set out early to catch the first light of the new day, its grass wet from a sudden shower:

Come, then, let us picnic on the greensward
With the passionate daughters of the vine!
(Chilly to the touch, they're inward fire,
Hot with sunshine hoarded in a pot
And poured from there into the finest crystal.)
We'll greet the dawn in a tree-shaded park,
Whose boughs weep softly from a last spring rain,
As through her tears she smiles and wipes away
The drops that fall like beads of glass unstrung,
Rejoicing with the vine's juice and the jays
And murmuring doves, and fluttering gaily,
Like a dancing girl, behind a veil of leaves.

Only now, the wind in the leaves imagined as a messenger from the poet's patron, do we get to the main point: the praises of Yitzhak ibn el-Yatom.

I fain would rise at such a sunrise to a breeze
That brings embraces from a dearest friend!

Yehuda Halevi

Let it play around the myrtle's branches
And bear their scent to cherished hearts afar
While palm trees clap their hands at the birds' song,
So that they wave and bow to Yitzhak,
Whose name means laughter and with whom all
                                        laugh.*
"It is a godly jest," the whole world says,
"To put the All in thrall to just one man!"
And I reply: Refute me if you can,
But Yitzhak's glory cannot be denied.
Although no ordinary grandee is all good
Without a modicum of bad, in him
Not a smatter of the latter's to be had.
My ears are gladdened when, thinking of him,
I hear his name; think then how seeing him
Would double and redouble my acclaim!

For you, Don Yitzhak, my voice flows in pure verse,
The pursuance of your praises my life's pledge.
Yet how win the race to add to these
When you are surrounded by such honors?
All the virtues have pitched camp in you,
And your wisdom rallies their joint forces;
Drinking deeply from discernment's sources,
You plumb the mysteries of things unseen,
Whose knowledge nests and frolics in your being.
Go forth and multiply, and give your progeny
The spirit of your generosity,

---

* Yitzhak, or Isaac, means "he laughs" in biblical Hebrew. The name is
explained in the Book of Genesis by Sarah's declaration when her son
is born: "God hath made me to laugh, so that all that hear will laugh
with me."

> And may their sons and sons' sons have more sons
> On whom God's grace rains down its benisons!

Unlike Halevi's poem to Moshe ibn Ezra, whose emotion is genuine despite the partial triteness of its imagery (nothing is more hackneyed in the poetry of the age than the flood of tears wept by longing friends and disappointed lovers), "The Earth's an Infant," with its lauding of a man distinguished only for his wealth, is sheer flattery. And yet it is marvelously well-crafted flattery, its first half weaving a rich tapestry in which the Mother Earth of approaching summer is seen first as a nursing baby, then as a housebound child, and next as a flirtatious adolescent before maturing into a seductive young lady. Shifting from her to Ibn Yatom, the last two stanzas extol him with a light touch that keeps them from being fulsome. If "The Earth's an Infant" was written in the 1090s, when Halevi was not yet financially independent, it shows a rapidly developing poet mastering longer and more complex forms that want only a deeper emotional palette to achieve expressive maturity.

Halevi also made a living in his post-Granada years by writing verse to order. Part of it consisted of elegies and eulogies. One, composed for a man known to the editor of the *divan* only by his first name of Avraham, was, to judge by its brevity, commissioned for a tombstone:

> Does the tear know whose cheek it runs down,
> Or the heart by whom it is turned?
> It turns to its light that is now in the ground,
> And the ground knows not who has returned.
> Returned is a grandee of our town
> Who feared God and was upright and learned.

Another, this time in rhymed prose, was of a fill-in-the-blank variety. A meditation on the brevity and mutability of life with lines like "The sun shines and we decline as it climbs," it concluded with a prayer that God shelter in Paradise the soul of "the honorable and esteemed _____." While literary royalties were not a feature of medieval life, it was presumably sold to more than one bereaved family.

Wedding poems were also a stock-in-trade. Often these give the impression of having been dashed off hastily, and Halevi may not always have known the couple whose marriage he was paid to celebrate. One suspects this to have been the case with lines like:

> Leave what was and what will be.
> Stick to what you plainly see!
>
> Every lad must hunt his lion,
> And each lass should keep her eye on
>
> Her young man: one look can bag him,
> And a single word may snag him.
>
> Yet when to a gem a gem engaged is,
> God joins them in a rock of ages
>
> Whose bright rays light up the dark
> And of this waste make Eden's park.
>
> By two such souls we now stand blessed
> As though by Levite and by Priest.

Although this is, one might say, the Hispano-Hebrew equivalent of a Hallmark greeting card, its deft wit explains why its author would have been much in demand for such occasions. Concentrate your minds, it tells the wedding guests, on the moment before you rather than (as do most wedding speeches) on tedious accounts of the bride and groom's family history, or equally tiresome homilies about what the future holds in store for them. And this moment, for all its ordinariness, is indeed a special one; for although proud and ambitious men may delude themselves into thinking that they have courted and won their wives when the truth is the opposite, every couple beneath a wedding canopy is an Adam and Eve, illuminating, if only briefly, a fallen world with new hope.

In speaking of the single look or word with which a husband might be snared, Halevi was alluding, not just to the usual enticements of flirtation, but to a social reality that every wedding guest would have been familiar with. This was the product of two values that were in conflict in the Andalusia of his age: the sequestration of women that was a feature of all medieval Muslim societies, and an ideal of courtly love that had begun to spread among the educated classes of the Arab world in the tenth and eleventh centuries. Since free contact between lovers was barred by accepted norms, romantic relationships, even if their goal was marriage, had to be conducted under a mantle of secrecy. The result was a code of romantic conventions that, while no doubt practiced more in literature than in life, was part of Andalusian culture.

The fullest literary treatment of these conventions was an Arabic work entitled *The Collar of the Dove*. Written by the eleventh-century Muslim politician, poet, and theologian Ali ibn Ahmad ibn Hazm, a personal acquaintance and ultimately bitter enemy of Shmuel Hanagid's, *The Collar* is a guidebook dealing at length with such topics as the nature of true love; the need for its dissimulation; the ways in which lovers can intrigue to meet; their strategies of communication in the presence of others; the aids and impediments to achieving private liaisons; the bliss of ultimate union, and so on. Two of the book's chapters deal with "verbal allusions" and "signs made with the eyes"—that is, with how lovers can cryptically convey their feelings and intentions to each other in a social setting.

This is the context in which "Leave What Was and What Will Be" needs to be understood. While its humorous comment on the singular power of looks and words must have made the wedding guests smile, it may also have produced a few sighs or heartthrobs. Although Andalusian Jews married young, and matches between them were almost always arranged and dependent on parental consent, some premarital romances surely existed.

In general, reading Hispano-Hebrew love poetry leaves us unsure how much it reflects the lives of the men who wrote it. (Of women, we can say even less. Jewish girls were not generally given a Hebrew education and could produce nothing like the stormy love letters written in Arabic verse by Wallada, the daughter of the next-to-the-last caliph of Córdoba, to her lover Abu-l-Walid ibn Zaidun.) A good deal of it was no doubt purely literary. When the young Yehuda Halevi composed the bantering quatrain,

> Ofra does her laundry in my tears
> And dries it in the sunshine she gives off.
> She doesn't need to take it to the trough,
> Or wait to hang it till the weather clears,

he need no more have had an actual woman in mind than did Martial when writing his Latin epigrams to Pontia or Gella. It is also possible, however, that he was alluding, under cover of a fictitious name, to a real if casual disappointment in love. Other poems from his bachelor years sound a similar theme. One, using the metaphor of sexual courtship as a form of warfare, depicts the woman who has jilted him as a victorious Amazon:

> Over this fallen soldier fight your war,
> Then make him burn still more as you withdraw.
> You have stopped loving me, so cast your spear
> And let it strike a heart that does not care.
>
> And yet, my sweet, I deem it not seemly
> That I should languish in captivity.
> Reverse your chariot and with one kiss
> Convert my sickbed to a bed of bliss!

The stricken lover was a stock figure of the age. "Every lover whose love is sincere but who is unable to savor love's union," wrote Ibn Hazm, "whether because of separation, his beloved's disdain, the need to keep his feelings secret, or some external circumstance, perforce grows haggard and gaunt and is prone to illness and may have to take to bed." Yet in contrast to such high seriousness, Halevi's "Over This Fallen Soldier" is lighthearted. In this respect it resembles most Hispano-Hebrew love poetry, whose debonair treatment of its subject lies halfway between the lofty Arab ideal of courtly love and the denigration of it by a rabbinic culture that interpreted even the erotic biblical love poem of the Song of Songs as a religious allegory untainted by sexual passion.

With one exception, Halevi gives the impression of having written such verse more to demonstrate a facility with the genre than from any compelling inner need. This exception is so remarkable, however, that it constitutes a major enigma, for the same poet who showed relatively little interest in love poetry has left us its greatest exemplar, not only from his own age, or even from the Hispano-Hebrew period as a whole, but in all of post-biblical Hebrew literature.

The theme of this poem is again a conventional one, that of separation—a fate so dreaded by lovers, Ibn Hazm observed, that he knew men faced with the prospect of it who deliberately provoked a rupture with their beloveds in order to avoid the pain of parting while in love. Halevi's poem is indeed pained. Yet despite its sea of tears, its metaphorically shed lover's blood, and its other borrowings from the repertoire of the times, it does not strike one as a literary exercise. The person it addresses is convincingly real, a woman who has gone away on a journey and left behind, without sending him word of herself, a man suffering from her absence. It begins:

> Why, my darling, have you barred all news
> From one who aches for you inside the bars of his own
> > ribs?
> Surely you know a lover's thoughts
> Care only for the sound of your hellos!
> At least, if parting was the fate reserved for us,
> You might have lingered till my gaze had left your
> > face.
> God knows if there's a heart caged in these ribs
> Or it has fled to join you in your journeys.

. . .

O swear by Love that you remember days of embraces
As I remember nights crammed with your kisses,
And that, as through my dreams your likeness passes,
So does mine through yours!
Between us lies a sea of tears I cannot cross,
Yet should you but approach its moaning waves,
They'd part beneath your steps,
And if, though dead, I heard the golden bells
Make music on your skirt, or your voice asking how I
                                                                    was,
I'd send my love to you from the grave's depths.

That you have shed my blood, I have two witnesses—
Your lips and cheeks. Don't say their crimson lies!
What makes you want to be my murderess
When I would only add years to your years?
You steal the slumber from my eyes,
Which, would it increase your sleep, I'd give you
                                                                    gratis.
My vaporous sighs are stoked by passion's flames,
And I am battered by your icy floes,
And thus it is that I am caught, alas,
Between fire and the flood, hot coals and cold deluges.
My heart, half sweetness and half bitterness,
Honeyed kisses mixed with hemlock of adieus,
Has been shredded by you into pieces,
And each piece twisted into curlicues.

But then, as the poet swings between opposite emotions,
a rush of tenderness sweeps away all recrimination:

Yet picturing your fairness—
The pearl-and-coral of your teeth and lips;

The sunlight in your face, on which night falls in
        cloudy tresses;
Your beauty's veil, which clothes your eyes
As you are clothed by silks and embroideries
(Though none's the needlework that vies with
        Nature's splendor, Nature's grace)—
Yes, when I think of all the youths and maidens
Who, though freeborn, would rather be your slaves,
And know that even stars and constellations
Are of your sisters and your brothers envious—
Then all I ask of Time's vast hoard is this:
Your girdled waist, the red thread of those lips
That were my honeycomb, and your two breasts,
In which are hidden myrrh and all good scents.

All that is left now is longing—and the hope for love's restoration:

O would you set me as a seal upon your arms
As I set you on mine! May both my hands
Forget their cunning if I forget the days,
My dearest, of our love's first bliss!
Hard for the heart made vagrant are the memories
Of your ambrosia on my lips—but could I mix
My exhalations with their perfumed essence,
I would have a way to kiss you always.
Are women praised for their perfections?
Perfection in you is praised for being yours.
The fields of love have many harvesters—
And your harvest is bowed down to by their sheaves.
God grant that I may live to drain the lees,
Once more, of your limbs' sweet elixirs!

Although I cannot hear your voice,
I listen, deep within me, for your footsteps.
O on the day that you revive Love's fallen legions
Slain by your sword, think of this corpse
Abandoned by its spirit for your travels!
If life, my love, will let you have your wishes,
Tell it you wish to send a friend regards.
May it bring you to your destinations,
And God return you to your native grounds!

The best translation cannot convey the sonorous beauty of this poem. I have sought to do so in part by ending each English line with an "s" in order to give some sense of the Hebrew mono-rhyme. But not only does this lack the musical effect of true rhyme, the rhyme it fails to reproduce is a perfect one. Consisting of the two syllables of the second-person singular, feminine, possessive suffix -*àyikh*, "your," it builds up slowly—*tsiràyikh*, "news of you" (literally, "your messengers"), *shlomotàyikh*, "your hellos," *panàyikh*, "your face," *masa'àyikh*, "your journeys"—until it becomes a haunted cry for the missing loved one. Moreover, since it is close in sound to *ayékh*, the feminine form of "Where are you?," this question repeats itself like a subliminal lament at the end of each line.

Who was she?

We haven't a clue. There isn't a shred of evidence in regard to her. She is biographically darker than Shakespeare's Dark Lady. All we can say is that she was someone with whom Yehuda Halevi, still single and most likely in his twenties, had a love affair. Almost certainly she was not his future wife, with whom his ties do not appear to have been romantic.

Someone else's wife? There is no indication of this in the poem.

An unmarried woman younger than him? If so, she must have been very brave, for well-bred girls did not behave this way in Andalusia, not even under cover of Ibn Hazm's codes of secrecy.

A slave girl, perhaps, as were many of the women to whom Arabic love poetry was written? (Sometimes cultured and educated, female slaves were more sexually available than others.) Although wealthy Jews did own slaves, the poem's description of a woman traveling independently does not lend itself to such a conjecture.

A purely literary creation, then, after all? This remains hard to believe. *Although I cannot hear your voice, / I listen, deep within me, for your footsteps*: These are the words of a man who knows what it is like to sit by an open window, waiting for a sound that never comes. They are different from anything else that Halevi ever wrote.

Did she return from her travels? If she did, separation had by then done its work, for he never wrote her another poem.

But his palette had deepened. Although we cannot accurately date its composition, if we had to guess when it was that Yehuda Halevi joined the ranks of the great Hebrew poets, we might plausibly point to the day on which he sat down to write "Why, My Darling, Have You Barred All News."

We also do not know when, or whom, Halevi eventually married. As a rule, Hispano-Hebrew poets did not compose poetry to or about their wives, nor was domestic life one of the themes they customarily dealt with. Yet even small families—Halevi's was to have just one grown daughter—needed to be supported. Living from patron to patron while writing verse on commission was not a dependable source of income. Most likely it was marriage or the prospect of it that made Halevi decide to acquire a profession. He chose medicine, a common occupation among Jews then as now.

Becoming a doctor in eleventh-century Spain was not accomplished by going to school. At the time there was only one medical school in all of Europe, that of Salerno in southern Italy. Learning to be a competent physician was a matter of independently mastering the available literature, especially the *Canon* of Ibn Sina, or Avicenna, as he was known in Christian Europe, and Arabic translations of the Greek works of Galen. (In a letter written to an acquaintance in these years, Halevi complained that his medical studies had taken him away from the writing of poetry and left him "black with the ink of Arabic and / sunk in the slime of the Greeks' quicksand.") Not even an apprenticeship with an experienced practitioner was required, there being no licensing procedures. Whoever thought he was ready hung out his shingle.

Medieval medicine was rudimentary by modern standards, both in its understanding of the body's workings and in its diagnostic capacities. Yet inasmuch as medical cures were limited, too, and restricted largely to herbal remedies, changes in diet and lifestyle, and psychological counseling, even inexperienced or incompetent doctors must have harmed fewer patients than they would today. Ultimately, those who were able to charm, impress, or help enough people gained a reputation and prospered. Yehuda Halevi was one of them. His professional success is attested to by a rhymed prose letter sent by him to the Provençal rabbi David Narboni. After apologizing for not replying sooner to a communication of Narboni's and for neglecting to carry out an unspecified request, Halevi explains that he has been busy with his medical practice, which he describes in self-deprecating terms:

> For some time now, my deeds have been weighed and great things of me said. I am praised to the skies with all kinds of lies, and many believe what they're told and think me as wise as Darda and Kalkol the sons of Machol,* when in fact I know nothing at all. I work day and night and in between at the vanity of medicine, which heals not a thing. The city I live in is large and its inhabitants huge, hard taskmasters, too. What can a slave do to serve such men but spend his days at their whim and his years treating them? Yea, we treat Babylon and cure none.†

Evidently, Halevi did not value the medical profession greatly, whether because he had come to be disillusioned by it, or because he had chosen it in the first place with no real belief in its efficacy. In this he contrasts sharply with another great Jewish figure born in Spain, one who was to be his antithesis in nearly every respect: Maimonides. For the latter, a physician, too, medicine was a sacred calling, a vocation second to none in its importance. For Halevi, it was a

---

* Legendary wise men mentioned in Kings I 5:11.
† This last sentence is taken from Jeremiah 51:9.

tedious way of making a living, even if his waiting room was crowded and he was well thought of by his patients.

But where was "Babylon," the "large city" with its "huge" inhabitants in which he was living when he wrote this letter? A series of poems points to Toledo, an identification consistent with our being told by other sources that he moved back at some point to Christian Spain.

These poems consist of four elegies written for a Toledan Jew named Shlomo ibn Ferruziel. Shlomo was the nephew of Yosef ibn Ferruziel, a minister at the court of Alfonso VI, the Castilian king who wrenched Toledo from Muslim hands and made it his capital. Yosef, known in Spanish as Cidello, was also Alfonso's personal physician, the leader of Toledo's Jewish community, and a man of great wealth and influence. A poem of Halevi's written on the occasion of a state visit by him to the city of Guadalajara began:

> When leaders assemble and kings seek advice,
> They give thanks to Yosef, their pride and their prize.
> He rules over men and to God's rule aspires.

A girdle song, this poem ended with a *kharja* in a mixture of Spanish and Arabic:

> *Des cuand mieu Cidyelo viénid*
> *tan buona albishara!*
> *Com' rayo de sol éxid*
> *En Wad-al-hajara.*

> When Cidello arrives,
> The news banishes all sorrow!
> He shines like the sun
> On Guadalajara.

Shlomo ibn Ferruziel was also an official at Alfonso's court. In the spring of 1108 he was sent on a state mission to the kingdom of Aragon, and Yehuda Halevi composed a poem in honor of his expected homecoming in which he described a city, obviously Toledo, "stricken with darkness" when Shlomo departed but "all radiant" upon his return. This poem was never read in public, however, for Shlomo was killed by highwaymen or assassins as he was traveling back through Christian territory. Toledo's Jews were plunged into mourning, and Halevi ended up writing one long and three short elegies in its place. One of the short ones, accompanied in the *divan* by the note that it was written "on hearing that he [Shlomo] had been killed," is addressed to the bearer of the news:

> Ah, me! You bring no good tidings, my friend,
> By telling me Shlomo is dead.
> O my heart, change your song to a dirge,
> For his welcome's an ill-come instead!

In the longer elegy, Halevi calls down the wrath of God on Christian Spain with a venom so disproportionate to the murder of a single man—"May He requite it with bereavement and widowhood, / And lay low all its idols and multitude," to cite two lines—that it can only be explained by a deeper anti-Christian animus. And yet why, if he felt that way, had he chosen to live in Toledo, a city whose Christian denizens, with their greater admixture of Visigothic blood, may indeed have seemed "huge" compared to the Andalusians, and that he disliked so much that he called it in another poem "a place of sepulchral darkness"?

Perhaps he did so because, its Muslim population greatly

reduced by the Christian reconquest, Toledo would have been suffering from a shortage of doctors. Medieval Catholicism's attitude toward medicine differed from Judaism and Islam's. Illness in the eyes of the Church was a punishment from God or an affliction of the Devil's, and in either case, to be treated by spiritual rather than physical means. The Council of Rheims, convened in 1135, actually forbade Catholic priests to practice medicine—a prohibition, given the clerical monopoly on education, that effectively barred all Christians from the profession. Yet ordinary Christians were not always happy to entrust their health exclusively to the altar and the confession box. When ill, they, too, wanted doctors. Toledo would have been an opportunity for a starting physician like Halevi to establish himself against weakened competition while staying as close to the Muslim south as possible.

Nor, southern prejudices notwithstanding, was Toledo a cultural wasteland in those years. Although the city's full intellectual flowering was still several decades away, Alfonso VI sought to attract Christian intellectuals, and its Jewish community was home to many educated Jews. Beside the Ibn Ferruziels, there was Moshe ibn Ezra, with whom Halevi could now renew a close relationship; Moshe's brothers, Yitzhak, Yehuda, and Yosef, the last of them a senior official in Alfonso's administration; the noted physician Yosef ibn Kamaniel; and such well-established and cultivated families as the Ibn-Shoshans (one of whose grandsons was to become a powerful figure at the court of Alfonso VIII), the Alfakhars, and the Abulafias—the latter the progenitors of a great rabbinical dynasty. Such men would have comprised Halevi's social circle.

Toledo's Jews inhabited a quarter known in Arabic as *medinet el-yahud*, "the Jewish town," and in Spanish as *la judería*. Its narrow streets and alleys were located near the northwestern section of the city wall, not far from the Tajo River and the San Martín Bridge, still the main approach to Toledo from Castile. While nothing is left today of anything Yehuda Halevi would have recognized, still standing near a house that was El Greco's in the years when he painted his magnificent Toledan landscapes is the most impressive Jewish architectural remnant in all of Spain: the stately Tránsito Synagogue, constructed in the fourteenth century under the sponsorship of Shmuel Halevi Abulafia, the treasurer of Pedro I of Castile. Halevi knew his ancestors.

Alfonso VI died in 1109 and was succeeded by his son-in-law, Alfonso I of Aragon, the husband of his daughter Urraca. In the period of the interregnum, a popular uprising broke out in the capital in which royal buildings were attacked and destroyed. Jewish homes and businesses were targeted, too, and Jews were killed. Although Alfonso of Aragon finally restored order, this was done by making concessions to the rioters, who were excused from payment of the customary blood money to the murdered Jews. (Henceforth, the new king also ruled, a Jewish life was to be assessed not like a Christian burgher's but like the less valuable one of a Christian peasant.) As everywhere in medieval Europe, the Jews of Spain lived under the protection of sovereigns who valued them for their skills and reliability; whenever royal power was weakened or challenged, their envied status caused them to be among the first victims. While the loss to Jewish life and property in Toledo in 1109 did not compare with the havoc wreaked in Granada in 1066, it was another reminder of how precarious, beneath the thin surface of *convivencia*, the Jewish situation in the Iberian Peninsula was.

Yehuda Halevi's residence in Toledo was a long one. Starting in the first decade of the twelfth century, it spanned the stormy years that followed Alfonso of Aragon and Urraca's estrangement in 1110, with its ensuing Aragonese-Castilian civil war that left the queen reigning in Toledo by herself, and it appears to have continued past her death in 1126. A canny and diplomatically astute ruler, Urraca led a sexually free existence that caused a contemporary chronicle, the *Historia Compostelana*, to call her a "wicked Jezebel," a reputation that has been seized upon to link her to an episode in Halevi's life. To explain the alleged connection, however, it is first necessary to digress to another time and place entirely—all the way to late-nineteenth-century Egypt.

I n 1896 the Jewish scholar Solomon Schechter, then a lecturer in rabbinics at Cambridge University, was shown some Hebrew manuscript pages acquired by two British tourists in Cairo. A cursory look sufficed for him to recognize them as belonging to the second-century B.C.E. book of Ben-Sira—or, as it is called in the Catholic Bible, Ecclesiasticus. Excluded from the Jewish canon, Ben-Sira had survived only in Greek translation. Now, correctly surmising that he was looking at part of its long-lost Hebrew text, Schechter set out excitedly for Cairo, where he traced the pages to the Ezra Synagogue, the city's most ancient place of Jewish worship.

What he found there surpassed all imagining. The thousand-year-old synagogue had a large attic loft, accessible only by ladder, that was home to a *geniza*, a storage place where were deposited discarded documents in Hebrew or Hebrew characters whose destruction was forbidden because they might contain God's name. From this loft had come the fragment of Ben-Sira, and in it Schechter discovered hundreds of thousands of other pages piled high from wall to wall. Realizing their potential riches, he negotiated their purchase, acquired the greater part, packed them in crates, and had them shipped back to England.

The Cairo Geniza proved to be one of the greatest archival finds in the annals of historical research. Since almost any medieval Jewish document might begin with an invocation of God's blessing, there was nothing a *geniza* could not hold. Squirreled away and forgotten for hundreds of years in the Ezra Synagogue were books of which no one had known; known books of which no copies had survived; the lost works of Jewish poets and philosophers; reams of rabbinical responsa; sacred texts and prayers with unfamiliar passages or variant readings; community records and protocols; files of personal correspondences; entire libraries of commercial documents—contracts, legal briefs, orders for merchandise, receipts for payment, bills of lading and of credit, statements of loans and investments, IOUs, partnership agreements, the letters and replies of far-flung merchants; notes, memoranda, lists, ledgers, title deeds, and account books. Some of this material was in Aramaic, Hebrew, or literary Arabic. The great bulk was in Judeo-Arabic, the vernacular tongue, written in the Hebrew alphabet and interspersed with Hebrew words and expressions, of the Jews of the Middle East, North Africa, and Andalusia.

It was a treasure large enough to keep scholars busy for generations. One of these stood out above the others: the German-born S. D. Goitein (1900–1985), a professor at the Hebrew University of Jerusalem and the Institute for Advanced Studies in Princeton, whose five-volume *A Mediterranean Society: The Jewish Communities of the Arab World as Portrayed in the Documents of the Cairo Geniza* is a monument of social and economic history.

Using the Geniza's material, which he spent a lifetime studying, Goitein was able to paint a remarkably detailed picture of the daily life of Jews in the medieval Islamic world. One of his discoveries was a cache of letters written to a wealthy Egyptian Jewish merchant and patron of literature named Halfon ben Netanel. Halfon traveled widely on business and made at least one voyage to Spain, where he spent two years between 1127 and 1129 and formed a close friendship with Yehuda Halevi. In some of the letters filed away by him, Halevi is mentioned; five of them, remarkably, were written by Halevi himself. Starting in the mid-1950s, Goitein published the most important of these in a series of articles, while a complete collection with extensive commentary was issued in Hebrew in 2001 by the Israeli scholars Ezra Fleischer and Moshe Gil. As a result, a number of previously unknown details from Halevi's life have been rescued from oblivion. Although most belong to its final year, two letters inform us of an incident that took place while he was living in Toledo.

Both are short, informal notes written by Halevi to Halfon in Judeo-Arabic and concerning a Jewish girl who was being held for ransom under unclear circumstances. The first asked Halfon to do something about a "remaining sum" owed to "the campaign for the captive girl." Even though,

Halevi wrote, the amount of money still missing was a small one, "we can no more proceed without it than we could if it were large." The letter ends with regards to a rabbi referred to only as "the bright candle of Israel" and asks Halfon to obtain from him "an answer to the people of Toledo," who "are depending on me, so that I cannot tell them that I am unable to intercede for them with the rabbi, may the Lord preserve him."

The main part of the second letter reads:

> I have already written to thank you for your contribution for the captive girl. Please have her father come here at once, because her case will soon be resolved to her satisfaction now that we in this city have put up ten dinars . . . and there is the dinar that you were good enough to contribute, and we are waiting for six from Malaga, and if we receive the ten from Lucena as agreed upon, the matter will be concluded . . . and we will free [the girl] before Sukkot [the Feast of Booths]. The wicked one has changed her mind about allowing her visits on Sabbaths and holidays. If her father can find a way of transmitting to us what has been collected, and of going to Granada [to collect more] should we fall short of the 32-and-⅔ dinars, have him do it. In my opinion, it's best to work quickly for her release. God will show us the way. The wicked one's deadline is the end of [the Hebrew month of] Tishrei and she won't extend it by a minute.

Read closely, these letters tell us the following:

- Halevi was writing to Halfon, then in Spain, from Toledo, whose Jewish community had previously turned to him for help in obtaining a reply to an unanswered query addressed to an illustrious rabbi, perhaps having to do with some matter of Jewish law. The woman called "the wicked one," who was holding the girl captive, lived in Toledo, too, since this was where Halevi wanted the girl's father to come for her release.

- The rabbi was most likely Halevi's friend Yosef ibn Megas, the head of the Lucena yeshiva, and Halfon, a learned Jew who may have taken time off from his business affairs to study with him, was residing in Lucena at the time.

- Halevi had taken on himself the task of raising the ransom money, which had to be handed over before the end of the autumn month of Tishrei, on the fifteenth of which fell the holiday of Sukkot. The sum demanded, nearly thirty-three dinars, was large but not enormous, it being estimated that a middle-class family in twelfth-century Spain needed twenty-five dinars a year to live on. As was the practice in the Middle Ages, in which the ransom of Jewish hostages (most commonly captured by pirates at sea) was considered a shared responsibility, different Jewish communities had been asked to contribute to the girl's liberation.

This leaves three questions: who was the girl, why was she being held, and who was the "wicked one" holding her? (The Hebrew word used by Halevi is *mirsha'at*, more colloquially translatable as "the bitch.") The first two mysteries have no solution. The answer to the third, Goitein suggested, was Urraca, the "wicked Jezebel" of the *Historia Compostelana*.

Goitein's identification has not gone unchallenged. Not

only is it based, its critics point out, on a far from rare epithet, it assumes that a ruler like Urraca would have stooped to kidnapping a Jewish girl for what was, by royal standards, a trivial sum. Moreover, whereas Goitein believed that Halfon had made at least one other visit to Spain prior to 1127, at which time Urraca was no longer alive, the evidence weighs against this. Very likely, the "wicked one" was someone else.

Yet the biographical importance of the incident lies not in the identity of the hostage holder but in its portrayal of Halevi as someone who, besides being a well-known poet and successful physician, was a recognized communal leader in contact with the influential Jews of his age. This is also borne out by his verse, in which there are many friendship poems written to prominent figures. It is noteworthy, too, that he is regularly referred to in the Cairo Geniza correspondence as Ravna Yehuda, "our master Yehuda," a title of affection and respect. In another of his letters to Halfon, he mentions a regular get-together held every Friday in his home, where he appears to have had held a weekly open house. At the onset of middle age, he was as sociable as when, "a humble youth from Castile," he had enjoyed staying up late at night with his friends, "making music on the wine cups."

Sometime before 1121, Moshe ibn Ezra's brother Yehuda passed away, the first of the four Ibn Ezras to die. Only Yosef remained in Toledo. On bad terms with him, Moshe had drifted back to the far north, alienated from his family. (It has been conjectured on the basis of a poem of his that the rift was caused by his having fallen in love with his brother Yitzhak's daughter.) Yitzhak, meanwhile, had moved to Lucena. For Yehuda, Halevi wrote a short, nostalgic elegy that recalled other days:

> Because it sees man is but a vain thing,
> Time turns on him. Like Abel killed by Cain,
> It lays the splendidest of our sons low
> And slays the darlings of our hearts.
> Souring our wine until our tears taste sweet,
> It has breached the Ibn Ezras' foursquare lines.
> For two of them, now far away, I pine,
> And for the days in which they won the palm,
> While asking for Yosef, I'm told to wait,
> And for Yehuda, "He is gone."

The poem begins with a pun, since *hevel*, the biblical word for "vanity," is also the Hebrew name of the biblical Abel. (Literally, the first two lines read: "Because it sees that man is *hevel*, / Time turns on him and becomes Cain.") Its penultimate line is a barb aimed at Yosef. Apparently, Halevi had gone to see him about some matter and been told he was too busy to receive him.

Yosef ibn Ezra died in 1128, and Halevi wrote an elegy for him, too, although cooler than the one for Yehuda. His most powerful poem of mourning, however, was for an unnamed girl. Its unusual dramatic structure has three voices—the bereaved father's, the mother's, and their dead daughter's—and with its refrain taken from the Book of Ruth (who tells Naomi, "Where thou diest will I die, and there will I be buried; may the Lord do unto me accordingly if aught but death come between you and me"), it is heart-wrenching. It goes:

Yehuda Halevi

My child!
Had you forgotten the way
To your own home
That your pallbearers strayed
To the underworld's gloom,
Leaving me with
(Since you are not here
To ask how you are)
A grave's clods to kiss
And your memory?
Ah, death has come between you and me.

O daughter torn
From her mother's rooms!
What life have I left when,
Shaped from my soul,
She makes my tears flow
Like a spring from split stone?
How can she be so changed,
Once white as the moon,
That she now wears the earth
As her bridal gown,
Its sod the sweets
Of her wedding feast?
Bitter is my own misery,
For death has come between you and me.

Plucked like a flower
Before her time,
She always will be
Before my eyes
Like a frontlet.

Yet were I to cry
Whole rivers for her,
Still she would lie,
A fallen star
In a wormy pit,
Deep-sepulchered,
Earth-bonneted.
My child, there is no clemency,
For death has come between you and me.

Languishing,
Her mother's voice,
Bereft, I hear.
(Ah, let her be!
She too grieves bitterly.
Death scaled her walls,
And pierced her side,
And drove her pride
From its abode,
And turned her joy
Into a dirge
The day it ripped
The vine she planted
From her heart.)
"What good, my child,
Does it to cry your name?
Your ears are deaf
And you are silenced utterly,
For death has come between you and me.

Alas, my child,
You have laid me low!"

"O mother, O!
You should not have had me
If you meant to spurn me,
And when my turn came
To Death's minion to wed me,
And with dirt to wreathe me
And cruelly lead me
Under doom's canopy.
Yet truly you did it not willingly,
For death has come between you and me."

May He
Whose judgments
None repeal
Unseal your bonds
And heal your sleep
With angels' song,
And be not wroth
With His own flock
And stop the plague
That He sent forth,
And comfort every heart
For what it lost!
And may you wake
On the Last Day,
To light like dew,
And rise in the arms of His mercy,
For death has come between you and me.

The final stanza tells us that the girl, who was of or close to marriageable age, died in an epidemic that was still raging when the poem was written. For the third time in this chapter, we find ourselves asking: Who was she? But this time there may be an answer. Although no note accompanies the poem in the *divan*, and Halevi's biographers have overlooked it, the child, I believe, was his own. It stands to reason that more children were born to him than the sole daughter who survived. Child mortality was high in the Middle Ages. He wrote many elegies, none more intense or terrible in its grief than this one. Can it be that what he had done for friends and strangers he would not have done for a child who was his?

Perhaps for two children. A son may have been over-looked, too.

All in all, Halevi wrote four more poems on the occasion of a child's death. Two of them, one spoken by a father grieving for an adolescent daughter and the other begun by him and continued by her from the grave, appear to be about the same girl. Another, three stanzas long, is for a small, nameless boy. It, too, has a dramatic structure, beginning in the third person and shifting quickly to the first:

Snatched was the child from its father's lap.
Shuddering, up from his vigil he leaped
And cried, "Cursed be the day on which I was
whelped
Into this world! Better not to have lived
Than see the death of my boy."

The father's concluding words are:

"Have pity, have pity on me, all my friends,
For God has taken, straight from my arms,
The light of my eyes and my chief of delights,
Whose body I washed with the wet of my tears,

And then buried deep in the crypt of my ribs.
Whenever I think of him—which is at all times—
In my depths—in my heart—heart of hearts!—
My heart is as dead as my boy."

The fifth poem, also a lament for the death of a young son, is in fragmentary form, only the first two of its stanzas having survived. In it as well, the child is described as having died in his father's arms. If this girl and boy were indeed Halevi's,[*] his feelings about the futility of medicine would be only too understandable.

Also nameless is the daughter who reached adulthood. She was married to the poet Yitzhak ibn Ezra (not to be confused with Moshe ibn Ezra's brother of the same name, to whom he was not related), the son of Avraham ibn Ezra—himself one of the great Hispano-Hebrew poets and a noted Bible commentator, mathematician, and astronomer.[†] Avraham was born about 1089 in Yehuda Halevi's hometown of Tudela, and his and Halevi's families must have been acquainted. Assuming that he was at least twenty when he fathered Yitzhak, the latter was probably born close to 1110. Since Halevi's daughter would not have been older than her husband and had, as we shall see, a son who was at least twelve or thirteen in 1141, she must have been born in Toledo, probably the last of his three children, not long after 1110, when Halevi was in his middle to late thirties, and married no later than 1128 or 1129.

---

[*] Appendix D deals with this question at greater length.

[†] Although the identification of Yehuda Halevi's son-in-law with Avraham ibn Ezra's son has been disputed, I believe it is correct. The issue is discussed in Appendix E—which I would recommend that the interested reader postpone consulting until referred to it at the end of Chapter 6.

As for Moshe ibn Ezra, his years after leaving Toledo were spent roaming unhappily in northern Spain, looking for a livelihood in a society that failed to recognize his worth. In a poem from this period, he writes that he has "trekked from sea to sea"—that is, from the Mediterranean to the Atlantic—without finding a resting place, so "blistered by the sun" and "blackened by the night" that "my own face no longer knows me and is unknowable." In the preface to his literary history *The Book of Discussions and Remembrance*, composed in the years before his death in 1138, he answers a friend who, he writes, had suggested that he produce such a book:

> Your request finds me tired, lethargic, and deeply depressed for two reasons. One is the fear that [if I were to write what you propose] the vulgar masses would think me mindless because of the hostility to culture that is their attitude. . . . The other is my long exile and the unending pain of life in this distant land and remote place to which fate has flung me at the end of my life, so that I am like a prisoner in jail—no, like a corpse in its grave.

Halevi missed Andalusia, too. The happiest time of his life had been spent there. Once, listening to the mournful gurgle of a nearby dove, he was moved to write a poem that began:

> A dove weeps in the treetops
> And her sobs make my heart sore,
> For its pangs are as her pain is
> And my fate is shared by her.
> I cry for kin and country,

She for old nesting grounds;
I for my lost dear ones,
She for scattered friends;
I for days long vanished,
She for youth now fled.

At some point during these years of fled youth, he also
wrote and sent a poem to Moshe ibn Ezra. Judging by the
distaste with which he described his surroundings, he was
still in Toledo, though as unreconciled to life there as he had
always been. Since setting out from Castile in his teens, he
had never had a home he could call permanent. Now, middle-
aged, he wrote:

Wander-life, you are an old friend—
And the River of Tears has flowed for long years.
Shall I quarrel with fate? But why fault what is fated?
Or with time that goes by? What else should time do!
Like a skein from the spindle it runs straight and true,
As does all made above. This may not be new;
But the world is not new and its laws are writ in God's
hand.
How expect them to change when they all bear His
stamp,
And all things run their course and each cause has its
cause?
Men are joined in order to part—that's how
differences start,
From which nations are born and the earth is peopled
with tribes.
Nothing is all good or bad; every potion is also a
poison,

And the day cursed as paltry by one man, others
                    praise for its bounty.
A rich dish is a treat if you're well, hot coals in your
                    mouth when you're ill,
And so black is the sight of the man who is vexed that
                    it darkens all light
As my eyes are clouded and wet because Moshe is
                    gone.

The source of all wisdom, his words were pure
                    nuggets of gold!
Our friendship is old; it goes back to when no one
                    harnessed or rode
The wagons of wandering's road, and my soul
Was unpracticed at parting, and our days were
                    unfractured and whole.
Time bore us separately, but Love, which bore us
                    twins,
Raised us in her spice garden and suckled us with
                    guzzled wines.
When I think of you, many mountains away (why, just
                    yesterday
You were my pleasure's peak!), the blood leaves my
                    cheeks
For the tears running down them. I think—and
                    remember the days
That once were. Were we dreaming? What a traitor
                    time is!
It has taken you from me and given me strife-minded
                    men
Who pretend to be friends. The more their manners

Stink like garlic, the more I miss the manna of your
                              speech.
Damn the fools who are so wise in their own eyes
That their own lies they deem the dogmas of true
                              faith,
And my faith sorcery! They sow and reap empty ears
                        and call it grain;
With the exteriors of fashion they cover up the gems
                           within.
But I will mine truth's storerooms for its rarest stones
And rest not till their sheaves bow down to mine.
"What? And cast my pearls before the swine?"
I'll say when they come knocking. "Why on seedless
                          soil
Let fall my rain?" No, all I need from this poor age is
                        what my soul
Needs from my body: a place to live in while it lasts,
And to abandon when it topples and we leave.

There is a world-weariness in this poem that we have not
seen in Halevi before. He had by now experienced his share
of sorrow. No longer, in addressing Ibn Ezra, was he the
younger poet writing to the master. Life's honors and life's
blows had made them equals.

Yet younger he remained. *I will mine truth's storeroom for its
rarest stones and rest not till their sheaves bow down to mine:* this is
the ambition of a man who, mentally at odds with his surroundings despite his social prominence, feels at the height
of his powers. The mention of "dogmas" and "faith" suggests that Halevi is referring in these lines to the writing of
The Kuzari, his great work on Judaism; those who "sewed

and reaped empty ears" were the Toledan Jews he was
friendly with but whose opinions he did not share. This
situation is also alluded to in the continuation of "A Dove
Weeps in the Treetops," where Halevi asks rhetorically,
"Why should I fear when mine is a soul / From whose cubs
lions cower," and answers:

> Should I hunger, it [the soul] has food;
> If I thirst, I have its streams.
> Its lute, when I am lonely,
> Plays its songs;
> No better conversation
> Than the wisdom of its words.
> Its quill makes music
> In the garden of my books.

These lines bespeak a period of intellectual isolation and
creative excitement that went together. If Halevi's "quill"
was at work on a book, it could only have been *The Kuzari*, of
which an early version, as we know from a letter of his to
Halfon ben Netanel, was indeed finished by 1129, toward the
end of his stay in Toledo.

Of Yehuda Halevi's return to Andalusia we are informed
by Moshe ibn Ezra's *Book of Disquisitions and Discussions*.
Writing in the 1130s, Moshe refers to both Halevi and Avraham ibn Ezra as residents of Córdoba. He would not have
done so had they not been living there for a while.

Perhaps because this is the only statement by a contemporary of Halevi's linking him to a specific place, Córdoba
alone of Andalusia's cities has taken a proprietary interest in

him. In the old *judería*, not far from the grand Roman bridge over the Guadalquivir, where the river makes a right-angled bend around the Barrio de Miraflores on its way to Seville and the Atlantic, is a Plaza Juda Levi with a Café-Bar Juda Levi on one corner. *"Fue filósofo, médico, y escritor de la época,"* its bartender answered knowledgeably when I asked him whom the establishment was named for. I chose not to probe him further.

Outside the café were some tables to which I took my coffee. It was a warm December day, and the oranges on the trees shared the branches with Christmas bulbs. Up the street from Plaza Juda Levi, on Calle Deanes, was the Pepe de la Judería tapas bar; beyond that were souvenir shops, a tacky emporium playing soft Moorish music, and—turning onto the Calle Romano—an ersatz Arab souk displaying nargilehs, Palestinian keffiyehs, machine-made Bedouin dresses, and cheap ceramic drums and shepherd flutes in a shabby mimesis of Córdoba's five centuries of Islamic rule.

Further on, the *judería* lapsed into a neighborhood of narrow streets and small whitewashed houses with barred window sills and geraniums on balconies. A door swung open on a brightly tiled courtyard. Orange and lemon trees, a fountain, potted palms. The door shut.

In the opposite direction from Plaza Juda Levi, Calle Abulcasis led to the little Plaza Tiberiades, in which a robed and turbaned statue sat meditatively on a stone bench. On the pedestal it rested its feet on, a Hebrew inscription in the Arabized script of the Cairo Geniza said *Moshe B'Rabi Maimon,* "Moses the son of Rabbi Maimon," better known in English as Maimonides. The statue was erected in 1964 for Córdoba's celebration, in a joint gesture to the spirit of *con-*

vivencia and the Jewish tourist trade, of a week dedicated to the great philosopher. A municipal brochure issued in 1985 explains that "in order to examine Maimonides, the illustrious polymath from Córdoba, [it was felt that] the best way would be by presenting him not as an isolated figure but inserted within his time and context, in the midst of those who, like him, felt as much Jewish as Cordobese or Andalusian and enjoyed the cultural privilege of living in Muslim Spain." *As much Jewish!* The tourist would never guess that in 1148, when Maimonides was ten years old, he and his family had enjoyed the privilege of fleeing from Córdoba, and soon after from Spain, as a new wave of Islamic intolerance swept in from North Africa.

From Plaza Tiberiades you can either walk a short way along Calle Salazar to Plaza Maimonides, in which you will find, in an elegant old building, a bull-fighting museum, or else follow Calle de los Judíos to the *judería*'s only identifiable Jewish remains, a medieval synagogue. Housed in a plain brick structure that served in different periods, after the expulsion of Spain's Jews in 1492, as a Catholic chapel, a rabies hospital, the office of a shoemakers' guild, and a school, the synagogue is no larger than a living room but has a lovely interior with graceful arches, lacelike stucco tracery, and the Hebrew inscription that it was built in 1315. You can then circle back via Calle Romero and Calle Deanes to Plaza Juda Levi by bearing right, or else turn left and come to the square of the magnificent Mezquita Cathedral, the "cathedral of the mosque." Here, Islam and Christianity face off in a remarkable architectural disputation.

It is a tale, not uncommon in the history of religion, of a sacred shrine built on a sacred shrine built on a sacred shrine, each faith simultaneously inheriting and disinheriting its predecessor. Originally the site of a Roman temple, the square of the Mezquita next housed the Visigothic Cathedral of St. Vincent, which was then converted, when Córdoba became the Umayyad capital, into one of the grandest mosques in the Islamic world; subsequently, following the Christian reconquest of the city in 1236, the mosque reverted to a cathedral. Today its original ground plan is still evident in its long avenues of columned arches, row after receding row, erected to frame men kneeling on a checkerboard of space in a minimal statement of the maximal, a patterned emptiness in which there was nothing to distract from the worship of an incorporeal Allah. Superimposed on it, the Christian cathedral is all clutter and gold, its naves, apses, altars, chapels, sacristies, sculptures, paintings, stained-glass windows, and crèches the fretful busywork of a religion that compulsively filled every cranny of the void with the story and splendor of its incarnate Savior.

Two conflicting theologies in stone, one overlying the other without erasing it. All over Andalusia are churches that once were mosques, the airy lightness of whose minarets now support the weight of Christian bells.

And Judaism? A room in Córdoba, a doorway in Seville. Yes, a doorway: the sole known Jewish feature left in that city is the former entrance to a synagogue that is now part of the church of Santa María la Blanca.

Standing in the Mezquita Cathedral, a Jew feels envy. How much *they* did for the glory of God, and how little we!

Of course, we never had the opportunity. Grand mosques were not built in Christian Spain, nor grand churches in

Muslim Spain, nor grand synagogues in either. And yet even when Jews have erected such structures where they could, as in nineteenth- and twentieth-century Europe and America, their hearts have not been in them. It is a striking thing about Judaism, a religion that codified everything expected of its practitioners in exhaustive detail, that it has almost no rules regarding a synagogue's appearance. Whereas mosques and churches have their architectural traditions, there are none for what the outside of a Jewish house of worship should look like. This remains true even in Israel, where, unless there is a menorah or Star of David on its roof, a synagogue cannot be distinguished from any other public building and need not be a building at all, since a plain room, large or small, will do as well.

And so another thought, ironic and dissident, came to me in the Mezquita Cathedral. *For whom*, it asked, *did you intend all this pomp, you who built and decorated this place? Did you think God was so easily impressed?* "Behold, the heaven and heaven of heavens cannot contain Thee," Solomon said in dedicating his Temple. "How much less this house that I have builded!" True, he went ahead and built it anyway, but this was a folly Jews committed only twice. Christians and Muslims have never stopped repeating it.

It was then that I thought, too, of a poem of Yehuda Halevi's, one known in the terminology of Hebrew liturgical verse as an *ofan*. In the great theophany of the prophet Ezekiel, the *ofanim* are the wheels that bear the heavenly chariots of God's angels, and in later rabbinic tradition, they are a kind of angel themselves. Thus, an *ofan* in Jewish prayer is a poem inserted into the description, found in the Sabbath and holiday morning service, of the angelic hosts worshiping God, right before their ecstatic crescendo of "Holy, holy, holy is the Lord of hosts; the whole earth is full of His glory!"

Halevi's *ofan* goes:

> Lord, where will I find You?
>   Your place is remote and concealed.
> And where will I not find You?
>   Your being fills the world.

> Creator of All, You are in all that is small.
> To the far You are near, to the near You are here.
> An ark was Your home—so is heaven's dome:
>   Its Hosts sing Your praises and You are host to
>   their clan.
>   The spheres cannot hold You, but a room can.

> Alone and unknown, above on Your throne,
> You are closer to man than his own skin and bone.
> His words proclaim that it was You who made him.
>   Who does not know You? Your yoke is his guide.
>   Who does not pray to You to provide?

> I have longed for Your presence, I have called You in
>   your absence,
> I have found You come to meet me as I set out to greet
>   You:
> In Your holiness I saw You, in the wonder of Your
>   glory.
>   Yet who has not seen You, if ever he saw,
>   In skies that are silent, stars loud with awe?

Did You truly decide to reside in man's midst?
O let him but trust in that, made out of dust,
Though You dwell in Your solitude, sacred and
                                        blessed!
    The seraphs extol You from their supreme
                                        height:
    They carry Your seat—and You, the world's
                                        weight.

The spheres cannot hold You, but a room can: the paradox of a God who is both transcendent and immanent, outside yet inside His creation, runs through Yehuda Halevi's religious thought. Although he was not a mystic in the full sense of the word, he knew the feeling of being close to the "alone and unknown." And yet what was a God who dwelled in solitude doing in man's midst? And not just in the midst of men but in the midst of a tiny group of them! The whole of *The Kuzari* is a grappling with the question of why the infinite creator of all things would choose to limit His revelation of Himself to a particular people such as the Jews, in a particular place such as the Land of Israel, in a particular form such as Judaism. Indeed, the omnipotent and omniscient Lord of the universe not only entered all that was small, He preferred it. The synagogue on Calle de los Judíos was just His size.

Córdoba must have received Yehuda Halevi enthusiastically. The most celebrated Hebrew poet of his day, he was a man who liked to mix with people. In Córdoba he had many old friends and acquaintances. There was Avraham ibn Ezra, a ruefully witty and financially unsuccessful wanderer who once joked in a poem that if he were to go into the candle trade, the sun would never set, and that men would cease to die if he sold shrouds. There was Yosef ibn Tsaddik, the recipient of Moshe ibn Ezra's girdle song that had enabled the young Halevi to extract an invitation to Granada; now a philosopher of note, he wrote a flowery poem of welcome to Halevi. There was the poet and rabbi Yosef ibn Sahl, a prominent product of the Lucena yeshiva. There was Maimonides' father, the rabbinical judge Maimon ben Yosef, a Lucena graduate, too. When Yehuda Halevi left Córdoba in 1140, Maimonides was two years old. There is nothing to prevent one from imagining him, a visitor in Maimon's home, gaily dandling the future philosopher on his knee.

Yet the overall mood in Andalusia was apprehensive. Almoravid rule was beginning to totter. Although the Almoravids had an administrative center in Seville, Muslim Andalusia was run as an overseas extension of their kingdom in Morocco, which was now on its last legs. A new armed movement of Islamic puritanism, founded by the Berber zealot Muhammed ibn Tumart, had risen in rebellion and was steadily closing in on the Almoravid capital of Marrakesh. Calling themselves *el-muwahidun*, "the worshipers of the one God," which became *los almohades*, the Almohads, in Spanish, the rebels turned the tables on the Almoravids by accusing them of the very vices they had come to power to uproot: laxity of faith, corruption, sinful materialism, and a reprehensible willingness to come to terms with Christian rulers instead of subduing them. The more inevitable an Almohad victory in Morocco appeared to be, the more clearly numbered were the Almoravids' days in Andalusia. Córdoba was the first Andalusian city to react. As early as 1119, when Almohadism was still in its infancy, an anti-Almoravid revolt broke out there and was crushed.

In the north, too, the Almoravids, their military push against Christian Castile exhausted, were on the defensive. Alfonso VII of Castile, the son of Urraca, was staging a series of increasingly daring raids into Andalusia. (In 1146 his forces would even seize Córdoba and briefly hold it.) In 1135 Alfonso had himself crowned "Emperor of All of Spain," a purely symbolic proclamation that nevertheless signaled his intention of conquering Andalusia if he could, thus delivering another blow to the dying spirit of *convivencia*. Never before had a Catholic ruler in Spain formally rejected the idea of Christian-Muslim cohabitation in favor of a fight to the finish.

The impending fall of the Almoravids sent shock waves through the Jewish communities of the Muslim south. Messianic expectations, easily roused from their dormancy in periods of historical instability and regime change, were stirred up. Messianic ferment had already broken out during the preceding decades in parts of the Jewish world, set off by millenarian hopes pinned on the thousandth anniversary of the fall of Jerusalem and the destruction of the Temple in 70 C.E. In 1060 a Jew declared himself the Messiah in the French city of Lyon and was killed by a Christian mob. Not yet born at the time, Halevi was later to write a heavily alliterative poem about the disappointment of such hopes in which he compared the Jewish people waiting in exile for God's deliverance to a bird lost in a forest and seeking her mate. It began:

> Far-wandering, the woodward-strayed dove
> Flails in the boughs and can't find her way out,
> Flounders and flings herself all about,
> Frantically beating her wings toward her love.
> A thousand years have now passed—yet her term
> Is not over, her dreams have been dashed.

But the messianic fervor kept up. In the 1090s, rumors of the Messiah's impending arrival, originating in Salonika, spread through Jewish communities in the Byzantine Empire. Several years later they reached Spain. Once again Córdoba took the lead. Close to the year 1100, a group of the city's Jews formed a secret society for the purpose of calculating the date of Redemption. As related seventy years later in his *Epistle to Yemen* by Maimonides, who knew of the episode from his father:

> There was in Córdoba a circle of prominent men who believed greatly in astrology and agreed that the Messiah would come that same year. Night after night they asked for divine guidance in their dreams as to whether he would be a fellow countryman [i.e., an Andalusian], and in the end they decided that he was a pious and reputable [Córdoban] Jew named Ibn Aryeh, a teacher of religion. They [supposedly] performed miracles and told the future . . . and so won the hearts of the populace. But when this became known to the heads and rabbis of the community, they had Ibn Aryeh brought before an assembly in the synagogue, where they flogged and punished him and declared him ostracized for having failed to speak out and having permitted these men to make use of his name without reproving

their sinfulness. All his followers were treated in the same manner—and thus they [the Jews of Córdoba] were saved in the nick of time from [reprisals by] the Muslims.

The Epistle to Yemen is also our main source of knowledge for a more extensive messianic movement that formed around a Moroccan Jew named Moshe el-Darri, who arrived in Andalusia in the late 1130s or early '40s with the tidings that he was the Messiah's herald. El-Darri, too, performed "miracles," such as predicting that on a certain day the heavens would rain blood—and indeed, Maimonides wrote, a "red and grimy" rain fell that day. (Red dust rain, originating in fine particles of airborne soil from the Sahara Desert, is a known meteorological phenomenon in southern Spain.) Many of el-Darri's followers obeyed his instructions to sell all their property and borrow money that would not have to be repaid because the Messiah was arriving on Passover, leaving them homeless and penniless when the holiday came and went. El-Darri himself fled to Palestine and died there.

There were still other messianic prognosticators, such as the Jewish astronomers Yohanan ibn Da'ud of Toledo and Avraham bar Hiyya of Barcelona, both of whom read the approaching End of Days in the stars; the latter's book *Megilat ha-Megaleh*, "The Scroll of the Unscroller," made public in 1129, laid out a detailed timetable for the Redemption. All this helps to explain a dream that Yehuda Halevi had in 1130, the Jewish year 4890, and a poem he wrote about it. The words italicized in my translation appear there in Aramaic and were taken by Halevi from the

Book of Daniel, traditionally mined by Jews for its cryptic predictions:

> Heart pounding, you wake. Is it as it seemed?
> What is this dream that you have dreamed?
>
> Did its vision truly show
> Yourself raised high and your foe laid low?
>
> Tell Hagar's son, then, "Cease to scorn
> The son of Sarah, higher born,
>
> For in my dream you were undone.
> Has your doom so soon begun
>
> That in the year 4890
> Your sway will end in naught also?*
>
> Proud tyrant! Assailant of heaven! Are you not the
> one
> Called 'wild ass of a man' and *pum memalel ravrevan*,
>
> The last to rise against God's Law,
> *Ḥasaf tina be-raglei farzela?*
>
> Suppose He struck you down with *avna di-meḥat
> Tsalma*, and paid you back for all that you begot!"

---

* "End in naught," which also punningly refers in my translation to the last cipher of "four-eight-nine-oh," reflects a numerical play on words in Halevi's Hebrew. There the line reads *u'shnat tatatz tutatz lekha kol ga'avah*, "And in the year 4890 [*tatatz*, whose letters *tet*, *tet*, and *tzadi* add up to 890] all your pride will be smashed [*tutatz*]."

Any educated Jew of Halevi's time would have understood this poem's allusions immediately. "Hagar's son" who is "laid low" is the biblical Ishmael, the father of the Arabs in biblical and rabbinic tradition, while the "son of Sarah" is his half brother Isaac, the second of Judaism's three Patriarchs. Although it would have been imprudent of a Jew publicly to accuse Muslim tradition of falsification in claiming that Ishmael, not Isaac, was Abraham's favored and nearly sacrificed son, Halevi did not hesitate to designate Isaac "higher born."

"Wild ass of a man" is an epithet for Ishmael in the Book of Genesis; he is "the last to rise against God's law" because Islam was preceded in its rejection of Judaism by paganism and Christianity. The phrase from Daniel, *pum memalel ravrevan*, "a mouth speaking high-and-mighty things," is sarcastically applied by Halevi to Mohammed's oracular style in the Koran. *Ḥasaf tina be-raglei farzela*, "feet of iron mixed with clay," comes from the Babylonian king Nebuchadnezzar's dream of a "great image" or idol, interpreted by Daniel to represent the four evil kingdoms of history; the fourth and last, represented by the idol's feet that symbolize a realm "divided . . . partly strong and partly broken," stands in Halevi's poem for the rule of the Almoravids, about to fall to the Almohads. *Avna di-meḥat tsalma*, "the stone that smote the image" (the verse in Daniel continues "upon its feet of iron and clay and broke them to pieces"), is taken as a foretelling of the Almoravids' approaching end.

Daniel's interpretation of Nebuchadnezzar's dream concludes with the eschatological prophecy that, after the destruction of all four kingdoms, "God in heaven shall set up a kingdom that shall never be destroyed." Did Halevi, too, believe he was living in messianic times? There is no real reason to suppose he did. A dream is only a dream—and like most Jews, he dreamed of the end of Muslim and Christian domination and the restoration of Jewish independence. As he was to argue in *The Kuzari*, however, he did not think, as most Jews did, that his responsibility ended there.

Both Halevi's "Lord, Where Will I Find You?" and "Heart Pounding, You Wake" have religious themes. Yet by Hispano-Hebrew criteria, they belonged to two separate categories. The first was *shirat kodesh*, "sacred poetry." The second was *shirat ḥol*, generally translated as "secular poetry."

The difference was thus not necessarily one of content. Although all "sacred" poems dealt with religious concerns, "secular" poems could do so also. On the whole, secularism did not mean to Hebrew poets of Halevi's age, who lived ritually observant lives like nearly all Jews, what it means today. It implied not a rejection of religion but the acceptance of another, parallel domain of experience and an exploration of the tensions between the two. These tensions were considered natural because human life was viewed dualistically, as the union of a mortal body and an immortal soul that collaborated at times and were in conflict at others. Each had its claims and responsibilities, and a poet could, at different moments, take the side of either or of both. When Moshe ibn Ezra writes in one poem "Pass the cup, which will banish sadness from my heart" while dismissing drink in another poem as unable to quench the "parched heart's" spiritual thirst, he need not have been writing at two different times of his life. He might have been, of course: as a poet grew older and his body became less reliable, he naturally sided more with the soul. But Ibn Ezra could equally well have written both poems in proximity as part of the body-soul dialogue, with no sense of being inconsistent. Both would have been considered secular.

Nor was the difference one of form; although the sacred poem was not obliged to be metrical and rhymed like its secular counterpart, it frequently was or else had an intermediate nature. The Hebrew of "Lord, Where Will I Find You?," for example, has biblical syllabic stress but the rhyme scheme and stanzas of an Andalusian girdle song. That the girdle song, commonly associated with levity and profaneness, should have lent its structure to such a poem is itself indicative of the reciprocity that existed between the realms of *kodesh* and *ḥol*.

At bottom, the distinction between the two kinds of verse was strictly functional. Sacred poetry, also known in Hebrew as *piyyut* (a word deriving, like the English "poetry," from the Greek *poietis*), was meant to be incorporated into the synagogue liturgy. Secular poetry was not. This is what puts "Lord, Where Will I Find You?," an *ofan* written for the morning service, in a different classification from "Heart Pounding, You Wake," which had no such purpose.

Almost all Hispano-Hebrew poets of importance who wrote *shirat ḥol* wrote *shirat kodesh*, too. As members of the Jewish community who participated in its religious life, they were expected to contribute their talents to it. In return, they were probably often, if not always, paid for their contributions. Although little is known about the financial aspect, it is unlikely that men like Shlomo ibn Gabirol, Moshe ibn Ezra, Yehuda Halevi, and Avraham ibn Ezra would have written the large amount of liturgical verse that they did had they not been well recompensed. *Paytanim*, or professional liturgical poets, were a feature of Jewish life as far back as the fourth or fifth century. Their task was not to compose any of the prayers regularly recited during the three daily services, whose different weekday, Sabbath, and holiday versions were by then largely standardized. Rather, it was to embellish the liturgy with additional, optional prayers that could be included or omitted as the cantor wished. Such *piyyutim* were generally written with a particular day of the year, part of the service, or weekly Torah reading in mind, and it was up to the cantor to set them to melodies of his own composition or choosing.

Many early *paytanim* were forgotten with time; others are numbered today among the great Hebrew poets. Some sought to be remembered by weaving their names into their poems, as did Menachem ben Saruk in writing to the king of the Khazars. In the Hispano-Hebrew period, this became a common practice. Though every new *piyyut* eventually entered the public domain, being the first congregation to introduce a poem signed "Shlomo" by Ibn Gabirol, or "Yehuda" by Halevi, must have had a cachet comparable to a contemporary American synagogue's acquisition of a stained-glass window by a well-known artist.

Such a signature of Halevi's can be found in a type of *piyyut* known as a *reshut*, the literal meaning of which is "permission." (Originally, a *reshut* was a prayer in which the cantor asked God's permission to pray on behalf of the congregation.) One variety of a *reshut* was a *nishmat*—a grammatically inflected word meaning "the soul of" or "the breath of" and commencing the part of the Sabbath and holiday morning service that begins *Nishmat kol ḥai tevarekh et shimkha adonai eloheynu*, "The breath of all that lives shall bless Your name, O Lord our God." A liturgical *nishmat* was a short poem sung by the cantor right before this section, and a *nishmat* of Halevi's went:

My soul!
Cross God's threshold at dawn and breathe to Him
                              sweet-incensed song.
How long will you follow Time's follies and think that
                              their witchcraft is truth,
Though your days' and nights' revels and mornings
                              slept softly away
Will soon leave you holding only the dead branch of a
                              tree?
Shelter under the wing of your Lord and your King,
May His great name be praised by all that lives from
                              His breath!

"All that lives from His breath" would have led directly into "The breath of all that lives shall bless Your name, O Lord our God," the cantor proceeding uninterruptedly from one to the other. Yet at the same time, this *nishmat* has a poetic unity of its own, starting with the breath of the worshiper as he enters the synagogue in the early morning and ending with God's breath of life in him. Prayer is depicted here as a divine circuitry in which God exhales, so to speak, into man and then inhales His own exhalation. (In the Hebrew, the second half of Halevi's opening line, with its literal meaning of "and offer your song like incense to His nostrils," makes this image more explicit.) But learning to breathe with God demands spiritual discipline. It cannot be done without throwing off the warm blankets of sensory pleasure and illusion in order to greet the dawn of a higher reality.

As is the case with "Lord, Where Will I Find You?," in which the poet searching for God finds God searching for him, "My Soul! Cross God's Threshold" is tinged by a mystical outlook that differs from that of older Jewish mysticism. There, the seeker of God, though able to approach Him in steps, can never really draw near Him. The closer he gets, the more terrifyingly transcendental God becomes.

In the poetry of Halevi and his Hispano-Hebrew peers, on the other hand, a genuine intimacy with God is attainable. Yet the idea of it, though owing much to the Islamic influence of Sufism, shies away from the belief in a union of the human and divine that was some Sufis' goal. A statement like that of the tenth-century Muslim mystic El-Hallaj, who wrote in a poem that "I am He whom I love and He whom I love is I," is inconceivable in Hispano-Hebrew verse. (For that matter, it was exceptional in Sufism, too. El-Hallaj was put to death by the authorities for blasphemy, and the lesson was learned. Even the remarkably daring thirteenth-century Sufi Jalaluddin Rumi, in declaring that man's answer to God's question of "Who are you?" should be "I am You," took care to put this in the form of a parable.)

Another variety of *reshut* was called a *barkhu*, a term taken from the invocation *Barkhu et adonai ha-mevorakh*, "Bless ye the Lord who is blessed," which begins the section of the prayer following the *Nishmat kol ḥai*. Halevi has left us *barkhu*s embroidered with his name, too. One reads:

My thoughts of You wake me at night and I muse on
                Your kindness to me.

It helps me to fathom the soul You have lodged in me,
>   which yet is beyond me.
I see and believe in You in my heart as though Sinai
>   rose over me.
I have sought You in visions and in their clouds Your
>   glory enveloped me.
And I think: my Lord who is blessed, let me rise at
>   day's dawning to bless You!

Here again we have a "soft" mysticism, a desire for close-
ness to God without the aspiration to submerge one's human
selfhood in Him. Indeed, the self is uniquely foregrounded
by such poems. As the scholar of medieval Hebrew literature Raymond Scheindlin has observed, many Hispano-
Hebrew *piyyutim* have a distinctive "personal flavor" that is
unprecedented in earlier Jewish liturgy. This is particularly
true of the *reshuyot*, which by definition stressed the "I" of
the cantor and of the poet standing behind him.

In other types of *piyyutim*, however, this "I" is little more
than a proxy for the congregational "we." One such type was
known as a *ge'ula*, a "redemption," because it was inserted
into the service before the words *Barukh ata adonai, ga'al yisra'el*, "Blessed are You, O Lord, who redeems Israel." The
tone of the *ge'ulot* was often anguished, since century after
century the prospect of national redemption had receded as
the Jews' subservient status grew worse. The question of
why God's chosen people should be made to endure an endless exile at the mercy of Muslim and Christian kingdoms
that scoffed at His law was a vexing one. The *ge'ula* was a
place for asking it, as Halevi did when he wrote:

Your will be done until your anger is gone.
Must I always be parted from You by my sin?

How long must I seek You and of You find no sign?
Why, O Ark-Dweller beneath cherubs' wings,
Have you enslaved me to strangers when You are
                                        mine?
Redeemer, look down on my folk from Your place and
                                        redeem!

The theology of this *ge'ula* is conventional: inasmuch as
God (characteristically described by Halevi as both near and
far, "Ark-dwelling" and "looking down" from above) has not
forgiven Israel for its sins, the chastisement of exile must be
borne. Yet the final line hints at rebellion. One would have
expected it to read, "Redeemer, look down on *Your* folk from
Your place and redeem." The unexpected "my" as though
declares to God: You say we are Your people—but You are in
Your place and I am in mine, and from where I am, Your
redemption is not discernible.

Closely akin to the *ge'ula* was the *ahava*, whose blessing of
Ohev amo yisra'el, "Who loves His people Israel," occurs in
the liturgy shortly before "Who redeems Israel." Several of
Halevi's *ahavot* also touch on God's perceived abandonment
of the Jews, but from a different perspective. Here the stress
is on His love, which is eternal even if it is felt to be with-
drawn. In one *ahava*, Halevi depicts God and Israel, in openly
sexual terms, as a temporarily estranged but ultimately
inseparable pair of lovers. This was a less bold metaphor
than might appear at first glance. Not only do the biblical
prophets frequently compare Israel to a woman, alternately
virginal and sluttish, courted and rejected, who is God's
great but unhappy love; rabbinic midrash, too, has recourse
to such imagery, particularly in its interpretation of the
Song of Songs. Other poets of Halevi's age followed in the

midrash's footsteps, and the last two lines of this *ahava* inset the Song of Songs' verses, "The coals [of love] are coals of fire, a godly flame. Many waters cannot quench love, neither can the floods drown it." The poem reads in its entirety:

> A rare beauty far from her place of high birth:
>> Why does she laugh when her lover is wroth?
> She laughs at the daughters of Edom and at
>> Arabia's mignons and at the thought
> That they covet her beau. Low-born sows!
>> Don't they know that she lay in his arms as his
>>> doe?
> Where are their Prophets? Where their Menoráh?
>> Where their Holy Ark and Shekhináh?
> Don't, my foes, don't hope to quench love's desire.
>> You will only be burned by its fire.

The "rare beauty" of this poem is the exiled Jewish people, while Edom is a rabbinic term for Christendom. (The mountains of Edom were the dwelling place of the biblical Esau, Jacob's brother, the ancestor of Rome and Christianity in rabbinic tradition.) Despite their degraded condition, "A Rare Beauty" affirms, the Jews can mock their rivals' pretensions in the confidence that they alone are God's true love. Only to them did He plight His troth with its dowry of Prophecy, the Holy Ark and seven-branched candelabrum in the Temple, and the Shekhinah, the divine presence dwelling in the Holy of Holies. No matter how long His quarrel with Israel lasts, God could no more lose His heart to the "low-born sows" vying with it than a king could choose a rude peasant girl over a princess.

"Low-born sows"—my translation of the Hebrew *pra'im*,

"wild desert asses"—is strong language. Yet Halevi was far from the only Hispano-Hebrew poet to resort to such terms. Even at the height of *convivencia*, in the first half of the eleventh century, the metaphor of Judaism as an elegant "gazelle" and Islam as a rude "desert ass" can be found in the poetry of Shlomo ibn Gabirol, and Hebrew poets in Andalusia routinely employed a wide range of biblically derived epithets, generally uncomplimentary, to refer to Islam and Christianity alike. Although they may have preferred life in the Muslim south of Spain to that in the Christian north, they were equally scornful of both religions.

On the whole, there is little basis for the common assertion that medieval Jews felt more comfortable with Islam than they did with Christianity because the former was rigorously monotheistic whereas the latter, with its doctrine of the Trinity, its man-God, and its dependence on visual icons was tainted by polytheism and idol worship. If anything, precisely because Islam was more like Judaism in its theology and religious outlook, the envy and humiliation inflicted by it were greater; psychologically, after all, it is those we most resemble whose success most wounds us when set beside our failure, since it suggests that our problem lies in being inferior rather than different. It was easy for Jews to rationalize the triumph of Christianity in terms of its compromises with idolatry, which allowed it to appeal to a world too weak and sinful to renounce pagan ways. It was far harder to explain the ascendancy of Islam, which was theologically as unitarian and anti-iconic as Judaism.

Nor can it be said that medieval Jews were less offended by Islam because it took a more lenient view of them. It is true that while Christianity accused the Jews of killing the son of God and bringing down on themselves an eternal curse, Islam merely blamed them for rejecting the revelation of Muhammed, a sin they shared with Christians and others. But the Christian argument with Judaism, while more bitter, was also more to the point and less demeaning from a Jewish point of view, since Christianity understood every word of the Hebrew Bible to be divinely given and true. Though the Jews, it believed, had misread the "Old Testament," they had not fabricated it or misrepresented its provenance, and its account of their history and chosenness up to the time of Jesus was correct. Inasmuch as the Catholic Church never denied Jews their own reality, the Jewish-Christian argument was profound and focused.

But Islam did deny Jewish reality, right from its starting point in the story of Abraham—which, according to the Koran, had been deliberately tampered with by the Book of Genesis. Nor was this so of Abraham alone. Adam, Noah, Jacob, Joseph, Moses, David, Solomon: the life of every major figure in the Bible is told differently by the Koran, which charges Hebrew scripture and rabbinic tradition with systematic distortion while raiding them for much of its material. "Woe," says Muhammed, "to those who wrote the Book [i.e., the Bible] with their hands and then said, 'This is from Allah.'"

To thinking Jews, this made Islam not a less but a more preposterous faith. If Christianity was an affront to rational monotheism, Islam was an insult to human intelligence itself, since who could take seriously a religion that, having come into existence two thousand years after its parent faith, accused the parent of counterfeiting a past of which it alone possessed the true version? The "mignons of Arabia" were even worse imposters than the "daughters of Edom." The sophistication of their culture was admired. Their language and literature were objects of emulation. But religiously, they were crass upstarts. No adherent of Judaism could hold otherwise.

In 1099 the army of the First Crusade, having fought its way overland from Europe, reached Palestine and conquered Jerusalem from its Seljuk rulers, Turkish Muslims who had taken it from the Egyptian Fatimids a few years earlier. The Crusaders' siege of the city ended with the mass slaughter of its Muslim and Jewish inhabitants, many of the latter herded into a synagogue in the Jewish Quarter and burned alive. Determined to Christianize Jerusalem permanently, the Crusaders barred Jews and Muslims from resettling there. Apart from a period following the failed Bar-Kochba Revolt of 132–135 C.E., when the Romans, too, had declared Jerusalem off limits to Jews, the city had never lacked a Jewish presence since the days of David and Solomon. Its Jewish community under Muslim rule, although small, had allowed Jews to feel they still had a share in it. Now the last vestige of them had been expelled.

This development ended a century whose closing decades witnessed an ominous decline in Jewish fortunes in both the Muslim and Christian worlds. First had come the massacre in Granada; then the anti-Jewish legislation of Gregory VII, the first pope to forbid, in 1078, Christian rulers to employ Jews; then the religious discrimination of the Almoravids; and finally, in 1096, as the First Crusade was getting under way, frightful pogroms in the Rhineland, where thousands of Jews were massacred. Although no one could have foreseen it clearly at the time, the long descent into the brutal anti-Semitism of the later Middle Ages had begun.

Symbolically, the slaughter in Jerusalem was the most disturbing of these events. Jerusalem was not Granada, Mainz, or Speier; it was the city Jews prayed for every day and turned to face in each of their prayers. Now, murdered in it and banned from it, they watched helplessly as Christians and Muslims jousted over it in a war that drove home the reality of Jewish impotence. On the Temple Mount, the most sacred of Jewish sites, the El-Aksa Mosque became the Church of St. Abraham, an image of the crucified Christ hanging above its altar. In an intricately punning *piyyut* written sometime after 1099, Yehuda Halevi called on his fellow Jews to pray for Jerusalem's welfare while imploring God to take vengeance on its conquerors and "roast them with coals made from their Cross [*u'tzlem be'gahaley tzelem*]." It was a punishment fantasized to fit the Crusaders' crime of burning Jews in their synagogues.

Most likely it was after 1099, too, that Halevi had a dream about Jerusalem. We know that, like most people of his age, he took his dreams seriously. In the medieval Muslim world, dreams were thought to have revelatory and predictive powers, and hundreds of manuals were written to codify and interpret their symbols. These guides, whose prototype was the second-century Artimedorus' *Interpretation of Dreams*, were of a general nature and treated dream imagery as invariable for all dreamers. Thus, for example, according to the Sufi author Abd-el-Malik el-Kharkushi, who died in the early eleventh century, a dreamed-of butcher signified impending hardship; a cook, joy and marriage; a turtle, a gift from a foreign land; and so on.

One dream manual probably read by Halevi was written by El-Kharkushi's younger contemporary Avicenna (980–1037). Avicenna's understanding of dreams was more psychological than El-Kharkushi's. The great majority, he held, reflected purely subjective mental states. Produced by the continued functioning of the imaginative faculty while the intellect was asleep, they might consist of jumbled memories of the previous day's events, expressions of unfulfilled desires, or the random associations of a mind freed from the restraints of reason. Yet some had a more objective reality. These were occasioned by a "divine force" that revealed hidden things to worthy individuals and informed them of future dangers or good tidings—the dangers being usually imminent, as God did not wish to keep the righteous in a state of prolonged anxiety, the tidings often of far-off events whose anticipation increased the dreamer's pleasure. Such "true dreams," wrote Avicenna, frequently assumed an explicit rather than a symbolic form and were sometimes sent to reassure persons in distress.

Halevi related his dream in a short poem:

Your dwellings, Lord, are places of love,
And Your nearness is clear as things seen, not guessed
                     of.
My dream took me to Your Temple's mount to sing
In all its lovely worshiping and bring
My offerings with their libations.
Around me swirled thick smoke and ministrations,
Sweet to my ears, of Levites at their stations.

I woke, but when I did You still were there
For me to thank You as befits my prayer.

Jerusalem and its holy places were despoiled. Comfortingly, Halevi dreamed that he had seen them in their erst-
while grandeur and taken part in the Temple's rites while
the smoke of sacrifice rose around him. Since he was a Levite
himself, his dream was also of his own sense of religious
vocation—and since he was a composer of sacred poetry, of
his literary calling as well. The Hebrew word *shir* means
both "song" and "poem," so that "to sing" in the poem's
third line can also mean "to make poetry."

"Your Dwellings, Lord" has another dimension, too. We
have seen how Halevi was drawn to the paradox that "the
Place of the world, which is not His place," to cite a rabbinic
epithet for God, could nonetheless dwell in the world. And
yet though this was a conundrum that human reason could
not resolve, God's dreamed "nearness" is as "clear as things
seen." What is unknowable to the intellect, "Your
Dwellings, Lord" proclaims, can be grasped by direct experience.

Halevi's dream was a powerful one. Like much in his
verse, it cannot be definitely dated. But if we look at his
remarkable sequence of poems about Jerusalem and the
Land of Israel that came to be known to posterity as his
shirey tsiyon, or "songs of Zion," "Your Dwellings, Lord" may
have been the first of them. This is because, unlike the others, it does not express the thought or hope of an actual
journey to Zion. It is as if, when Halevi wrote it, such a hope
did not yet exist—or, going a step farther, as if the hope
were engendered by the dream. In the language of Avicenna,

the dream was the tidings; the hope, the anticipation of their fulfillment.

In the language of Freud, of course, a dream is the expression of an unconscious wish that already exists. (Avicenna, too, knew about such dreams; he just did not attribute any higher significance to them.) But whichever came first, wish or dream, the idea of a journey to Crusader-ruled Palestine now took hold of Halevi and steadily tightened its grip on him. In the shortest and most frequently translated of his songs of Zion, he was to write:

> My heart in the East
> But the rest of me far in the West—
> How can I savor this life, even taste what I eat?
> How, in the chains of the Moor,
> Zion bound to the Cross,
> Can I do what I've vowed to and must?
> Gladly I'd leave
> All the best of grand Spain
> For one glimpse of Jerusalem's dust.

My translation of this poem is a fairly free one.* A more literal rendering, appearing beneath a transliteration of the Hebrew text, would be:

> *Libí*   *v'mizráḥ*   *v'anokhí*   *b'sóf*
> My heart is in the east and I am at the end of
>   *ma'aráv*
>   the west.

---

* For a discussion of my approach to translating Halevi's poems, see Appendix F.

Yehuda Halevi

Eykh   et'amá   et ashér okhál   v'éykh
How will I taste what I eat and how
    ye'eráv?
  will it be sweet?

Eykhá   ashalém   n'daraí   ve'esaraí,   b'ód
How   will I pay my vows and my oaths when

Tsiyón   b'ḥével   edóm   va'aní
Zion is in the domain of   Edom   and I am
    b'khével   aráv?
  in the chain of   Arabia?

  Yeykál b'eynaí   azóv
It would be easy for me to leave
    kol tuv s'farád,   k'mó
  all the goodness of Spain, as

  Yeykár b'eynaí   r'ót
It would be precious for me to see
    afrót d'vír   neḥeráv.
  the dust of the Shrine that is in ruins.

In formal terms, "My Heart in the East" is easily described. It has three long lines, each consisting of twenty-eight or twenty-nine syllables and breaking into two hemistiches. Its Arabic-style meter can be notated as long-long-short long-long-short long-long-long-short long-long-short-long; however, as this does not always coincide with natural syllabic stress, I have indicated the latter with accent marks above the stressed vowels. The poem's three lines rhyme in -ráv, as does its first hemistich. It has one pun, a double play on *ḥevel*, "domain" but also "rope," and *khevel*, "chain," and three phonetically linked pairs of words: *mizraḥ*, "East," and *ma'arav*, "West," *yeykal*, "it would be easy," and *yeykar*, "it would be precious," and *tuv s'farad*, "the goodness of Spain," and *d'vir neḥerav*, "the Shrine [i.e., Temple] in ruins."

All this is cut and dried. But "My Heart in the East" is a living poem—and a perfect one. It is a miniature marvel of balance in which opposites tug in different directions while remaining musically joined; an answer to a riddle that asks what, though torn in two, remains whole; the last moment of equipoise in a man tensing his muscles to jump and to take Jewish history with him.

In small numbers, Jews had journeyed to the Land of Israel before Yehuda Halevi's time, too. Groups of pilgrims, generally from nearby countries like Syria and Egypt, came annually to Jerusalem, most often for the autumn festival of Sukkot. There was a custom of ascending on the holiday to the Mount of Olives in order to mourn the lost glory of the city and its Temple Mount, which lay spread out in full view below. Sometimes these pilgrimages were made in fulfillment of vows of penitence or thanksgiving.

The pilgrims almost always returned home. Few settled in Palestine, where a small Jewish population had continued to exist under Muslim rule. During much of the early Islamic period, the country's largest Jewish community resided not in Jerusalem but in Ramle, the local administrative capital of the Abbasid and Fatimid caliphates. Yet damaged by earthquakes in 1033 and 1067, Ramle, too, had declined in importance by the time Yehuda Halevi was born.

Poorer and less developed than neighboring lands, Palestine had nothing to offer Jews economically. The rabbinic Judaism of the age attached little importance to inhabiting it and did not urge its adherents to do so.

A different position was taken by the Karaites. Eager to gain a foothold in Jerusalem, they emphasized the religious duty of taking up residence in the city, in which they had established a congregation as far back as the ninth century. Many of its members belonged to a group known as the "Mourners of Zion," which practiced an ascetic lifestyle in token of their grief for Jerusalem's fallen state. Their most articulate spokesman was the Karaite polemicist Daniel el-Kumisi, who sent epistles to his co-religionists in the Diaspora calling the latter an "unclean place" in which even synagogue prayer was no better than idol worship. Holiness, Daniel insisted, was to be found only in the Land of Israel and Jerusalem—a city frequented by Christians and Muslims but forgotten by Jews. At the very least, he proposed, every Karaite community should send five of its congregants to live there and should provide for their livelihood.

It was perhaps just as well that El-Kumisi's call for a corvée of settlers went unheeded, because the Karaites of Jerusalem perished together with their Rabbinite rivals in 1099. Elsewhere in Palestine, Jews fled or were killed, too. Although the country's small Jewish community was gradually rebuilt in the following decades, the process was slow. The Spanish Jewish traveler Benjamin of Tudela, visiting Palestine in the late 1160s, found fewer than a thousand Jews scattered in different places, and they must have been even more scarce when Yehuda Halevi was writing his songs of Zion decades earlier. Moreover, at the beginning of the twelfth century, Jewish pilgrimage to the Holy Land came to a halt. Long overland and sea voyages were dangerous, threatened by highwaymen, pirates, and storms, and even Jews prepared to brave them feared the Crusaders, whose edict barring Jewish residents from Jerusalem remained in force for some time. Besides having to put up with the hostility or mockery of its Christian inhabitants, a Jewish pilgrim to the city would have found no Jewish home to stay in, no synagogue, and no kosher food. It was a daunting prospect.

Yet Halevi clung to it. In a poem to Jerusalem, he wrote:

O fair of view! World's joy! Great monarch's home!
For you, from earth's far end, my spirit yearns.
Compassion stirs in me when my mind turns
To your lost cloister and its splendor's doom.
Would that on an eagle's wings I flew
To mix the water of my tears with your parched clay!
Always I think of you—and though your king's away,
And snakes and scorpions scuttle where once grew
Your balm of Gilead, your stones and earth
Would taste, when kissed, like honey in my mouth.

The dust that the poet sought a mere glimpse of in "My Heart in the East" was now imagined as a more intense sweetness, the taste of a lover's kiss. Indeed, "O Fair of View," with its beauteous queen banished from her "cloister" of the temple by the God-king who has abandoned her, has the motifs of a romantic love poem. Its pining lover, its beloved he has been torn from by a cruel fate, its hope for a blissful reunion with her: each has its chapter in Ibn Hazm's *Collar of the Dove*. It is just that she is now a city and a land. As in his *ahavot*, Halevi had Jewish tradition to fall back on in this, for Zion, like the people of Israel, is often personified by the biblical prophets as a woman. Yet Zion's lover in the Bible is God alone. The prophet is her rebuker and comforter, no more.

Halevi's songs of Zion were thus not simply an extension of Jewish tradition. They were a romantic reformulation of it—and the first to realize this was another great Jewish poet, Heinrich Heine. In Heine's long verse narrative "Jehuda Ben Halevy,"* there is a passage that, its whimsicality notwithstanding, is wonderfully astute. Comparing Halevi to the medieval French troubadours and their German counterparts, the minnesingers, Heine called him "in every way the equal / Of Provence's best lute strummers." Then, briefly digressing from him to that "sweet orange-tree land of Christian gallantry," the troubadour country of southern France, he continued:

> O lovely world of nightingales
> In which, in place of the true God,
> Men worshiped Love's false deity
> And to the Muses turned in prayer!
>
> Christian priests with wreathes of roses
> Round their tonsures sang new paeans
> In the limpid Langue d'Oc;
> And their flock, knights in bright armor,
>
> Trotted proudly on their horses,
> Cantillating rhymes and verses

* By the time he wrote this poem, which appeared in 1851 in his volume *Romanzero*, four years before his death, Heine had come to regret his conversion to Christianity. He inserted the "Ben" of "Jehuda Ben Halevy" for metrical purposes. The translation from the German is my own.

In adoration of the Ladies
To whom they gladly kneeled in homage.

(No Lady meant there was no *Minne*,★
Which is why the minnesingers
Had as much need of their women
As a slice of bread needs butter.)

Our celebrated hero also,
Our Jehuda Ben Halevy,
Had the Lady of his heart strings;
And yet she was of an odd sort.

She was not another Laura,
Whose clear eyes, those mortal jewels,
In the cathedral, on Good Friday,
Lit the famous flame in Petrarch—

Nor was she a blushing chatelaine
At the height of youthful blossom,
Who, when the tournament was over,
To the winner gave the laurel.

No, she who our rabbi fell in love with
Was a sorrowful, poor maiden,
The very soul of lamentation:
A damsel called Jerusalem.

At this point Heine digresses again, this time more
lengthily, to relate the ancient legend of how Alexander the

★ "Love" in medieval German.

Great, after defeating the Persian king Darius in battle, found in Darius' tent an exquisite casket used to hold the king's perfumes and declared that he would place in it something even more precious—his copy of Homer's *Iliad*. In Heine's retelling of this story, the casket, passed down through the ages as a jewel box, comes into his possession and is used to hold a poem of Yehuda Halevi's. Whereas, Heine writes, the world's most precious pearl is "But the slime of a poor oyster / Sick and helpless on the seabed,"

> The pearls placed within this casket
> Were by a great man's soul secreted,
> One beautiful and even deeper,
> Far, far deeper, than the seabed.
>
> Yes, they are the pearls of teardrops,
> That Jehuda ben Halevy
> From his weeping eyes let trickle
> For Jerusalem's destruction—
>
> Pearls of teardrops strung together
> On the golden thread of rhyming,
> Crafted into glowing verses
> In the smithy of a poet.
>
> And this pearly teardrop poem
> Is the famous lamentation
> Sung in each and every one
> Of the far-scattered tents of Jacob
>
> On the Ninth of Av, the Hebrew
> Fast day of commemoration

For the holy city's sack by
Titus, son of Vespasianus.

The lamentation Heine had in mind was Halevi's *Tsiyyon halo tish'ali bishlom asirayikh*. Not originally written as a *piyyut*, it is Halevi's only poem to have been incorporated into the Ashkenazi liturgy of Central and Eastern Europe, in which it is recited on Tisha b'Av, the day of mourning for the Temple. Although unable to read it in Hebrew, Heine would have come across a reference to it in Michael Jehiel Sachs' *Die Religiöse Poesie der Juden In Spanien*—the book, published in 1845, that first aroused his interest in Halevi— and may also have remembered it from his childhood visits to synagogue. Addressed to a femininely imagined Land of Israel, the poem begins with a description of Jewish exile and of the poet's yearning for his people's lost homeland:

Zion! Do you wonder how and where your captives
Are now, and if they think of you, the far-flocked
remnants?
From north and south, east, west, and all directions,
Near and far, they send their greetings
As I send mine, captured by my longings
To weep like Hermon's dew upon your mountains.
Mourning your lowliness, I am the wail of jackals;
Dreaming your sons' return, the song of lute strings.
My heart stirs for Peniel, and for Bethel, and all those
places
With their pure traces of God's presence, where your
gates,
Facing the portals of the highest heavens,
Stand opened by your Maker. You He illumines

Not with the sun, or moon, or stars, but with the rays
Of His own glory. Gladly I would choose
To pour my soul out where your chosen ones
Stood in a downpour of God's effluence.

With their strong lyrical sweep, these lines declare that
the Land of Israel does not differ from other countries solely
because of its sacred history. It has a sacred geography as
well, a unique place in the cosmos. And yet this makes its
having fallen under the sway of usurpers even bitterer.

You are the throne of the Lord, His royal house—
How then are slaves enthroned in your lords' houses?
If only I could wander past the way points
Where God appeared to your appointed and your
                                                    seers,
And, flying to you with a bird's wings,
Shake woeful head, remembering the throes
Of your dismemberment, my face
Pressed to your earth, cherishing its soil and stones—
Yes, even so, the graves of patriarchs.
Wondrous in Hebron at your choicest tombs,
I would cross Gilead and Carmel's woods,
And stop to marvel at your lofty peaks
Across the Jordan, on which, illustrious,
Lie buried the two greatest of your teachers.
Your very air's alive with souls;
Your earth breathes incense and your rivers
Run with balm. I would rejoice
To walk with my bare feet, in tatters,
Upon the ruins of your Sanctuaries,

In which, before it was removed from us,
The Holy Ark stood guarded by its Cherubs
Posted at the innermost of chambers—
And then, all worldly pomp cast off, I'd curse
The fate that did defile your peerless pilgrims.
How could I eat or drink, seeing the dogs
Make off with the remains of your proud lions?
How find the daylight sweet when my two eyes
Were forced to witness crows feast on your eagles?

"The two greatest of your teachers" are Moses and
Aaron, buried, according to the Bible, across the Jordan; the
"dogs" and "crows," the warring armies of Christendom
and Islam. Yet the poem ends on a note of consolation.
Zion's fate is not like that of other civilizations, which
flower only to perish. God's promise to it is eternal. Its day
of redemption will come:

Enough, desist from me, O cup of sorrows,
Drained to the dregs of all its bitterness!
Zion! God's love, combined with Beauty's grace,
Has bound to you the souls of all your friends,
So that they joy when you're at peace
And weep when you're all wounds and wilderness.
Imprisoned, they yearn for you, each from his place
Turning to bow in prayer to your gates—
Your many flocks, dispersed to distant hills
Yet ever mindful of their vows
To reascend to you and reach your heights,
As the palm tree, rising above all else,
Is scaled by the bold climber. Who compares
To you? Not ancient Babylon, nor Greece:

What are all their empty oracles
Beside your Prophets and the breast plates of your
priests?
The heathen kingdoms lapse, collapse, and pass,
But you remain forever, crowned for the ages.
God makes His home in you: blesséd are those
Who dwell with Him, residing in your courts.
Blesséd is he who comes, and waits, and sees
The rising sun illuminate your dawns,
In which your steadfast share the happiness
Of your lost youth, restored as it once was.

For Jerusalem's lover, the "bold climber" who ascends to her heights like a daring suitor scaling a balcony, the "poor, sorrowful maiden" of Heine's "Jehuda Ben Halevy" has never ceased to be a beauteous queen. Yet Halevi was, as Heine saw it, not only romanticizing Zion. He was also Judaizing the troubadour's cult of devotion (which, as Heine may have known, reached southern France in Halevi's life-time via the Arabic poetry of Andalusia) by replacing its idealized woman with a divinely chosen holy land. If the new European feminolatry had taken the biblical commandment to love God "with all one's heart and all one's soul and all one's might" and transferred it to a human object, Halevi was now returning it toward its sacred source.

Would Halevi have agreed with Heine's judgment? A comparison of "Zion, Do You Wonder?" with "Why, My Darling, Have You Barred All News?" strongly suggests that he would have. In his entire corpus, "Why, My Darling" 's mono-rhyme of *-ayikh* can be found in only one other poem—and that is "Zion! Do You Wonder," in which the submerged cry of "Where are you?" reverberates in the same way. (I have once again, in my translation, used a final "s" in place of it.) The two poems, moreover, are almost the same length and follow the same progression of emotions. In composing the greatest of his songs of Zion, Halevi was clearly aware of having modeled it on the greatest of his love poems, whose "sea of tears" was now a real body of water dividing Spain from Palestine.

Perhaps Yehuda Halevi did not at first relate to the idea of leaving Spain as anything more than a poetic fantasy. But fantasies either strike root in real thought or atrophy. By 1129, at the latest, he was making practical plans to settle in Palestine.

This information comes to us from a brief Judeo-Arabic letter sent in that year to his Egyptian friend Halfon ben Natanel, who was either spending his last days in Spain while preparing to embark for Egypt or had already sailed. Noting that he was writing hurriedly while "surrounded by people" at one of his open houses, Halevi told Halfon:

> Your warm, dear letters have reached me and soothed my longing [for you]. But God, may He be exalted, may soon provide a solution. . . . I don't mean this metaphorically, but quite literally, as I publicly announced in your presence. My greatest hope is to head east as soon as I can, if only Providence will assist me. As you know, I'm doing all I can [to make it possible].*

---

* For the dating and circumstances of this letter, see Appendix G.

The purpose of "heading east" could not have been just to visit Halfon in Egypt. Besides being risky, sea travel was arduous; medieval ships were small, slow, and uncomfortable, and only adventurers, religious pilgrims, and international traders chose to travel long distances in them. Halevi's plan, as he had already informed Halfon and others at a social gathering, would have been to continue from Egypt to Palestine, which could only be reached via Egyptian ports, with the intention of settling there.

Although this gathering may have been the first occasion when he spoke of his departure as imminent, the direction Halevi was leaning in must have been known to his friends for some time. It could only have met with shock and bafflement. He was the most renowned Hebrew poet of his age, a member of its social elite, a universally liked and admired figure. He was also economically well off, his income from his medical practice having been multiplied by business investments. (A Geniza letter to Halfon from a merchant in Almería informs us of the impressive sum of 150 dinars that was forwarded to Halevi on one occasion, apparently as his share of the profits from a commercial venture.) To give up his way of life, family, friendships, and comforts for a voyage of no return to a country where nothing awaited him but danger, loneliness, and hardship would have seemed akin to madness. He was not a young man. Even if he reached his destination safely, what would he do there? How would he live? There would be no one to welcome or honor him, no Jewish community worthy of its name to take him in. What was he thinking of?

What?

Of an existence, evidently, radically different from the

one he had led until then. We have spoken of the weariness that came over him during his years in Toledo. One might call it a midlife crisis were it not that midlife came earlier for medieval man than it does for us. (Dante, *nel mezzo del camin di sua vita*, was thirty-five.) But a crisis of some sort it was—a need to get away, the feeling of time running out, a sense of something left undone. Halevi disliked the city he was living in. His medical practice was onerous. Two of his three children were dead; he, the doctor, had been unable to save them. His relationship with his wife, however troubled or smooth, shows no signs of having been a deep one. The one woman he had loved passionately had been lost to him long ago; she was now only a distant memory. All the honors and adulation merely weighed on him. They stood between him and himself. Growing old, for most people a process of accommodation to who they are, had become for him the anxiety of who he still was not.

This is of course a modern way of putting it. The Middle Ages thought in terms of body and soul. When the body is young and its passions are strong, the soul is on the defensive; as the body ages and weakens, the soul gains the upper hand. It demands more, is less compromising, more aggressive on its own behalf—but the person it belongs to remains a body and soul yoked together in a single self and must, even if exhausted by the long struggle between them, go on living with both. There is a poem of Halevi's, antedating his songs of Zion, that begins with an expression of extreme religious devotion coupled with a fatigue so great that it is couched as an open death wish; pulls back from this brink with the reflection that, despite the poet's sense of having lived enough, he is unprepared to cast off a world in which he has not yet fulfilled, or even clarified, his true mission; and ends with the confession that this failure makes him as frightened as the next man of the death he thought he had longed for:

> Lord, You are my sole desire,
>> Though I keep it my soul's secret.
> Could I but do Your will and die
>> That moment, I would seek it.
> Placing in Your hands my spirit,
>> I would sleep—and sweet such sleep is.
> Far from You, all life is dying;
>> Death is life with You beside me.
>
> And yet I know not how to further
>> Most my faith or best to serve it.
> Instruct me in Your ways, then, Lord,
>> And free my mind from folly's service.
> Teach me while I have strength to suffer,
>> Nor despise my suffering
> In the time still left before,
>> Myself a burden to myself,
> My cankered bones fail to support me
>> And, my only choice submission,
> I make the voyage to my fathers,
>> Stopping to rest at their last stop
> Deep in the earth, I who once was
>> A sojourner upon its surface.
>
> My young years thought of naught save themselves.
>> When will my world-sated soul save itself?

How worship my Maker when all He has made
    Makes me passion's captive and slave,
Or strive for the heights when at the day's end
    Sister worm awaits my descent?
How, even, be glad in glad times,
    When none know what the future will spell,
And the days underwrite my decay
    With the nights, half of me to dispel
To the wind and half to the dust?
    What can I plead when I am pursued
By my lust from my youth to my wane?
    What of this world but Your will is my share,
And if You are not mine, what is mine?
    What more can I ask or declare?
I am naked of deeds, Your justice my only attire.
    Lord, You are my sole desire.

"Heading east" was the deed he chose to clothe himself in. Friends sought to dissuade him. He argued with them. To one, he wrote an angry poem. "Your words were salved with smoothest myrrh," it began with a touch of sarcasm, which quickly changed to the accusation that the friend's remarks, while "sweetly stated," concealed "stinging bees, their honeycomb a bed of thorns." Although we are not explicitly told what these were, it is possible to reconstruct their two main points from Halevi's reply.

The first was that it was foolhardy to put himself at peril by journeying to a country that was in the hands of barbarians. Although the love of Zion was praiseworthy, one had to be sensible. It was reckless to "seek the peace of Jerusalem" when the city belonged to "the blind and the lame"—an allusion to the Crusaders taken from the Book of Samuel, where the words contemptuously refer to Jerusalem's Jebusite rulers before David's conquest of the city.

Halevi made short shrift of this argument. Was Abraham being sensible, he asked, when he left everything at God's bidding for a promised land? If personal safety came first, "our forefathers erred in being strangers" in a land in which "unjustifiably they built their altars / and sacrificed upon them to no end." To challenge his, Halevi's, decision on such a basis was to accuse the biblical Patriarchs of recklessness.

The friend's second point concerned Spain. In no other country was Jewish life more thriving or secure. How could one abandon it for a wilderness where there was hardly a synagogue to pray in, much less the amenities of civilized life? How could Halevi reject the home in which his ancestors were buried and his family had lived for generations? Surely loyalty to Judaism and its traditions called for remaining in Spain, not leaving it.

The poem's response to this was scathing. The dead, it declared, command our loyalty not by virtue of being dead, but only by virtue of being models for the living. "Are we to haunt old wormy graves," it demanded,

> And turn away from life's eternal source?
> Are synagogues our sole inheritance,
> And is God's holy mount to have no heirs?
> And where, in East or West, are we more safe
> Than in the land whose many gates all face
> The heavens?

Continuing in this vein a while longer, the poem veers off in its final lines on a different tack:

See here, my friend—see here and understand.
Beware of pitfalls, snares, and traps,
And don't be fooled by wisdom of the Greeks,
Which bears flowers but no fruit, its only crop
The crabby apples of an uncreated earth,
A tent of heaven no one pitched,
Time begun at no time, and no end
To the endless cycles of the moon.
Listen to the ramblings of the wise,
Their writings plaster slapped upon a void,
And they will leave you with an empty heart
And a mouthful of vain thoughts and theorems.
Why then should I take the crooked road,
As you would have me do, and lose my bearings?

Though powerful, this is puzzling. Why end a defense of a voyage to the Land of Israel with an attack on ancient Greek philosophy and its doctrine of an eternal universe? What does one thing have to do with the other? Any answer to this question must look at Halevi's own philosophical thought in *The Kuzari*, the subject of our next chapter.

"Your Words Were Salved with Smoothest Myrhh" is the statement of a man who has decided. Indeed, we now know from the Cairo Geniza that within a year of telling his friends he was about to "head east," Halevi said his final goodbyes to them. This is revealed to us by a letter to Halfon, now back in Egypt, from a Granadan acquaintance, Yosef ibn el-Lakhtush. After mentioning that he is writing in the Hebrew month of Sivan (May–June) in "the year 90" (that is, the Jewish 4890 and the Christian 1130, the same year in which Halevi had his dream about the downfall of Islam), Ibn el-Lakhtush extended his condolences for the recent death of a brother of Halfon's, inquired about the latter's activities, and continued:

> Please be so kind as to tell me everything and may you have pleasure, happiness, and benefit from it. Surely God, may He be exalted, knowing your distinguished and superior nature, has been good to you in sending you the very quintessence of our land, our bastion and leader, that honored paragon of erudition and virtue, the peerless Yehuda Halevi. It is our misfortune that we have parted from him and your good fortune that you will be reunited with him. May God grant you pleasure from each other's company and bring us happy tidings of your encounter.

Halevi, as far as Ibn el-Lakhtush was concerned, was already on his way to Egypt. And yet he never reached Egypt, let alone Palestine, in that year—nor do we know why he didn't. Fleischer and Gil, citing his poems, contend that he sailed from Spain to North Africa with the plan of continuing to Egypt by land and turned back. Yet nowhere in his poetry is there an explicit reference to such an expedition, and he could just as well have changed his mind at the last moment while still in Spain.*

What made him change it? It might have been a specific impediment, and it might have been a more generalized fear. Tearing himself away from everything familiar on the threshold of old age was more easily said than done, and he had perhaps internalized his friends' arguments against it more than he cared to admit. Instead of traveling to Palestine,

---

* For further discussion of this episode, see Appendix H.

he moved back from Toledo to Andalusia. In the Cordoban period that followed, he neither gave up the idea of his journey nor, as far as is known, made a second attempt to undertake it. From year to year he put it off while his impatience and aggravation with himself mounted. He was standing, so it seemed to him, before an ultimate test that he lacked the courage to submit to.

Sometime in his fifties—that is, no later than the early 1130s—he wrote a poem about this. In it he takes himself to task for clinging to material pleasures and social enjoyments in disregard of the duty to set out. The distractions of a busy life have encouraged him to postpone what needs to be done, even to question whether he need do it or whether, as some seek to persuade him, he is making unreasonable demands on himself.

He is afraid. Not for the first time, he imagines the sea voyage ahead of him. A fierce storm rages. His ship, its crew paralyzed, threatens to capsize. The passengers pray for their lives.

But at this juncture, as all is about to founder, the poem turns on itself. Or rather, it is the poet who turns—toward Jerusalem. Remembering his destination, where so many of God's miracles have taken place, he is calmed by the thought that one is possible now, too. And with the sudden quieting of his soul, as if the storm's awesome eruption were but the outer manifestation of his inner turmoil, the winds die down and the sea grows still. A serene evening descends. The sun sets on docile waves; a crescent moon, night's "silver-sworded captain," shines in a sky bright with stars; reflected in the water, where they are far from their native land like the pilgrim regarding them, they are now his companions and guides. His heart brims with grateful emotion.

The poem goes:

A man in your fifties—and you still would be young?
Soon your life will have flown like a bird from a
                                        branch!
Yet you shirk the service of God, and crave the
                                        service of men,
And run after the many, and shun the One
From whom the multitudes of all things come,
And laze about instead of setting out
On your true way, and for a mess of pottage
Sell your immortal part. Has not your soul had
                                        enough?
Why then yield each day to its lusts?
Leave its counsel for God's, put the five senses aside,
And make amends to your Maker before your last days
                                        rush away.
Don't pretend you have to seek to know His will,
Or wait for auguries. Will but to do it!
Be bold as a panther, swift as a deer!
Fear not the open sea, though mountains of waves
                                        crest and crash,
And hands shake like rags in a gale,
And speechless ships' carpenters quail,
And crews leap to the task and in dismay stagger
                                        back,
Trapped in an ocean with nowhere to flee
While the sails flap and crack, and the deck creaks and
                                        groans,
And the wind whips the water into haystack-high
                                        bales.
One day it towers like ricks and the next it's flat as a
                                        field,

A ripple of snakes without even a whisper or hiss.
Yet when roiled to a prideful of lions, each hot on the
                    other one's heels,
Mighty fleets reel and are wrecked. Masts totter and
                    fall;
Bulwarks are breeched; the tiers of great triremes are
                    pierced,
Unmanning their oarsmen; men, women, grow faint
                    with dread;
Sailors stand stunned by their shrouds; the living
                    would rather be dead;
The heft of the yards counts for nothing, for nothing
                    the tricks of old tars;
Tall spars are no stronger than straws; cedar beams
                    snap like stems;
The ballast cast out is but chaff; keels have the
                    resistance of grass.

At such times, when each man prays to what is holy to
                    him,
You turn to face the Holiest of Holies.
Recount, then, stamped in men's memories,
The wonders of the Red Sea's parting,
And of the Jordan's in the days of Joshua.
Praise the Soother of the storms that stir the depths,
The Pardoner of stained souls, who for His sainted
                    Patriarchs' sakes
Will pardon yours. Sing Him a Levite's song while He
                    renews
His awesome world, restoring souls to bodies, life to
                    dry bones.

Now the waves subside; like flocks of sheep they graze
                    upon the sea.
The sun has set, departing by the stairs
Up which ascends the night watch, led by its silver-
                    sworded captain.
The heavens are an African spangled with gold, blue-
                    black
Within a frame of milky crystal. Stars roam the water,
Flare and flicker there, outcasts far from home.
The seaward-dipping sky, the night-clasped sea, both
                    polished bright,
Are indistinguishable, two oceans cupped alike,
Between which, surging with thanksgiving, lies a
                    third, my heart.

One of Halevi's most magnificent creations, "A Man in Your Fifties" can be read as a waking dream in which the poet masters his anxiety by letting the worst happen in his thoughts, so that his heart beats as wildly as a ship tossing in high seas and then, the winds subsiding as he regains control of his fears and his breathing becomes regular again, reassuringly slows to the steady pulse of the certitude of being in God's hands.

Meanwhile, however, he was still in Spain.

5

The only explicit mention of Yehuda Halevi's *Kuzari* to have come down to us from his lifetime was made by Halevi himself. At the end of the same answer to Halfon ben Natanel in which he announced his intention of "heading east," Halevi referred to a manuscript that Halfon had heard about from a certain Yosef ben Barzel, a doctor and minor Hebrew poet of the age. Apologizing for not having informed Halfon of its existence, Halevi promised to bring it with him to Egypt:

> And as for the *Book of the Kuzari*, surely that eminent physician and scholar Yosef ben Barzel has been kind to me in praising whatever foolishness comes from my pen, which otherwise I would refrain from showing to you. It all began with a request from a sectarian in Christian lands; he asked me about certain matters, and I sent it [the book] to him and later repudiated it. When we meet again, you shall see it.

And so a book that was to become a classic of Judaism first appears in the historical record as "repudiated" by its own author for its "foolishness"! Is this merely the same sort of self-deprecation with which Halevi dismissed his reputation as a physician? An attempt to soothe Halfon's ruffled feelings at having been kept in the dark about a book Halevi was writing? Or an indication of genuine discontent with a work that was begun, so Halevi's letter tells us, as a casual reply to a Karaite living in Christian Spain who apparently asked Halevi for his views on Karaism and Judaism?*

These possibilities are not mutually exclusive. Halevi was not above a show of modesty, especially if he thought it might mollify Halfon. But *The Kuzari* is also a book whose text, divided into five parts, shows clear signs of having been rewritten and enlarged more than once, with its original critique of Karaism ending up in the second half of Part III as a mere tenth of the whole. It is likely, then, that the version called "foolish" in 1129 was an early one that Halevi was unhappy with and proceeded to revise.

Certainly, had *The Kuzari* not been expanded beyond the short treatise it was begun as, it would not have touched on philosophical matters at all. The dispute between Rabbinism and Karaism was a purely historical one, having to do with whether the Oral Law of Jewish tradition was the unbroken chain going back to Moses that the rabbis held it to be or, rather, as the Karaites maintained, a rabbinic invention. Both sides agreed that the Torah was God's permanently binding revelation to mankind; their dispute was over how to read it. Yet while this quarrel might be compared to the Catholic-Protestant schism of later centuries, with rabbinic Judaism claiming a divinely sanctioned authority to interpret Scripture freely and the Karaites insisting on every individual's right and obligation to arrive

---

* Writing in Arabic, Halevi described this man with the Hebrew phrase, into which he inserted an Arabic definite article, *ehad mi-nitkaley al-minut*, "someone tripped up by sectarianism." In the context of medieval Spain, this could only have meant a Karaite, as is also clear from the use of the word *minut* in *The Kuzari* itself.

at a more literal understanding of his own, Rabbinism and Karaism were never separated by the deep theological gulfs that split Christianity. Their differences were confined to specific laws and rituals, with the Karaites often taking the more stringent view—as when, for example, they challenged the rabbinic ruling that the biblical prohibition on making a fire on the Sabbath allowed the warming or cooking of food if the oven was lit before the day of rest commenced.

Halevi's reply to his Karaite interlocutor was historically oriented, too. Essentially, it was three-pronged. To begin with, it argued, the Mosaic law could not have been observed even in Moses' day without an interpretive approach, since its many general precepts had to be amplified and clarified if they were to serve as the basis for a concrete way of life. Second, the Karaites' insistence that every Jew should be his own biblical commentator cannot possibly have been Moses' intention, since this would have led to a proliferation of different Judaisms in his own lifetime, let alone in subsequent ages. And last, inasmuch as a normative tradition of interpretation was necessary, there is no reason to doubt the rabbis' tracing of it from Moses' disciple Joshua through the biblical Judges, the Prophets, Ezra and Nehemiah, and the early Pharisees to its eventual codification in the Talmud and its commentators. This is a reliable narrative that no single person or group could have counterfeited, as it was handed down by communities of reputable men who would not have tolerated the falsifications of innovators. The stricter constructionism of the Karaites is only proof, Halevi wrote, of the weakness of their position, since the Rabbinites are "at ease in the traditions they possess and have confidence in them, as does a man walking in city streets without fear of being waylaid, whereas [the Karaites] are like one who ventures into the wilderness with no idea of what may befall him, so that he must be armed and ready for battle at all times. Let it not surprise you, therefore, that their exertions are greater, nor disappoint you that the bearers of tradition—that is, the Rabbinites—strike you as more lax."*

Halevi began his anti-Karaite critique while living in Toledo, the likely venue of a meeting between him and a "sectarian in Christian lands." Subsequently, he decided to expand it and give it a fictional setting and a dialogue form that would appeal to a wider audience. For this he chose a story that he knew from the letters of Hasdai ibn Shaprut and King Joseph: the conversion to Judaism, sometime in the eighth century, of the pagan king of Khazaria, the "Kuzari" of the book's title. (Halevi may also have met and spoken to descendants of Khazar Jews in Toledo, for, writing several decades later, the chronicler Avraham ibn Da'ud speaks of a number of them living there.) And at the same time, he broadened the book's focus: no longer restricted to the argument for rabbinic Judaism against Karaism, it now made its case against all comers. This is reflected in the rhymed Arabic subtitle that Halevi gave *The Kuzari*'s final version, *Kitab al-Haja w'ad-Dalil Fi Nasr ad-Din ath-Thalil*, "The Book of Proof and Demonstration in Defense of the Despised Faith."

---

* All quotations from *The Kuzari* in this chapter have been translated into English by me from two Hebrew versions of Halevi's Arabic: Yehuda ibn Tibbon's twelfth-century rendition and Yehuda Even-Shmuel's 1994 one. I have also consulted, and at times borrowed language from, Hartwig Hirschfeld's 1905 English translation.

Rabbinic Judaism's principal "despisers" in twelfth-century Spain were Christianity and Islam—and indeed, whereas spokesmen for these two religions appear in *The Kuzari*'s prelude, the Karaites, though mentioned in it, are unrepresented.

This prelude begins:

> I have been asked about the arguments and rebuttals known to me that might be useful in replying to those who attack our religion, whether they be adherents of philosophy, believers in other faiths, or Jewish sectarians. This caused me to recall what I once heard about the arguments made by a rabbi to the king of the Khazars, who became a Jew some four hundred years ago.

The narrator-author continues:

> This king—so it is said—had a dream that kept recurring. In his dream appeared an angel, who spoke to him and said: "Your intentions are worthy in the eyes of the Creator, but your deeds are not." Now, the king was a scrupulous observer of the religion of the Khazars, so much so that he personally officiated in their temple and offered sacrifices with all his heart. Yet no matter how scrupulous he was, the angel kept appearing night after night and telling him: "Your intentions are worthy, but your deeds are not."

Taking his dream as seriously as Yehuda Halevi took his dream of Jerusalem, the king resolves to discover what it requires of him. Since the angel has spoken in the name of a monotheistic Creator, the king does not bother to investigate other forms of polytheism. The first person he asks to talk to is a philosopher, a man representing the Neoplatonic school of thought that was intellectually fashionable in Muslim and Jewish circles during Yehuda Halevi's age. The philosopher, whose formal religious affiliation is unstated, tells the king that all three monotheistic faiths are equally valid symbolic systems meant to represent a higher reality that the ordinary man cannot comprehend without the aid of religious dogmas and rituals for which the philosophic mind has no need. The God of the philosophers is not the rewarding and punishing figure that He is imagined as being by Judaism, Christianity, and Islam, which must entice or frighten their followers into compliance. There is nothing that He needs or wants from mankind, because

the Creator has neither a will nor [likes or] dislikes. He is beyond all desire and intention, since desiring indicates a lack on the part of the desirer, who is incomplete until his desire is fulfilled. Similarly, He is, in the philosophers' opinion, beyond all knowledge of individual details, because these change from moment to moment and the Creator is unchangeable. He therefore has no knowledge of you, much less of your deeds or thoughts, and He certainly does not hear your prayers or observe your activities. And if the philosophers say that He created you, this is merely a metaphor, because although He is the First Cause in the process of creation, nothing is deliberately created by Him, including mankind, the world being eternal and every human being having been born from a predecessor and bearing the features, characteristics, and temperament of his father, mother, and other relations.

These remarks, which sum up the thought of such early Islamic philosophers as Al-Farabi (870–950) and Avicenna, represent the "wisdom of the Greeks" alluded to in Halevi's poem "Your Words Were Salved with Smoothest Myrrh." Although such men preserved in their writings the terminology and outward trappings of Islam, both to protect themselves from charges of heresy and in the belief that the average Muslim required such things, their God presided over a cosmos that ran by rules He was powerless to change. True worship of Him had nothing to do with what religion one practiced or how one lived. It consisted solely of an intellectual contemplation of Him and His "creation"—or, as Al-Farabi and Avicenna put it, borrowing a term from Aristotle, of raising one's mind to the level of the "Active Intellect," the cosmic principle of reason.

The king quickly realizes that philosophy is not the answer to his quest. If the angel has told him that his deeds are unworthy in God's eyes, God must know and care about deeds. Determined to discover which of them are acceptable to Him, he dismisses the philosopher and summons a Christian priest and a Muslim qadi. There is no need in his opinion to speak to a Jew, since the Jews' "lowly state, small numbers, and hateful reputation" rule out their possessing the truth.

The Christian arrives first with a statement of his creed. As opposed to the philosopher, he tells the king, he believes that God alone is eternal; that the world was created in six days, as the Bible says; and that its Creator has emotions and desires and speaks to His prophets. "In short," the priest declares, "I believe all that is written in the books of the Jews. There can be no doubt of the truth of it, because it was revealed to a large mass of people and has been widely known for ages." However, Christians also believe that, subsequently, "the divine essence became embodied in an embryo in the womb of a virgin." The child born was the Messiah, and the Jews earned God's wrath for rejecting him and were replaced as God's chosen by the Messiah's followers. Men's duty is to worship this savior and "exalt the cross on which he was crucified."

The king, unable to conceive of the Creator of the universe being born from the womb of a virgin, let alone crucified, is unimpressed. "Such a religion," he dryly tells the priest, "does not leave much room for logic." Of course, seemingly illogical phenomena do exist; students of nature encounter them all the time without doubting the evidence of their senses. But the Christian doctrine of the Incarnation has no evidence to support it. Therefore, the king declares, sending the Christian away and calling for the Muslim, he cannot accept it.

The Muslim, too, has prepared his presentation. Like the Christian, he informs the king that he believes in the biblical account of creation, the descent of the human race from Adam, and God's revealing Himself through His prophets. However, he differs first in denying all corporeal qualities to the Deity, who could not have assumed human form, and second in holding that the ultimate revelation, superceding all its predecessors, was granted to the greatest of all prophets, Muhammed, in the guise of the Koran. Whoever accepts the Koran, whose language is too divine to be anything but God's own, will enter paradise after death. Whoever does not will suffer eternal punishment.

The king is not convinced by the Muslim, either. Why, he asks, should he believe that the Koran is God's word? As he knows no Arabic and can only read it in translation, its linguistic superiority is not apparent to him. Had its composition been accompanied by a miracle or other unusual event attested to by eyewitnesses, its divine origins might be more creditable. But Muhammed was alone when, as he claimed, God spoke to him, and his followers have to rely on his testimony alone. He, the king of the Khazars, sees no reason to join them. Why would God, "the Creator of this world and of the next world and of all the angels, and the Maker of the heavens and their luminaries," have chosen to communicate with a particular representative of "lowly matter," a single, arbitrarily chosen human being like Muhammed?

The Muslim seeks to parry the king's challenge. One must not, he replies, think of Muhammed in isolation, since he was the last in a long line of prophets. "Our holy Koran," the Muslim argues, "is full of stories about Moses and the Children of Israel, whose truth cannot be called into question . . . and also of what happened before that, such as the Flood and the destruction of Sodom and Gomorrah. Aren't such things so well known that they are beyond all doubt or suspicion of being hoaxes or imaginative delusions?"

The king listens—and draws his own conclusion. If both the Christian and Muslim, he reflects, are forced to fall back on the Jewish Bible in order to defend the veracity of their faith, perhaps he should consult a Jew after all. "I now see," he declares, "that they [the Jews] are the only proof that God has given a law to mankind." And so, *The Kuzari* tells us, "The king then sent for a rabbi and asked to hear about his religion."

The rabbi, too, arrives promptly. Yet his opening words

strike the king as impromptu and disjointed. Rather than begin like the Christian and Muslim at the beginning, he plunges directly into what should logically come later, and then, as if quickly exhausted by his first long sentence, stops short. "I believe," he declares,

> in the God of Abraham, Isaac, and Jacob, who delivered the Children of Israel from Egypt with signs and wonders and sustained them in the desert and gave them the land of Canaan after bringing them safely across the Red Sea and the Jordan with many miracles, and who sent them Moses with His Torah, and thousands of prophets after him, all of whom preached His Torah while promising a reward to those who obeyed them and punishment for those who disobeyed. We believe in everything this Torah has written in it—but it's a long story.

The king is offended. Surely the rabbi could have been expected to make a long story short! Huffily, he replies:

> I see now that I had good reason not to inquire of the Jews, because I knew all along that they no longer remember or think clearly, their poverty and abasement having left them no good qualities. Don't you suppose, Jew, that you should have begun by telling me that you believe in a Creator of the world who orders and oversees it, and who made you and gives you your daily bread, and has other divine attributes such as are credited to Him by all religious people, so that they strive for truth and justice in their desire to be like Him?

The rabbi is unfazed. "What you say," he replies, "applies to all religions based on human reason and the needs of society." Though no argument for or against any of them can ever be decisive, this is not the case with Judaism.

This piques the king's interest. "What you say now, Jew," he declares, "is more to the point than what you said at first. I'm ready to hear more."

"But what I said at first *is* the point!" the rabbi answers—and with that, philosopher, priest, and qadi vanish, and we are left with the king, the rabbi (or "friend," as *The Kuzari* calls him*), and the case for Judaism, which the rest of the book proceeds to make.

The rabbi's opening statement is indeed the point. While *The Kuzari* is an intricate book with many themes, its central motif is that Judaism is a fundamentally different kind of religion from Christianity and Islam. The latter are soteriological. They make claims for a single savior or prophet that cannot be empirically justified and demand an act of faith on the part of the believer, whether this takes the Christian form of the Nicene Creed, with its affirmation that "Jesus Christ, son of God . . . for us men and our salvation came down and was incarnate and was made man," or of the *shahada*, the Muslim profession of belief that "there is no God other than Allah and Muhammed is His messenger." In return for such avowals, the believer is promised everlasting life.

---

* The Hebrew word for "friend," *ḥaver*, was occasionally used in Judeo-Arabic, as it is in the Mishnah, to denote a member of the rabbinical elite, one belonging to its most select circles.

But Judaism, the rabbi argues, is based not on faith but on historical experience. While it shares with Islam and Christianity the belief they took from it in a divine Creator, its truth does not depend on any single personage. Its first patriarchs may have been solitary figures, but the God who approached them subsequently gave His Torah publicly at Mount Sinai—and the number of Israelites at the base of the mountain, which "quaked greatly" and "smoked like a furnace," was, the Bible says, six hundred thousand. So many people and their descendants cannot possibly have been victims of autosuggestion or self-delusion, which is why the biblical account is accepted by Christians and Muslims as well as Jews.

Eventually, it is accepted by the king of the Khazars, too. Midway through his first conversation with the rabbi, he concedes:

> A Law given with so many miracles cannot but be consented to by those witnessing it, since none of them could have suspected that he was the victim of sorcery or charlatanry or of his own imagination. And by the same token, it could no more have been only in their imagination that the Red Sea split for them and that they passed through it than it could have been in their imagination that they were liberated from slavery and their enslavers were killed. . . . Only the most incorrigible skeptic could entertain such a notion.

By the end of Part I of *The Kuzari*, much of which is devoted to the rabbi's review of biblical history, the king has been won over completely. Of the three monotheistic faiths, Judaism alone, he now admits, passes the bar of evidential proof. And so, the reader is informed by the opening paragraph of Part II, which stresses the risks the king has taken by adopting a religion so looked down upon that it must be practiced in secret:

> After all this, as is related in the history of the Khazars, the king confided his dream to his vizier, and in its next repetition he was told to seek the God-pleasing deed in the mountains of Varsan. Traveling to these mountains, which are in a desert by the sea, he and the vizier came one night across a cave to which certain Jews repaired every week to keep the Sabbath. They disclosed their identity to them, embraced their religion, were circumcised in the cave, and then returned to their country, their minds at rest because they had become Jewish. However, they kept their conversion secret until they found a way to reveal it, at first to a small, chosen group, and then, as their numbers increased, to more and more people until a majority of the Khazars accepted Judaism.

Of course, not only is Yehuda Halevi's account of the Khazars' conversion to Judaism largely fanciful, the rabbi's appeal to biblical history is less than satisfying to the modern mind. Its reasoning can only strike us as circular: we know, it says, that there were six hundred thousand Israelites at Sinai because the Bible tells us so—and we know that the Bible is telling us the truth because six hundred thousand Israelites could not have been wrong! Wasn't Halevi aware, one wonders, of the faultiness of such logic?

How could it have failed to occur to him that the biblical account of Sinai, let alone of the Patriarchs, the Flood, and the Creation, might have been written long after such supposed events took place and been imagined, not by a multitude of Israelites, but by a small number of biblical authors?

There are two ways of defending him against this objection. One is to cite *The Kuzari*'s opening lines, in which, after speaking of "the arguments made by a rabbi to the king of the Khazars," the author-narrator adds: "And as many of the rabbi's arguments seemed right to me and were in accordance with my own opinions, I decided to record them as they were set forth—and the discerning will understand." This, as some commentators on *The Kuzari* have observed, is a sly statement, for if "many" of the rabbi's arguments are "in accordance" with the author's opinions, it follows that some are not and that Halevi is not automatically to be identified with the rabbi or his views. There may be places in *The Kuzari* in which these views, put in the rabbi's mouth for dramatic or didactic purposes, are not Halevi's own—and if so, the appeal to biblical history could be one of them.

In fact, there is much to be said for distinguishing between Halevi and the rabbi. In this respect, the dialogue of *The Kuzari* differs from the question-and-answer format found in the writings of many Muslim theologians of Halevi's age, or from that resorted to by a Jewish philosopher like Shlomo ibn Gabirol in his Neoplatonic work *The Fount of Life*. The discussants in these exchanges are little more than stick figures with neither personalities nor voices of their own. In *The Kuzari*, on the other hand, as in many of the Socratic dialogues of Plato that were known to Halevi in

Arabic translation, the dialogue forms part of a story that must be read for its fictional nuances. Precisely our ability to relate to it in this fashion would seem to be the "discernment" that Halevi asks of us.

And yet to read *The Kuzari*'s appeal to biblical history as intended ironically, presented for our consideration so that we might realize its absurdity, would be undiscerning on our part. The argument is too sustained and thematically important to be viewed in such a light, and we need to assume that it is indeed one of the rabbi's opinions with which Halevi *does* agree and to ask why this is so.

Let us suppose for a moment that someone were to maintain that Julius Caesar never existed or crossed the Rubicon, all this being the fabrication of later historians. We would consider such a claim too preposterous to rebut, but if pressed to do so, we would point out first that we possess descriptions of Caesar and his career by contemporaries of his like Cicero; next, that even though our only full biographies of him were written by historians born after his death, such as Plutarch, Tacitus, and Suetonius, these men lived too close to his lifetime to tell major lies about him without being exposed; third, that the Rubicon is a real river in northern Italy that can still be seen and crossed; and last, that the basic facts concerning Caesar's life and death are so universally taken for granted that it is inconceivable they could be imaginary. The only recourse left the Caesar denier would be to argue that Cicero, Plutarch, Tacitus, Suetonius, and a host of others, along with all their works, are also fabrications by which we have been bamboozled—and by then the patience of the most forbearing listener would have been exhausted.

Now, Julius Caesar lived and acted roughly 2,000 years

before our time. Moses, according to biblical chronology, lived some 2,200 years before Yehuda Halevi's time—and from Halevi's point of view, the case for him and Sinai was as solid as the case for Caesar and the Rubicon seems to us today. After all, Joshua, who knew Moses intimately, speaks of him often in the Book of Joshua; in the Book of Judges, which relates events immediately following Joshua's death, the prophetess Deborah proclaims that "the mountains melted before the Lord; this was at Sinai, before the Lord, God of Israel"; Samuel, who was born close enough to the time of Deborah to have known people who knew her, proclaimed to the Israelites of his age, "It is the Lord who made Moses and Aaron, and that brought your fathers out of the land of Egypt"; and David, whom Samuel crowned king, relates the entire story of the exodus from Egypt in his 105th psalm. Moreover, Mount Sinai was a real place in the Sinai desert, its authenticity attested to by Bedouin tradition, and the entire nonpagan world acknowledged that Moses had received the Torah there. Only a perversely stubborn mind (Halevi could not have envisioned the modern bible critic) could believe that this was all a deliberate swindle.

The appeal to history, then, would have seemed to Halevi a valid way of defending Judaism. The need for a work that did so was great. By the early twelfth century, Jewish fortunes were on the decline everywhere. Weakened by the Karaite schism and increasingly hounded by Christianity and Islam, Judaism also had to fend off the inroads of philosophy—which, by dismissing the truth of all religions, temptingly offered the educated Jew a quickly achieved parity with his Muslim and Christian peers. Moreover, apart from Sa'adia Gaon's *Beliefs and Opinions*, a tenth-century work that influenced Halevi but was dated from a twelfth-century perspective, there were no intellectually sophisticated arguments for Judaism available. Ibn Gabirol's *Fount of Life* lacked specific Jewish content, while Ibn Gabirol's follower Bahya ibn Pakuda was still writing his more Jewishly oriented *Duties of the Heart* when *The Kuzari* was begun.

There was a breach to be stepped into—and Halevi took the step. The idea of casting his book as a conversation with a Khazar king was a clever one. Although the kingdom of Khazaria was a shadow of its former self by the time Halevi was born, having been largely destroyed by its Slavic neighbors in the course of the tenth century, news of its demise, like light from a distant star, had yet to reach the Jews of Spain. Its legend continued to be a bright spot in a darkening exile, a proof that the "despised religion" could, if given the chance, successfully compete for the allegiance of great potentates and their subjects.

The Kuzari, though, was prompted by more than just Halevi's desire to strike a blow for Judaism. If that had been its sole aim, it would have concentrated on refuting Christianity and Islam. Yet once its prelude is concluded, these two religions no longer play a role in it. From this point on, the book focuses on philosophy, "the adversary par excellence," as Leo Strauss put it, "of Judaism from Halevi's point of view." On the face of it, this may seem strange: philosophers, after all, were not attacking Jewish privileges in Andalusia, murdering Jews in the Rhineland, or massacring them in Jerusalem. But intellectually, Halevi did not feel threatened by Islam or Christianity because he was never attracted to either. To philosophy, he was—as were many

Jewish admirers of "Greek wisdom" whom he knew. Viewed as the final stage of a work that was in progress for many years, *The Kuzari* tells the story of Halevi's disenchantment with philosophical thought, his attitude toward which, analyses of the book's different strata show, became increasingly negative over time.

A veiled account of this process can be found in Part IV of *The Kuzari*, in what is at first glance a puzzlingly long discussion of a Hebrew text called *Sefer ha-Yetsirah*, "The Book of Creation"—a slender work of mystical cosmogony most probably dating from the fifth or sixth century C.E. but purporting to contain esoteric knowledge going back to the time of Abraham. Despite its occultism, *Sefer ha-Yetsirah* was read as a philosophical work by its rabbinic commentators, starting with Sa'adia Gaon, who took it as evidence that Judaism possessed an ancient Neoplatonic tradition predating the Greeks. Such is also the view of the rabbi in *The Kuzari*. The Jews, he explains to the king, are in no way the Greeks' inferiors, since all of Greek philosophy derives from them. They just never bothered to develop their philosophical insights systematically, because while *Sefer ha-Yetsirah* represents "Abraham's opinions after the unity and sovereignty of God had dawned on him [intellectually], this was prior to God's revealing Himself to him, after which he gave up all philosophical reasoning and strove only to do God's will."

In other words, once Abraham became a prophet who was in direct communication with God, philosophy ceased to interest him. And yet why, if he turned his back on it, does the rabbi go to such lengths to prove to the king that *Sefer ha-Yetsira* is a philosophical work? This can only be because Abraham's change of mind was not part of *The Kuzari*'s earlier versions, in which philosophy had not yet been rejected and in which Halevi sought to demonstrate that the Jews were its original founders. Abraham's abandonment of philosophy in *The Kuzari* was Halevi's, too.

This is one side of Halevi's identification with the biblical patriarch. There was another. Not only does Abraham go from an intellectual acknowledgment of God to a direct experience of Him, this experience first comes in the Book of Genesis in the form of the divine command: "Get thee out of thy country, and from thy kindred, and from thy father's house, unto a land that I will show thee." The blind journey to the Land of Israel that God requires of Abraham is a radical action that, to his friends in Ur of the Chaldees, must seem unjustifiably rash—and it was this same action that was chosen by Halevi in order not to be, as he says in his poem "Lord, You Are My Sole Desire," "naked of deeds."

Naked of deeds? We have heard that somewhere else:

> Th[e] king—so it is told—had a dream that kept recurring. In his dream appeared an angel, who spoke to him and said: "Your intentions are worthy in the eyes of the Creator, but your deeds are not."

The Kuzari, then, is not only in some ways a work of fiction, it is a work of autobiographical fiction in which the philosopher, the rabbi, and the Khazar king represent different aspects of the author at different stages of his life. It is worth keeping this in mind as one reads it.

I n *The Kuzari*, Yehuda Halevi put aside poetry for religious philosophy. Yet he remained enough of a poet to be an anti-philosophical religious philosopher, one convinced of philosophy's inadequacy to deal with religious experience. In this he is the reverse of Maimonides, and if *The Kuzari* and Maimonides' *Guide for the Perplexed* became paired with each other in the Jewish mind, this is not just because they are the two most influential works of Jewish religious philosophy ever written, but because they fit together as only opposites can.

The medieval philosophy that Halevi ultimately rejected was an attempt to harmonize biblical and Koranic monotheism with classical Greek thought as represented by Aristotle, Plato, and such Neoplatonists of the early Christian era as the third-century Plotinus and Porphyry, the fourth-century Iamblichus, and the fifth-century Proclus. This was not easily done. The God of monotheism, though not a person, had many features of one. He thought, planned, decided, acted, and sometimes regretted His actions; felt love, anger, jealousy, disappointment, and other emotions; talked to human beings and listened to what they said.

The God of Greek philosophy did none of these things. He was an "it," not a "he"; a principle, not a personality. This principle was Aristotle's "First Cause," the primal something from which the universe proceeded and by which all existence was generated, much as—to take a rough analogy from contemporary science—a Unified Field Theory could generate not only all the laws of nature but every single event in the cosmos resulting from them, past, present, and future. And just as science forms both a descending and ascending ladder, so that as scientists work out the laws governing the world in ever greater detail they also strive to find an ever more unitary source for them, so later Greek philosophy elaborated a steadily increasing number of stages, or "emanations," in the language of Neo-platonism, by which the First Cause, or "the One," engendered the multiplicity of phenomena and the multiplicity of phenomena reverted to the simplicity of the One.

It is historically debatable why Islam, the last of the three major monotheistic religions and therefore also the last to be exposed to Greek philosophy, was the first to be so profoundly affected by it. After all, both Judaism and Christianity were, in the centuries before Islam's appearance, primarily religions of the Graeco-Roman world. Yet though both were well aware of Greek thought and—Christianity especially—borrowed ideas and concepts from it, they never grappled with it methodically. This was precisely what, starting with the ninth century, Muslim thinkers felt compelled to do. Perhaps, having discovered Greek philosophy in Arabic translation late in the day, when Greek pagan religion no longer existed, they were less wary of it or prone to associate it with a sinful polytheism. Perhaps, too, Islam having emerged from the desert with little intellectual baggage of its own, they were more impressed, even overwhelmed, by the scope, logical rigor, and systematic approach of the Greeks. Whatever the reason, they threw themselves into the study of them, causing Judaism and Christianity to follow suit.

This led to different schools of Islamic thought. On the one hand, there were the pure philosophers, or Falsafa, as they were called in Arabic, men like Al-Farabi and Avicenna who believed that philosophy was the indispensable key to a full understanding of reality, with which the Koran had to be shown to be compatible in order to be defended. Over against them were the Islamic theologians, or Mutakallimun.

Among these were the Mutazilites, who sought to synthesize philosophy with religion while using its formal logic to uphold Muslim precepts that clashed with Greek ones; the Asharites, who pressed such logic into the service of a Koranic fundamentalism; and still others who, paradoxically, made use of it to deny its utility completely.

What all sides had in common—itself a legacy from the Greeks—was a commitment to rational argument and dialectical dueling. Although the questions they debated may seem abstruse to the modern mind, which tends to regard medieval philosophy as the occupation of hair splitters, they were not very different from those that scientists (and children) still argue about today: Did our universe always exist? If so, how can time recede infinitely back into the past? And if not, how did the universe begin, and what came before it? Can there be anything beyond it? Will it last forever—and if it won't, what will come after it? Are time and space real or illusory? Do things happen the way they do because they have to, or could they just as well happen differently?

For example: we have seen how, in his remarks to the Khazar king, Yehuda Halevi's philosopher states that God is "beyond all knowledge of individual details, because these change from moment to moment and the Creator is unchangeable," so that "He has no knowledge of you, much less of your deeds or thoughts, and He certainly does not hear your prayers or observe your activities." This was the position of the Falsafa. God is omniscient only in the sense that all things derive from Him. He "knows" them in a general way, not by hearing or seeing them but by being their causal antecedent, just as Newton's law of gravity "knows" that all leaves will fall in a forest but not which leaf will fall at what moment. Gravity is mathematically simple and has a high level of generalization. To predict the fate of a particular leaf, however, one would need to invoke a large number of secondary, more complex, and less comprehensive laws dealing with plant physiology, biochemistry, meteorology, aerodynamics, kinetics, probability, etc., and then apply them to a vast amount of physical data—and then too, it is theoretically uncertain whether one could ascertain even a second in advance, let alone at the creation of the universe, the precise moment of this or that leaf's falling.

For Al-Farabi and Avicenna, God had to be maximally simple while logically prior to the universe. Moreover, if He "knew" at one point in time that a particular leaf was going to fall, at a second point that it was falling, and at a third point that it had fallen, He would "know" it in three different ways, which would be inconsistent with His unity and immutability. When the Koran proclaimed, therefore, "And He knows what is in the land and the sea; and there falls not a leaf but He knows it," it was using ordinary human language to convey a philosophic truth that the average man was incapable of grasping.

To the more conventionally minded Muslim, a God whose involvement with the world was a mere figure of speech was unacceptable. Yet a God who *did* know where and when every leaf would fall posed an equally great theological problem, since the same omniscience that made Him cognizant of each leaf's future also made Him cognizant of each human being's future, thus depriving mankind of both freedom and responsibility. How hold anyone responsible for an act that he has no choice but to commit because God knows he will commit it? And if he has no choice, how can a just God reward or punish him, as the Koran says He does?

This was a conundrum shared by all the monotheistic religions. Rabbinic Judaism had been aware of it for centuries, as illustrated by Rabbi Akiva's well-known pronouncement, "All is foreseen [by God], but permission is granted [to choose freely]." Yet far from trying to puzzle out the paradox, Akiva was declaring its two contradictory halves to be an unfathomable mystery that must simply be accepted. The authority of Greek philosophy precluded such an option for Muslim intellectuals of Halevi's age, who felt committed to solving the problem by rational means. This they sought to do in various ways. The Mutazilites maintained that foreseeing the future is not the same as making it happen, so that God's knowledge that a person will do something does not preempt that person's decision to do it. The Asharites held that God does not act through chains of causality but rather re-creates the universe and everything in it anew at each moment; thus, human deeds are not predetermined as effects are by causes. The determinists known as the Jabrites contended that, while freedom of will indeed did not exist, this did not compromise divine justice, which operated differently from human justice. Although all these solutions may strike us today as equally sophistical, they were vigorously disputed by those who advanced them.

And where does *The Kuzari* stand? For this we must turn to its final pages. There, after listening to the rabbi describe some of philosophy's doctrines and explain why they are not to be trusted (they are unsupported by empirical evidence; the same logical methods used to confirm them can also be

used to refute them; their proponents disagree among themselves and challenge one another's conclusions, and so on),
the king remarks rather dismissively that the rabbi is obviously not a philosopher himself and is simply repeating
things heard from others. And yet, he goes on, there is
one philosophical issue about which he insists on knowing
the rabbi's personal opinion, since "all human deeds depend
on it"—namely, that of "human choice versus predestina-
tion."

It is obvious why the king is so interested in this, since he
has staked his life on a dream about his own deeds. The rabbi
replies without hesitation. "Only a stubborn dogmatist," he
tells the king,

> would deny the category of possibility—and even he
> would be saying what he doesn't believe. Why, just
> look at such a person: he [too] makes efforts to attain
> what he desires and to avoid what he fears! You can
> conclude from this that he believes that the thing in
> question is possible and that his efforts can help bring
> it about, because if he thought it was predestined he
> would accept it and not bother, say, to arm himself
> against his enemies or to look for food when he is hun-
> gry. . . . And if he is honest rather than obstinate, he
> will admit that his will is free [to choose] among possi-
> ble things. . . . He can do them if he wishes and refrain
> from them if he does not. . . . Choice, to the extent
> that it is choice, has no antecedent cause, because if it
> had one, it would become necessity and a man's speech
> would be as constrained [by forces outside his control]
> as his pulse; yet this would contradict what is self-

evident, since your speech and your silence are decided on by you alone.

In a word, the rabbi says, we know we are free to choose because we instinctively feel that we are and act in accordance with our feeling. This is not something that can or needs to be proven by philosophy; it is an empirical reality on which we base our behavior, the denial of which would be as foolish as denying the existence of our bodies or of the world around us. And by the same token, the rabbi continues, philosophical reasoning tells us nothing of value about God's omniscience; for although it is clear that everything but human will must have a cause, and that every cause must have another cause, forming a chain leading back to the First Cause, there is no way of deducing which of these causes is a direct intervention of God's and which is independent of Him, and thus no way of establishing what He does or does not know. All our notions about such things, which vary "from people to people, individual to individual, time to time, place to place, and set of circumstances to set of circumstances," are pure speculation.

The king falls silent, either because he is satisfied with the rabbi's answer or because he sees no point in arguing about such things with someone who sees no point in it himself. From the perspective of philosophy, indeed, the rabbi's approach is disappointingly naive. The entire enterprise of late Greek and medieval philosophy starts with a distrust of experience and its illusions, which are viewed as stemming from the body's dependence on misleading sensory impressions that the mind must emancipate itself from by means of pure thought; the intuitive "knowledge" that we have freedom of will is thus no knowledge at all, just as the refusal to think logically about a metaphysical problem like God's omniscience is an abdication of the obligation to use our powers of reason. In so doing, the rabbi is rejecting, not just this or that philosophical school, but philosophy itself.

It would be wrong to claim too much originality either for him or for Yehuda Halevi in this respect. In part, Halevi was returning to Rabbi Akiva and rabbinic tradition, with its oft-quoted statement that there are four things men should not waste their time pondering: "what is above [the nature of the Divinity], what is below [the secrets of Nature], what is before us [the eschatological future], and what is behind us [the details of Creation]"; in part, he was influenced by an anti-philosophic reaction that had occurred in the Islamic thought of his age, especially in the work of his Arab contemporary Abu Hamid al-Ghazali (1058–1111). Al-Ghazali's *The Incoherence of the Philosophers* is a dialectical tour de force in which, one by one, twenty leading philosophical doctrines that are incompatible with Islamic beliefs are dissected and shown to be internally inconsistent, starting with the affirmation of the world's past eternity and ending with the denial of the body's resurrection on Judgment Day. Compared with Al-Ghazali's precision reasoning against reason, the rabbi's arguments are primitive. He is, as the king points out, no philosopher, although he does have a good knowledge of the field.

So, of course, did Yehuda Halevi, who would have read the Greek and Islamic philosophers in the course of his medical studies had he not, as a cultivated young poet, been familiar with them before then. As his religious poetry makes clear, he never fully identified with the Falsafa; God was always too real for him to be reduced to an abstract First Cause. Yet for a long while, it would seem, the God of Israel coexisted in Halevi's mind with the philosophical thought that ruled out His existence. By the time *The Kuzari* was finished, this conflict had been resolved. The God of Israel, proclaims the rabbi, exists. Philosophy is merely a way of thinking about existence, one subject to all the limitations of the human mind.

The rabbi's philosophical relativism clearly speaks for the position Halevi himself arrived at in the end. Since human ideas about the unknowable vary from "people to people . . . and sets of circumstances to sets of circumstances," our intellectual interpretations of reality are socially and culturally determined (or "constructed," in the language of postmodernism). In the final analysis, philosophical disputes are less about the truth than about what we find useful or convenient to think is true.

But this does not mean there is no truth. There is, and it is called Judaism, and the reason we can be sure of it, like the reason we can be sure our wills are free, is human experience. The difference is that free will is the experience of everyone, while Judaism is the experience of a particular people. In either case, however, we know what we know because of the lives in which it has been lived.

The Khazar king is told in his dream that his deeds are unworthy. As Judaism is preeminently a religion of deeds—of *mitzvot*, or "commandments," as it calls them— he is being pointed in its direction even before he is aware of it. Philosophy, the rabbi maintains in *The Kuzari*, is a matter of what one thinks; religions like Christianity and Islam, of what one believes; Judaism, of what one does. To the philosopher, the Christian, and the Muslim, intentions are crucial; the subjective state of the individual is what counts most. In Judaism, it is the objective actions that he performs.

Of course, Christianity and Islam have their commandments, too. But not only does Judaism have many more of them, enumerating 613 in the Bible alone, it has a far greater number that are rationally inexplicable. When, for example, a religiously observant Jew dresses in the morning, he must first see to it that there is no mixture of linen and wool in what he wears; next, he must don a ritually fringed undergarment beneath his shirt; after that, he straps leather thongs to his head and arm before praying. He then sits down to a breakfast that may consist of certain foods and not others, and upon leaving his home passes through a doorway to which an amulet with parchment verses from Scripture must be attached. None of this makes rational sense—and his day has just begun.

Why Judaism has so many seemingly arbitrary regulations was a question first addressed in the Middle Ages by Sa'adia Gaon's *Beliefs and Opinions*. Sa'adia divided the commandments into two categories. One, the "rational commandments," serve some obvious social or ethical purpose and can be found all over the world. Mosaic laws like "Thou shalt not steal," "Thou shalt not commit adultery," and "If a fire break out and catch in thorns, so that the stacks of wheat or the standing wheat be consumed, he that kindled the fire shall make restitution" are all rational. Societies everywhere can and do understand the need for them without the aid of divine revelation.

The nonrational commandments were called by Sa'adia "commandments of obedience." These are unique to Judaism; had they not been revealed to Moses at Sinai, there would be no way of knowing what they are. Their justification, Sa'adia thought, is pedagogic and didactic—that is, to inculcate habits of discipline and devotion to God. In itself, there is no reason why wool should not be worn with linen; precisely the irrationality of the ban tests our readiness to obey it; were it exchanged for another, similar prohibition—one, say, on wearing red clothes with blue clothes—the same end would be served. This holds true of many of the Mosaic commandments, such as circumcision, the dietary laws, some of the laws of purity and contamination, the laws of sacrifice in the Tabernacle and the Temple, the priestly regimen, and so on. All call for the performance of acts whose value Sa'adia considered symbolic, each bearing some message or lesson.

Sa'adia's position was adopted by most medieval Jewish thinkers, including Maimonides. In his *Guide to the Perplexed*, the latter states:

> Every one of the 613 commandments serves to inculcate some truth, to remove some erroneous opinion, to establish proper relations in society, to diminish evil, to train in good manners, or to warn against bad habits. All this depends on three things: opinions, morals, and social conduct.

If Maimonides differs from Sa'adia, it is only in his tendency to find a hidden utility in many of the "commandments of obedience," thus making them more like the "rational commandments." Of the dietary laws, for instance, he maintains that "the food which is forbidden by the Law is unwholesome"; of circumcision, that it "counteracts excessive lust" by curbing "the power of sexual excitement"; of animal sacrifice, that it was a necessary step in getting the biblical Israelites to worship God, since

> the custom which was in those days general among all men, and the general mode of worship in which the Israelites were brought up, consisted in sacrificing animals. . . . It was in accordance with the wisdom of God, as displayed in the whole Creation, that He did not command us to give up and to discontinue all these manners of service; for to obey such a commandment would have been contrary to the nature of man, who generally cleaves to that to which he is used.

God, in other words, does not need sacrifice, and mankind is better off without it. It was strictly a temporary educational device designed to help the Israelites make the transition from polytheism to pure monotheism.

This is not the standpoint of Yehuda Halevi. Indeed, so utterly different is Halevi's conception of the "commandments of obedience" that it has more in common with medieval Jewish mysticism than with medieval Jewish religious philosophy. His understanding of sacrifice illustrates this well. We find it stated toward the end of Part I of *The Kuzari*, after the king has turned to the rabbi and said:

> [What you have been telling me] strengthens the opinion I have arrived at, which was also confirmed by my

dream, namely, that no man can attain contact with the divine except it be . . . by deeds God commands him to perform. For otherwise this would be something that could be accomplished by anyone striving to worship God according to his understanding, including the stargazer, the sorcerer, the fire and sun worshiper, the Manichean, and many others.

To which the rabbi replies:

True enough! Such are the commandments of our Torah. All were spoken by God to Moses, and all were written by Moses and transmitted to the great multitude gathered in the desert. . . . Even the descriptions of the sacrifices, how they were offered, and where, and facing what direction, and how [the animals] were slaughtered, and what was to be done with the blood and cuts of meat—all this was explicitly stated by God without omitting the slightest detail, which would have rendered everything unfit. It is the same as in the world of nature, whose parts are composed of the most unimaginably precise proportions [between the different elements], the slightest inexactitude in which would put an end to their existence by making each plant, animal, and organ unsustainable.

The smallest aspect of any "commandment of obedience" is crucial because, the rabbi continues, "there is no room in the worship of God for guesswork, logic, or considered judgment. If there were, the philosophers would have achieved by means of their intellects twice as much as did the Israelites." The commandments, if executed correctly, have an objective impact on things, just as—to resort again to a scientific analogy—combining hydrogen and oxygen in certain proportions and no others yields water, and heating water to a given degree and not a lesser one produces steam. Earlier, the rabbi has related a parable in which God is compared to the king of a far country who sends a gift of medicines—the laws of the Torah—to heal the ailments of distant allies. Now, this parable is returned to in order to explain the difference between the God-given laws of Judaism and their counterfeits in other religions. The counterfeiter, the rabbi declares in a metaphor drawing on Halevi's medical experience, is comparable to

a mountebank who breaks into the medicine chest of a doctor known for his cures, and, seeing the many people waiting outside the doctor's office for the medicines that will help them, starts handing these out in whatever containers he can find, with no knowledge of each drug or of its correct dosage for different people . . . [and without realizing that] its effectiveness depends on the wisdom of the physician who prepares it and prescribes the right amount for every patient, supplemented by diet, exercise, rest, regular hours of waking and sleeping, fresh air, and so forth.

Only God knows why the "commandments of obedience" work as they do on the individual or on the universe—which was conceived of by Halevi, as by every educated person of his age, as hierarchically structured. At its apex was God; at its base, primal matter, most simply manifested in the four elements of earth, water, air, and fire, from the differing combinations of which, each endowed with its formal attributes by a higher spiritual emanation, or "influence," all physical bodies were composed. At the lowest, mineral level, these attributes were the qualities of color, taste, hardness or softness, and so forth; at the vegetative level, of growth, the absorption of nutrients, and reproduction; at the animal level, of sense perception, desire, and motility; and at a still higher, human level, of speech, rational thought, and imagination. Yet only a small number of human beings developed these capacities to the full. In the eyes of philosophy, these were the philosophers, whose understanding of the universe was so great that their minds were a reflection of its laws; for religion, the prophets, whose mental, moral, and imaginative perfection made them vehicles of divine inspiration. Such men were the pinnacle of human achievement. They represented God's return to Himself, a reascent of the ladder of Being from matter to spirit after its descent in the opposite direction.

With one alteration, this schema is also that of *The Kuzari*, in which the prophet is described as a kind of divine poet, a man with an "inner eye" that sees what others cannot. But the alteration is momentous, for it consists of the introduction of an additional rung on the ladder to stand midway between humanity and the prophet. This rung is the Jewish people, whose elevation by Halevi to a place of its own in the cosmic order of things took him out of the realm of even anti-philosophical philosophy and helped pave the way for that medieval mythicization of Neoplatonic thought that eventually came to be known as Kabbalah. (Indeed, with its ten Sefirot or divine emanations that unfold downward from an infinite and unknowable God to the material world, Kabbalah—which projects onto this abstract process a semi-personified drama of sin and redemption in which the

Jews are the key human actors—might be said to be Neoplatonism's last surviving historical form.)

Let us return to the rabbi's initial remarks to the king about the historical transmission of religious truth. Its uninterrupted chain, he explains, goes back to Adam, after whom came a long line of biblical descendants, each separated from his contemporaries like a kernel of wheat from its chaff and many granted the prophet's relationship with God. This continued through Noah, who was followed by nine more generations leading up to Abraham, Isaac, and Jacob. Only with Jacob's sons did the vertical line of descent expand horizontally, growing into the twelve tribes of Israel that left Egypt in the Exodus. A single family tree thus extends from the Garden of Eden to Mount Sinai and from Mount Sinai to the rabbi and the king's own age.

Were this all the rabbi says, there would be nothing new in it from a Jewish point of view. But he says more, for he then proceeds to make the claim—never before put forth in the name of Judaism—that the Bible is not just about a family *history* of prophecy but about a family *capacity* for prophecy as well. No one but a Jew is biologically able to be a prophet. Not only can a Gentile, however spiritually developed, never attain such a level, but no convert to Judaism can, either, since prophecy's form-giving "influence" can only be bestowed on those high enough on the ladder of Being to receive it. The born Jew alone is on such a level.

Needless to say, this is not a tactful thing to tell a potential convert, and the king of the Khazars shows considerable self-restraint when all he asks upon hearing it is, "But would it not have been better and wiser had God guided all men in the truth?"

Bluntly, the rabbi retorts:

And would it not have been better if all the animals had the power of speech? If you think so, you have already forgotten what was said to you about the inheritance passed down . . . to Jacob's sons, each of whom was special and [like] the kernel of wheat, so that they were distinguished from the rest of humanity by godly attributes that made them like another, angelic species.

Here, too, the king fails to protest. Clearly, though, he is irked by the suggestion that animals are to human beings as human beings are to the Jews, because a short while later in the conversation, he finds an opportunity to strike back. Told by the rabbi that Judaism assigns no intrinsic merit to suffering, which does not automatically earn the sufferer a reward in the life to come, the king replies sarcastically that this is a great shame, since suffer is all the Jews seem to do in this world.

Now it is the rabbi's turn to be stung. "I see you are reproaching us for our lowly state!" he complains while seeking to persuade the king that the Jews' continued devotion to their religion despite their downtrodden condition is proof of its power. They are content with their lot because they are close to God.

The king finds this sanctimonious. "That might be true," he says, "if your lot had been chosen by you. But in fact it has been forced on you, and if only you could, you would slaughter your enemies as they slaughter you."

This hurts even more. "You've struck home, king of the Khazars!" the rabbi admits. "If only most of our people had accepted its degradation out of true submission to God and

His Torah, the divine influence would not have abandoned us for so long." Prophecy might then have continued as a feature of Jewish life instead of disappearing in the time of the Second Temple, after which it existed only as an unfulfilled potential.

But at this point the tension subsides, the difference between the convert and the born Jew having turned out to be purely theoretical. For all practical purposes, the rabbi assures the king, converts can be as close to God as other Jews are. Moreover, if prophecy ever returns, the children converts have with other Jews may be eligible for it, too. Therefore, while the convert is, in a sense, a second-class citizen in Judaism, he is less so, say, than the naturalized American who is denied the right to become president by the Constitution, since the United States still has presidents, while the Jews no longer have prophets.

With this, Part I of *The Kuzari* ends. Since Part II, as we have seen, begins with the king's conversion, he obviously has not remained rankled for long.

Yehuda Halevi was a doctor. Just as he looked for the bodily expression of all mental and emotional complaints, so he believed that every spiritual phenomenon had its physical substratum—not in the name of the scientific reductionism that characterizes our own times, but as part of the medieval inquiry into the relation of form to matter. Since prophecy, according to Judaism, had historically been limited to Jews, it was not necessarily outrageous to propose that a propensity for it might be inherited.

Still, this was not the best nor the most obvious explanation. Maimonides, for instance, believed that "any human being can be a prophet who has a proper physical constitution and has been duly trained and educated," so that whether he becomes one depends only on "the will of God who is to prophesy and when"; although Jews alone have risen to such a rank, Gentiles can in principle attain it, too. Why could Halevi not have taken a similar position? If biological Jewishness has no practical consequences, why make such a point of it in *The Kuzari*? Why run the risk of alienating the king with a harsh doctrine lacking any prior basis in Jewish thought?

Only a sense of historical desperation can account for this. The "despised faith" was at a nadir. Physically at the mercy of Muslims and Christians, Jews had become their intellectual and cultural vassals as well, taking from them far more than they gave. The very fact that *The Kuzari* had to be written in Arabic, presumably because Halevi felt that Hebrew lacked the vocabulary and stylistic resources for the task, was a humiliating admission of this. So was the powerful influence of Arabic poetry, which *The Kuzari* deplores. Declaring to the king that Hebrew, the noblest language of mankind, has fallen into disuse among Jews and "grown feeble," the rabbi attacks its adoption of Arabic meters, thus reviving the old argument between Dunash ben Labrat and Menachem ben Saruk by taking Menachem's losing side. Inasmuch as Yehuda Halevi went on composing Arabic-style poetry during and after the years in which he wrote *The Kuzari*, he was attacking himself in its pages as well, an irony that would not have been lost on his readers.

Nor could the Jews of Halevi's age claim, as Jews could do before the appearance of Christianity and Islam, that they were needed to spread the belief in one God. Who indeed would miss them if they disappeared entirely? How refute the assertion that Judaism had become an irrelevance? Rabbinic thought held that the faith of Israel would be vindicated in messianic times, when the world would turn to it. But Yehuda Halevi had lived through an age of messianic disappointments. The trumpet of the Messiah had come to have a hollow sound.

Hence, it would seem, Halevi's recourse to biology, or—there being little difference in medieval terms—to ontology. By making the Jewish people a discrete building block of the universe whose removal would compromise the entire structure, he was seeking to anchor it to a metaphysical reality that could withstand the buffeting of history. Moreover, he was providing a "scientific" explanation of Judaism's temporary eclipse. It is well known, the rabbi points out to the king, that inherited traits often skip one or more generations before reappearing; many of Abraham's ancestors in the Bible were not subject to the "divine influence" at all. Similarly, the Jews of the rabbi and king's own era, however unimpressive their achievements, carry within them the seed of past and future spiritual greatness and will bring forth prophets once again. Without them, mankind could never reascend the ladder of Being to the top. It would be comparable to a body without a heart, which is, "like Israel among the nations, the most vital to health and the most prone to illness of all the organs." The Jews are the sick heart of humanity.

Yet for this heart to regain its health and for prophecy to reappear, the rabbi tells the king, Jewish exile must first come to an end. A Jew can only prophesy in the Land of Israel, which is to other countries as Israel is to other peoples. It, too, is part of the hierarchy of Being, which has its own geographical pyramid. "It should not strike you as strange," the rabbi explains in Part II of *The Kuzari*,

> that a given land should excel at something more than others. Anyone can see that one place may be more suitable than another for a certain plant, or a certain mineral, or a certain animal, and its human inhabitants may also differ in appearance and behavior from people elsewhere on account of their physical constitutions, on which all spiritual perfections and imperfections depend.

The king listens skeptically. He is obviously unhappy to hear another country praised so lavishly at the expense of his own, and when the rabbi begins to enumerate the Land of Israel's many virtues, the king interrupts him to observe tartly that if this is so,

> you are disobeying a commandment of your Torah by not going to that land and living and dying there. . . . All your genuflections [to it] in your prayers are either unthinking or hypocritical, especially since your first ancestors chose to live there above all other places and to be sojourners there rather than natives in their birthplace.

There are no stage directions in *The Kuzari*. Still, one can only give the rabbi's response to this charge its due weight by imagining a pained silence on his part. When he speaks again, it is to say:

> Indeed, you have shamed me, king of the Khazars! This is the same sin because of which we failed to fulfill our divine destiny in the days of the Second

Temple. . . . Had only all [the exiles in Babylonia] answered the call and returned to the Land of Israel unhesitatingly [in the days of Ezra], the divine influence would have been bestowed on us again. But only a few of them responded, and most, including their leaders, remained in Babylonia and accepted exile and enslavement rather than lose their homes and businesses. . . . Had we been ready to approach the God of our fathers with a whole heart, He would have delivered us as he delivered our ancestors in Egypt. But this has not happened and the prayers we utter, such as "Bow down to His holy mount," "He who restores His presence to Zion," and the like, are like the starling's caw, since we do not mean what we say, as you have so justly observed, O Khazar king!

There is a barbed allusion here that Halevi's readers would have understood. Although the rabbi speaks of Babylonia, where the people of Judea were exiled after Nebuchadnezzar's destruction of the First Temple in 586 B.C.E., Spanish Jews were proud of their legend that their ancestors had reached the Iberian Peninsula in Second Temple times from the Babylonian dispersion, to whose leading families they had belonged. *The Kuzari*, they would have realized immediately, was talking about them, too.

Just as it begins with a prologue, so *The Kuzari* ends with an epilogue. We are told:

After all this, the rabbi made up his mind to leave the land of the Khazars and journey to Jerusalem. The king was vexed at his departure. "What is there to seek today in the Land of Israel when God's presence is no longer there?" he asked. "He whose heart is pure and whose desire is great can be close to God anywhere. Why expose yourself to the dangers of deserts, seas, and hostile peoples?"

It is easy to understand the king's vexation. Never once in the course of their conversations has the rabbi intimated that he might leave someday. Because of him, the king has set his life and the life of his kingdom on a new course. He has assumed that the rabbi would remain by his side to guide him. Now, feeling abandoned, he tries talking him out of his plan.

The rabbi answers the king point by point. It is true, he says, that the *visible* presence of God, as manifested by the signs and wonders granted to the prophets and their coevals, no longer dwells in Zion. But there is an invisible spiritual presence that continues to accompany every Jew who is "unsullied of deed and pure of heart"—and just as no Jewish heart can be fully purified except in God's land, so no Jewish deed can be complete elsewhere. Moreover, while the journey there is indeed dangerous, men undergo similar risks for less noble ends, such as hazardous business enterprises or wars fought for booty or glory. Should he, the rabbi, perish on the way, he will at least know that his death has atoned for his sins.

Rebuffed, the king tries another approach. Referring to the special ritual obligations, such as tithing, that life in the Land of Israel entails, he taunts the rabbi: "Until now I have considered you a lover of freedom. Now, though, I see that you wish to make a slave of yourself by assuming the extra duties of the many commandments that the Land of Israel imposes on you and that you are not subject to here."

The rabbi fends this off easily. "The only freedom I seek," he answers, "is from enslavement to others, whom I have no desire to please anymore—and even if I spent my life trying to, I could never succeed, and if I succeeded, it would get me nowhere." He wishes to serve only God, "enslavement to whom is freedom and submission to whom is true honor."

A conventional enough expression of religious piety, this can only upset the king even more. Is the rabbi saying that he regrets having gotten involved with the Khazars in the first place, since this has "enslaved" him to them?

That is certainly what it sounds like. The king, in any case, now resorts to his last argument. "Precisely," he declares, "because you believe in everything you say, God knows your good intentions, there being nothing hidden from His sight." Surely, then, there is no need for the rabbi to voyage to the Land of Israel. His intention is enough, and he can remain in Khazaria.

Poor king! Poor rabbi! Have all their conversations been in vain? Did not these begin with the king's dream in which he was told by an angel, "Your intentions are worthy in the eyes of the Creator, but your deeds are not"? From this, everything followed. Now, months or years later (*The Kuzari* has no stated time frame), the king insists that the rabbi's voyage is unimportant because deeds matter less than the intention behind them. For a moment we, the book's readers, feel we have returned to its starting point.

The rabbi must feel this way, too. Yet for once he is tactful. Putting the best possible light on the king's remark, he replies, "You are right—but this is only when a deed is not performable." He then patiently explains once again that:

> The commandments need to be carried out in full in order to be worthy of recompense. . . . Only when a deed is impossible is there any merit in concentrating on its intention while begging God's forgiveness for not executing it.

The journey to the Land of Israel, though difficult, is possible; therefore, it must be undertaken. But at the same time, the rabbi does feel responsible for the Khazars. Having made Jews of them, he cannot leave them thinking that he disapproves of the kind of Jews he has made them. And so he says in his parting words:

> But he who arouses love for the holy place in the hearts of others also does something meritorious, for he, too, hastens the arrival of the day we hope for, as it is written [in Psalms 102]: "Thou shalt arise and have mercy upon Zion, for the time to favor her, yea, the set time, is come. For Thy servants take pleasure in her stones and cherish her earth." This means that Jerusalem will not be rebuilt until the day when all Israelites so yearn for her with all their hearts that they cherish her stones and earth.

A cunningly ambiguous conclusion! On the one hand, it reassures the king that encouraging an emotional attachment to the Land of Israel is an acceptable deed, too; if the Khazars do this, they can be Jews in Khazaria in good conscience. And yet can one cherish stones and earth from a distance? One is reminded of the movement from thought to act in Halevi's poem "O Fair of View":

Always I think of you—and though your King's away,
And snakes and scorpions scuttle where once grew
Your balm of Gilead, your stones and earth
Would taste, when kissed, like honey in my mouth.

The rabbi's remarks, in any case, have far-reaching implications. Up to the time *The Kuzari* was written, normative Jewish tradition had held that ending the Exile was the sole prerogative of God. He had driven Israel from its land in punishment for its sins and would bring it back when "the set time" arrived. At most, Jews might seek to shorten their sentence through repentance and piety. Now the rabbi suggests something else: a passionate caring for the Land of Israel, expressed by the readiness to live there, can bring about exile's end.

Resigned to the loss of his friend, the king has no arguments left. Keeping a stiff upper lip, he declares: "Well, then, it would be a sin for me to stand in your way, and the performance of a commandment to help you. May God be with you, and be your shield and savior, and bestow His mercy on you.

"Fare you well!"

And so the rabbi departs for Jerusalem because he must, and the king and his subjects stay in Khazaria because they may: it is at once a satisfyingly evenhanded and frustratingly evasive way for Yehuda Halevi to have ended his book. Has the king really learned anything? For all his intelligence and desire to know the truth, *The Kuzari*'s last pages suggest that he has not internalized all he has been taught. He has a kingdom to rule and cannot break the habit of thinking expediently.

But it would be a mistake to think that *The Kuzari* is only about the king's education. It is also about the rabbi's. Indeed, although the king has been given many lessons in Judaism and the rabbi but one, it is this one that matters most.

The Kuzari begins with the king's dream. And yet for a long while, the rabbi has no inkling that this dream is meant for him, too. Although the entire logic of Judaism as explained by him demands the deed of living in the Land of Israel, he has never done anything about it. It is the king, ironically, who points out his inconsistency—and even then, getting over his embarrassment, the rabbi fails to act. He prefers to rationalize his inaction, which he proceeds to do twice in *The Kuzari*. The first time is in Part III, where, toward the end of a description of the *ḥasid*, the ideal Jew, he tells the king that such a person bears misfortune with fortitude and adds:

All this is true of his private misfortunes. But he behaves identically toward the misfortunes of his people: for when his thoughts lead him into religious doubt on account of the length of the Exile, and the extent of the dispersion of the Jews, and their diminution and enfeeblement, he will take comfort, first, in the thought that God is just; second, in [the exile's] atoning for our sins; and third, in the reward [for those who bear it patiently] of life in the world to come and of contact with the divine in this world.

This is the traditional rabbinic position. Yet in light of the king's criticism, the rabbi, it would seem, is no longer comfortable with its doctrine of passivity. And so, in Part IV of *The Kuzari*, he returns to his failure to journey to the Land of Israel, which clearly has begun to bother him, with a different justification—an entirely original one in the history of Jewish thought. (Today, when modern variants of it have long been part of standard Diaspora apologetics, its having been first introduced by *The Kuzari* tends to go unnoticed.) Comparing Judaism to a seed that needs to be scattered in as many places as possible, the rabbi says:

> Furthermore, God has a secret purpose in keeping us in exile, which is like the secret contained in a grain of wheat. When the grain is absorbed by the ground, it seems to disappear, swallowed by earth, water, and mud; yet in reality, it transforms these elements until they come to partake of its nature and to change, stage by stage, until they are transubstantiated and become like it, growing bark and leaves and so on. . . . The same holds true of the religion of Moses: every religion that comes after it is transformed by becoming like it, even if it appears to be different. Such religions are a preparation for the hoped-for coming of the Messiah, which can be compared to the fruit at the end of days. . . .

Poor rabbi! Has he, too, learned nothing? Although he has changed the king's life, he is too reluctant to change his own life to remember what he has taught the king. *Philosophy is about what one thinks; Christianity and Islam, about what one believes; Judaism, about what one does.* If Christianity and Islam have sprouted from Judaism's seed and "become like it," the resemblance consists of their belief in God the Creator, not in their "commandments of obedience." How can the cause of Judaism be furthered by disseminating a mere belief, especially one that now vigorously disseminates itself? This, too, is a pure rationalization of exile.

Ultimately, the rabbi comes to realize this. We are not privy to his inner struggle any more than is the king. We are only made aware that it has taken place because, like the king, we are informed of its outcome. But once we are, we know what has happened. The rabbi has been forced to admit to himself that he has been living a lie. Nothing he has taught the king has the slightest value unless he decides to live in the Land of Israel. If he does, his teachings are meaningful; if he does not, they are the foolishness Halevi called them in his letter to Halfon ben Natanel. The rabbi proves worthy in the end of having been the king's teacher only because he has been willing to be the king's pupil.

6

Sometime in the summer of 1140, Yehuda Halevi finally sailed for the East. He was between sixty-five and seventy years old and had probably finished his final version of *The Kuzari* earlier that year. The book's opening paragraph informs us that the Khazar king converted "about four hundred years ago," and later on in Part I, in a discussion of the Jewish calendar, the rabbi tells the king that they are living in the year 4500, the Christian year 740.

Even if "about" does not mean "exactly," *The Kuzari*'s epilogue, at the very least, must have been composed during Halevi's last weeks or months in Spain, since the book would have been laughably compromised had it concluded with its rabbi departing for the Land of Israel and its author remaining in Spain. Rarely indeed have a book's end and a life's end wagered so heavily on each other. Franz Rosenzweig, himself a translator of Halevi, put it well when he said: "If ever a life went into the ripening of a single deed, it was this one."

Halevi has left us two poems about leaving Spain. One describes a hurried leave-taking, followed by a voyage by land and sea:

> Driven by longing
> for the living God
> to hasten to where
> His anointed ones dwelt,

I had no time
to kiss my friends
or family
a last farewell;
no time to weep
for the garden I grew,
the trees watered and watched
as they branched and did well;
no time to think
of the blossoms they bore,
of Yehuda
and Azarel,
or of Yitzhak,
so like a son,
my sun-blessed crop,
the years' rich yield.

Forgotten are
my synagogue,
the peace that was
its study hall,
my Sabbaths
and their sweet delights,
the splendor of
my festivals:
I've left them all.
Let others have
the idol's honors
and be hailed—
I've swapped my bedroom
for dry brush,

its safety
for rough chaparral,
the scents
and subtle fragrances
that cloyed my soul
for thistles' smells,
and put away
the mincing gait
of landlubbers
to hoist my sail
and cross the sea
until I reach
the land that is
the Lord's footstool.

The second poem relates of his departure:

I thought neither of wealth nor the world,
nor of losing all I accrued,
but alone of my loin's only fruit,
my soul's sister, and of her child,
from whom parting still pierces my craw,
my progeny and dear boy,
his memory my one joy.
Can Yehuda forget Yehuda?

Halevi's "loin's only fruit" was his daughter, and Yehuda
was her son and his grandson. (Unlike Ashkenazim, Spanish
Jews permitted the naming of grandchildren after living
grandparents.) Yet the two other names in the first poem are
problematic. Whereas no Azarel is known to us from Halevi's
milieu, Yitzhak, "so like a son," begs to be identified with

Halevi's son-in-law Yitzhak ibn Ezra. There is, however, a difficulty with this identification, since we know from the Cairo Geniza that Yitzhak ibn Ezra accompanied Halevi on his 1140 journey and did not part from him in Spain. This has led Fleischer and Gil to propose the theory that the first poem was written in 1130 and the second alone in 1140. This would also, they contend, account for the first's allusions to the "dry brush" and "rough chaparral" of an unsuccessful land trek assumed by them to have taken place in North Africa.

Apart from her possible inclusion as "family," Yehuda Halevi's wife is not mentioned in either of these poems. Perhaps she was no longer alive when they were written, although in that case, her death did not elicit from him an elegy, or even a line of verse, that has come down to us. One way or another, she meant less to him than did his daughter, to whom he was evidently extremely close. Called by him "my soul's sister," she could not have expected to see him again. He was setting out not as a pilgrim intending to return home but as a man leaving home forever, and an old one at that. Only the "idol's honors" of which he had had his fill would follow him—or rather, travel ahead of him and be waiting in Egypt when he arrived.

Twelfth-century sea voyages across the Mediterranean were uncomfortable. Ships averaged fifty to a hundred feet in length, the same as a medium-sized to large modern yacht, but often carried hundreds of passengers and their belongings in addition to large crews, commercial cargo, foodstuffs, water, and animals slaughtered for their meat along the way. The more spacious quarters in the forecastle and poop were generally reserved for officers and crew, leaving the passengers packed into an unventilated hold, where each slept on a pallet spread over his traveling trunk, head against his neighbor's feet. Sanitary conditions were atrocious, and rats so abounded that no ship sailed without its complement of cats. Halevi described the ship he sailed on in (apart from its last lines) a wryly humorous poem framed as a mock letter to those left behind by him in Andalusia:

To sisters, brothers, family, and friends:
  Greetings from one,
    a prisoner of hope sold to the sea,
      his spirit hostage to the winds
        that blow from west to east and back again!
Between him and death is nothing more
  than a thin sliver of a board
    (unless death already has occurred,
      since he is buried in a wooden box
        six feet under water without a coffin's
          worth of space).
Seasick and scared of pirates, tempests, and
        Mohammedans,
  he sits because there isn't room to stand,
    lies down and has no place to put his feet.
The captain is a brute, the crew are no-accounts,
  yet they're this kingdom's king and counts
    with whom no education counts if you can't
      swim.
I'll tell you, though, what makes them glum:
  it's when I smile because I know

> that soon I'll lay my soul in my Lord's lap.
> There, where once His ark and altar stood,
>> I'll thank Him, requiter of men's guilt with good,
>> with all the song and praise I can bestow.

Travel was slow. Large ships were square-rigged, so that their sails could be angled only slightly and were incapable of being close-hauled. Able to run before the wind or sail on a broad reach, they could make little progress in a head-wind and had to stray off course or cast anchor when one blew. Nor did their shallow keels ensure against capsizing in the Mediterranean's winter storms and high seas. Consequently, long voyages were undertaken only from late spring, when the rainy season ended, to midautumn, when it began again, and ships tended to hug the coast, frequently put into port for shelter and provisions, and sailed in convoys held back by their slowest vessel. The three-thousand-kilometer voyage from Spain to Egypt could take two months or more. In addition, keeping close to land made ships more vulnerable to pirates, who lay in wait along the shore and launched their boats when sighting a target, and offered only partial protection against the siroccos that whipped out of the North African desert. Halevi's ship was caught in at least one of these dry-weather squalls that fill the air with dust, a frightening experience of which he wrote:

> Wheeling across the water,
> The waves ran thick and fast.
> Beneath a darkening sky,
> The sea churned loud;
> Then, surging from its depths,

It made a sound
As a pot makes when it boils.
Cries filled the air,
And stout hearts fell
And failed to quell the fear.
The world was half abyss,
Half precipice,
The ship that reeled from that to this
Sick with the staggers.

On other days, the prevailing westerlies of summer would have driven the ship steadily on in fine weather. It was then, while the captain risked a course farther out to sea, that Halevi, sitting or standing on deck, must have written the half-dozen sea poems that are among his finest work. Even today, when the Mediterranean is crowded with large and small craft, the yachtsman often finds himself alone on it, with nothing but water as far as the flat horizon. The world seems utterly empty, one's boat a tiny speck on its surface. Halevi has given us a fine description of this:

Has a new Flood drowned the land
And left no patch of dry ground,
Neither bird, beast, nor man?
Has nothing remained?
A strip of bare sand
Would be balm for the mind;
The dreariest plain,
A pleasure to scan.
But all that is seen
Is a ship and the span
Of the sea and the sky, and Leviathan

> As he churns up the brine,
> Which grips the ship as the hand
> Of a thief grips his find.
> Let it foam! My heart bounds
> As I near the Lord's shrine.

The ship sailed on and docked safely in Alexandria on September 8, the twenty-fourth day of the Hebrew month of Elul. Halfon ben Netanel, who lived in Fustat—today the old section of Cairo, far inland up the Nile—was waiting anxiously for news of Halevi's arrival, and his Alexandrian cousin Amram ben Yitzhak wrote to tell him about it. He had not yet seen Halevi, Amram wrote, because the poet was still aboard the docked ship, whose approach had been advertised by a companion vessel putting in ahead of it. He had kept Halfon uninformed of this because "I did not want to overexcite you. Since then we have been waiting, no one more frantically than myself, and praying to God, may He be exalted and praised, that he [Halevi] is in good health and that you may soon be granted [the reunion with him] you long have wished for."

It was a week before Rosh Hashanah. From then until Halevi sailed for Palestine in the month of May, we have, in large measure thanks to the Cairo Geniza, a more detailed record of his whereabouts, moods, thoughts, and relationships than from any other period of his life. Considering that his Egyptian sojourn was largely an enigma for eight hundred years after his death, this is a remarkable example of how, gazing through the telescope of historical research, it is sometimes possible to know far more about distant events than did those who lived soon after them.

I had thought it would be handier to speed through Alexandria," Yehuda Halevi wrote in a rhymed prose letter sent sometime after his arrival in Egypt to Shmuel ben Hananiah, the *nagid*, or official head, of Egyptian Jewry, who lived in Fustat. The Nagid had written to request the honor of a visit from Halevi, whose reply stated that he had originally intended to remain in Egypt as briefly as possible, only long enough to find a ship with which to continue his eastward journey.

Yet the passage from Spain had taken longer than he had counted on, and he had arrived in Egypt late in the year. The summer was nearly over. The High Holidays were at hand. Even had an eastward-bound ship been available immediately, he would not have wanted to spend the most solemn days of the Jewish calendar at sea, especially as this would have been an affront to Alexandria's Jews, who expected to host him for the holidays. After Rosh Hashanah came Yom Kippur and Sukkot, the eight-day Feast of Booths, and by the time they were over, it would be well into October, with the rainy season about to begin.

True, bad storms rarely hit the eastern Mediterranean before November; a few last ships might still be setting out. But at this point, a new factor intervened in the person of Aharon el-Ammani, a wealthy and cultivated rabbinical judge and prominent member of Alexandria's Jewish community. Acting on instructions (or so Halevi thought) from Shmuel ben Hananiah in Fustat, El-Ammani persuaded Halevi to extend his stay, showering him with largesse and offering him the hospitality of his spacious home.

Halevi's lengthy letter to the Nagid began with a polite refusal of what was probably an offer to defray the expenses of a trip to Fustat, followed by a description of his situation:

> I have been blessed by God's giving and am not pressed for a living. Indeed, having all that I need and more to pass on, I wished only to push on and be a credit to myself and a burden to no one else. And so I thought it would be handier to speed through Alexandria and proceed on my way without further delay. Yet soon I met a man who defeated my plan, a wise judge in your employ, Your Grace's envoy, that scholar of eminence and companion par excellence, our very own Rabbi Aharon. . . . He plied me with munificence and regaled me in magnificence, with a feast for each repast and a house that is vast, full of alcoves and larders and quarters for boarders with beds to alight on and tables to write on. His kindness surrounded me and his goodness confounded me, for the more I was cold, the more he cajoled, and the greater my resistance, the more stubborn his persistence, until it ended in my failing to keep him from prevailing. And so I and my kin and company who came with me across the sea are now ensconced in his home, sheltered under its dome and consuming its treats and digesting its meats and imbibing its fine collection of wine.

Halevi's "kin and company" were Yitzhak ibn Ezra and an otherwise unknown figure named Shlomo ibn Gabbai, who had come along as his personal attendant. Aharon el-Ammani had an urban estate of impressive proportions. In a poem addressed to his friends in Spain, Halevi told them he was living "in a castle . . . a place of ponds and jetting water." The lavish grounds boasted (as described in a different poem) a gardened pool; a fountain from which "Water shoots up from below / And falls like rain from on high, / As though vying to make the slow clouds / Look cumbersome in the sky"; and an outdoor sauna, its stone floor heated by hot coals.

Despite its light tone, which the jingly nature of rhymed prose tended to impose on its writer, Halevi's letter to Shmuel ben Hananiah reveals a troubled state of mind. He and his two companions had just concluded a long, grueling sea voyage. They would have arrived in Alexandria exhausted and in need of rest. The opportunity to recuperate in luxury as pampered guests during the Jewish holidays must have seemed a stroke of good fortune. Comparing his trip across the Mediterranean to the Children of Israel's crossing of the Red Sea, Halevi thanked Aharon el-Ammani in a poem for having raised him "from the cursed and bitter deep" and brought him to a "splendid house" surrounded by exotic plants and waterworks.

Yet it wasn't so simple. Breaking with a lifetime in Spain had demanded every bit of resolution that Halevi could muster. Not only had he abandoned everything familiar, he had leaped blindly into a future whose only certainty was how difficult it would be—and now he had landed not on the hard reality of the Land of Israel, but in a soft bed in Alexandria. Although this must have come as an instinctive physical and emotional relief, it must also have been a mental shock to a man who had steeled himself for every imaginable trial except that of having to steel himself once more to soon leave yet another life, however brief, of feted comfort.

Moreover, he had failed the first test. In the remaining weeks of generally clear October weather, he could have continued on to Palestine and hadn't. His clenched will had relaxed its grip, leaving him feeling weak and fearful that he might have missed his chance. The premonition that he did not have long to live began to haunt him. His letter to Shmuel ben Hananiah—much of it an explanation of his voyage that summarized the arguments put forth in *The Kuzari*—ended with a poem as earnest as his opening remarks were buoyant:

> If you, my lord, would do my will,
> Let me travel to my Lord,
> For I will have no peace until
> I make my home in His abode.
> Do not, my footsteps, linger while
> Death overtakes me on the road.
> Beneath God's wings, I ask to rest
> Where my ancestors were laid.

"Let me travel to my Lord"—*shalḥuni ve-elkha le'adoni*—is one of the many biblically encoded allusions in this letter, *shalaḥ* being the Hebrew verb used by Moses in declaring "Let my people go." Halevi knew he would be received even more royally in Fustat than he had been in Alexandria and, in his concern about being detained there, did not shrink from comparing the Nagid's invitation to him to Pharaoh's holding the Children of Israel in bondage.

Of course, everything could be rationalized. Aharon el-Ammani had been a generous host; it would have been rude to spurn his magnanimity. Moreover, the caravan routes to Palestine across Sinai, while even more arduous than sea travel, were open all winter. They originated not in Alexandria, which lay at the Nile delta's western edge, but farther east, or else in Fustat, at the delta's southern tip. Why not, then, set out from the latter? This would also make it possible to bring Halfon ben Netanel his promised copy of *The Kuzari* while spending time as his guest instead of forcing him to come for a hurried rendezvous in Alexandria.

It must have seemed the best solution: a few more days of luxury in Alexandria, the journey upriver, a brief stay in Fustat, and Halevi would be on his way. Besides, he had become involved in a commercial venture that he needed time to complete. And so, he answered Shmuel ben Hananiah, although happy to accept the invitation, he would not depart for Fustat just yet. "May Your Grace," he wrote, "forgive my slow pace, for I first need to seal a business deal. (You might call it a steal, although it's from me the men I'm dealing with are stealing.) Meanwhile, here is my letter to go ahead of me and arrive instead of me to exculpate my coming late." It may seem strange that a man who had renounced "wealth and the world" now found himself conducting a dubious transaction with unreliable partners. But Halevi had invested his money with merchants for much of his life. A perceived opportunity for profit having come his way, the force of habit had apparently proved irresistible.

Remaining in Alexandria had gotten him into another predicament, too. Excited by his presence and wishing to make the most of it, the city's wealthier Jews vied in inviting him to gatherings and dinners in his honor. Yet he was in no mood to socialize. For years he had complained that human company had become burdensome. In the long weeks at sea, he had been anonymous for the first time since his youth, unrecognized by his fellow passengers and relieved of the need to be friendly or charming. Now, the prospect of having to revert to all that and make small talk with admiring guests at dinner parties must have seemed insufferable. Turning down all overtures, he clung to the solitude of Aharon el-Ammani's home. The public distress aroused by this can be gauged from an Arabic letter written to Halfon ben Netanel by an acquaintance, the Alexandrian businessman Abu Nasr ben Avraham. Halfon had asked Abu Nasr for an account of Halevi's activities, and Abu Nasr replied on the tenth of Heshvan, October 23, 1140:

> He [Halevi] has been to see no one except the "old man" [the reference is unclear] on the eve of Rosh Hashanah before the holiday began, and also, a certain Kuram el-Shama, who came on the same ship with him and was promised a visit, which he briefly paid him on the day of his arrival. . . . Subsequently, it also happened that the honorable Abu el-Karm ben Matruh tried to get him to come, imploring and pressuring him by means of the judge [Aharon el-Ammani] and of a messenger from the governor of the city, until he [Halevi] went to his [Ben Matruh's] home on a Sabbath eve, no one else being present but the judge and the son of our master Avraham [Ibn Ezra]. Otherwise, on the holidays and on the fast [of Yom Kippur] and on Sabbaths, he [Halevi] has been with our esteemed friend [Aharon el-Ammani]. . . . I myself, though I see poorly in the dark, went to pay a night call on our master Yehuda Halevi [at El-Ammani's], so as to keep peo-

ple from entreating him by saying, "How come you visited so-and-so and not me?" I am now waiting for Your Excellency, God preserve you, to come yourself, and I'm counting the minutes in the hope of meeting him [Halevi] again together with you. I am surprised at you [for not coming to Alexandria], because this headache needs to be dealt with and you, who have the authority and ability to solve greater problems, can surely cope with it.

Abu Nasr paints an almost comic picture of a Jewish community so eager to entertain Halevi that it did not balk at using its connections with the Muslim authorities to compel him to accept its invitations. (Did the governor, one wonders, threaten to have Halevi put in irons unless he dined with Ben Matruh?) Halevi himself was aware of the stir he was causing and regretted it. In a short letter to Halfon, he declared:

The [Alexandrian] community has shown me great respect, friendship, and cordiality, but so many wordy praises and encomia have embarrassed me. Although I have sought outwardly to go along with it all, it has inwardly been most difficult. I did not, after all, come [to Egypt] for any of this. I wanted the opposite, to be alone and by myself, because I am almost like one at death's door. But as you know, my natural instincts do not allow me to be rude to my well-wishers and I try to be as friendly as possible. And as for our friend the judge [Aharon el-Ammani], he persists in trying to own me and make me his slave. . . .

There are lacunae in this letter, and the remainder of the passage is unclear. Certainly, its disparaging reference to Aharon el-Ammani needs to be taken with a grain of salt. Although a part of Halevi may have resented El-Ammani's proprietary attitude, he also knew that Halfon would be jealous of the relationship: here he was, after all, spending his time in Egypt with a new friend in Alexandria while an old one awaited him impatiently in Fustat. Blaming El-Ammani for "enslaving" him was a convenient excuse.

On the whole, Halevi felt genuine warmth and gratitude toward El-Ammani, to whom he wrote over a dozen friendship poems. Coming on the heels of the intense expectancy of the weeks at sea, his first days in Alexandria could only have been anticlimactically disorienting. Nor would the Jewish holidays have helped; separation from family and friends is never felt more keenly than on the occasions one is accustomed to celebrating with them. Aharon el-Ammani's erudite and witty company was the one thing that restored Halevi to a sense of himself, and the days when the judge was absent were hard for him to get through. Once, when El-Ammani, who had five sons, was away for the Sabbath, Halevi sent him a verse note that said:

> This Sabbath was not the same for me;
> Its leisure lacked all splendor.
> When I don't see
> The son of Zion* and his sons,
> How can I take pleasure?

* An allusion to El-Ammani's having been born in Jerusalem.

A few months later, while in Fustat, Halevi sent El-Ammani an appreciative rhymed prose letter telling him how much he missed him and thanking him for his help. El-Ammani's home had been for him, he wrote, "a city of refuge." The judge had protected and defended him at a time when

> my muse had gone away and my thoughts had gone astray. I could not find the rightful creatures of my mind and grieved they ever were conceived. They betrayed and disobeyed me; the more I swore to lay down the law, the more they jeered, pretending not to see or hear. Alone and on my own, I tried to stalk and catch them but could not match them or bend them to my will—not until I called out in your name and they grew tame. Now they come and go again as bidden; inspiration is no longer hidden.

These words describe a period of nervous exhaustion that Halevi felt helpless to extricate himself from. (The temporary loss of his poetic powers, coming after his prolific output of verse at sea, is also referred to in his letter to Shmuel ben Hananiah, as well as in some lines to El-Ammani that begin, "See how the clouds that bring my dew and rain / Are stopped by drought.") He seems to have been suffering from what today would be called an agitated depression, an emotional flatness and creative barrenness accompanied by a high level of anxiety and an inability to concentrate.

It took him a while to recover his equilibrium. If in the end he stayed in Alexandria for two and a half months, it was not just to conclude a business deal. In Fustat, he knew, he would be forced to be far more convivial. He needed to get a grip on himself before facing that prospect.

By mid-November, he felt up to it. The trip to Fustat was made with Halfon ben Netanel, who came to fetch him. Halfon had a consignment of imported merchandise that needed to be transported by pack animal from Alexandria, and rather than sail upstream against the Nile's current, he and Halevi joined a caravan organized by an Alexandrian shipping agent known as Abu el-Ala. The late-summer floods that annually inundated the fields along the river and its canals, swollen by Africa's rains, had receded by then. It was the season of autumn planting, when the rich soil of the delta, newly watered and fertilized by fresh silt, was plowed and sowed. A first green fuzz covered the earth. Such a vista was new to Halevi. Andalusia was a land of wild mountains and farmed valleys. The alluvial plain of the delta, every inch of it cultivated, must have seemed to him like the "garden of the Lord" that the Bible compares it to, an immense *karm* stretching as far as the eye could see.

Egypt's history spoke to him even more than its scenery. No other place outside the Land of Israel had been the site of so many biblical events. In the land of Goshen, as the Bible calls the Nile delta, Jacob and his sons had settled; there the Children of Israel had become a people and been enslaved until God sent Moses to free them; had celebrated their first Passover and smeared the blood of its paschal lamb on their doorjambs; had set out to cross the Red Sea, led by cloud and fire, and proceeded to Mount Sinai.

Halevi felt that he was on semisacred ground. Passing

through the mud-brick villages along the Nile on his way from Alexandria to Fustat, he wrote:

> These great cities, these country villages,
> Were of old lived in by Israel.
> All honor then to Egypt!
> Tread gingerly in streets
> Through which God's presence roamed,
> Seeking His blood pact on the doors.
> Columns of fire, columns of cloud,
> Seen by every eye!
> The people of the Covenant carved out,
> Its mighty cornerstones
> Cut for the ages!

Another poem speaks of his initial encounter with the Nile, which was stricken in the first of the Ten Plagues by the same staff of Moses that had become a serpent at Pharaoh's court:

> From age to age Your wonders, God, are told
> And not denied by father or by son.
> This river Nile has always testified
> To how its waters were turned into blood.
> No hierophants performed the magic trick,
> But only Your name and Moses and Aaron's rod,
> Transformed by You into a hissing snake.
> Help then Your trusting servant to make haste
> To a place more wondrous yet than this.

This poem harks back to a major theme of *The Kuzari*. The stories of the Bible are believable, it states, because they have been passed down from generation to generation:

between the peasant plowing his field by the Nile and his ancestor thousands of years ago, horrified by the sight of the great river flowing red, there are no gaps in time through which a false account could have crept. So memorable were Egypt's sites that Halevi had to remind himself that an even greater experience lay ahead of him in the Land of Israel.

From Alexandria to Fustat by caravan took close to a week. It may have taken Halevi and Halfon a bit longer, since a subsequent letter from Abu el-Ala hints at mishaps that occurred along the way. By early December, in any event, the two men had arrived. This is documented by a poem Halevi sent from Fustat to Aharon el-Ammani that began, "My thoughts this Hanukkah are sad / And sigh to be without you, sir." The first candle of Hanukkah was lit that year on the night of December 6.

F ustat was at the bottom of the V of the Nile delta, near the site of ancient Heliopolis—the point of connection between Upper Egypt, in which the Nile flows in a narrow valley hemmed in by hills, and Lower Egypt, where, released from its confines, it branches out on its way to the sea. The city was founded as an administrative capital after the Muslim conquest of Egypt in 641 C.E., while adjacent to it a royal precinct called el-Kahira was established in 969 by the first Fatimid caliph, El-Mu'iz li-din Allah.

The Fatimid caliphate was Shi'ite, and distrust between it and Egypt's Sunni majority caused it to rely heavily on Christian Copts and Jews for support and administrative manpower. As a result, apart from a period of persecution in the early eleventh century under the "mad caliph," Abu-Ali Mansur el-Hakim, Egypt's Jews enjoyed a high degree of security and religious tolerance. Because they lived under a more centralized regime than did the Jews of Spain, their own institutions were stronger, too. Shmuel ben Hananiah was a powerful ruler in his own right, wielding an authority that no Spanish Jewish leader could have claimed since the days of his namesake, Shmuel Hanagid, the eleventh-century poet-politician of Granada. Ben Hananiah had only recently been elevated to the office by the caliph, succeeding his predecessor, Moshe ben Mevorach.

In the mid-twelfth century, Fustat, with an estimated population of 200,000, was one of the world's great metropolises. While Cairo housed the caliphate's palaces and royal residences, Fustat continued to serve as its commercial center, and whereas Alexandria commanded Egypt's access to the Mediterranean, it was Fustat that consumed most of the port city's imports and supplied it with goods for export from Africa and Asia. Much of the spice trade, the most lucrative business of the age, passed through Fustat's warehouses. Jewish merchants like Halfon ben Netanel played an important role in such activity, ranging as far west as Spain and as far east as India, and using their extensive connections with Jews elsewhere to build global networks of commerce.

Compared to his self-imposed isolation in Alexandria, Halevi's stay in Fustat was indeed highly social. Already on the third night of Hanukkah, he attended a reception at Shmuel ben Hananiah's official residence, which had been renovated before the new Nagid moved into it. (Of this we are told by a poem of Halevi's written in the Nagid's honor that starts, "And there was light for the people of the Torah / In three branches of the Menorah.") The occasion was probably a public housewarming, as befitted a holiday commemorating the restoration of the Temple. We know such a celebration took place during Halevi's stay in Fustat, because he wrote another poem for it with the line "Sing a song of dedication for [*l'ḥanukkat*] this house."

Halevi saw a good deal of Shmuel ben Hananiah and of his secretary, Natan ben Shmuel, and the time the three spent together went well beyond the formal nature of the Nagid's office. On one such occasion, apparently a festive dinner, Halevi was prevailed on by Natan to take part in the old pastime of verse competition that, once unrivaled at, he had long ago sworn off. In a rhymed prose letter later written to Natan, he compared him to a magician at Pharaoh's court who had bewitched him into something that, at his age, he had not believed he would indulge in again:

Though your powers alarmed me, your magic so charmed me that every vow I had taken was forsaken. My youth was restored; new verses poured forth; no longer recalling that evening was falling, I forgot my fear that my end is near with so much still left to do. Challenged by you, I reached for my lyre; I couldn't let your gauntlet just lie there.

He was being complimentary, having had no more reason to fear Natan's poetic powers than does a chess grandmaster a challenge from a park bench. In fact, if this was the same evening that Halevi wrote about in the continuation of his letter from Fustat to Aharon el-Ammani, he was not quite sober at the time. After telling El-Ammani about his cordial welcome by Shmuel ben Hananiah and the excellent impression the Nagid had made on him (Halevi calls him *ish ḥamudot*, "the most lovable of men," borrowing a phrase from the Book of Daniel), he described the circumstances of Natan's challenge:

> I've all but gone back to my old carousing, as once when every woman was arousing and I could have loved a thousand had any loved me back. How lovely were those days that never came back! Do you remember the poems you and I would pen as young men? Would you believe such times could come again, now that the disheartened heart is old, and our heads are gray and bald, and we look about and see that the lights have gone out and no rain breaks the drought? And yet the other night, as your well-wishers were drinking and hotly thinking of their longing for you, I—a memory come alive!—was plied with such strong brew and got so high and grew so spry that I began to versify. Attended by the most lovable of men, I wrote a poem to a friend that I now send. May you not be offended by how I start it or end it, and may you comprehend it as the gift that I intend it!

It is a singular scene: the renowned poet on his way to a solitary life in the Land of Israel and his newfound friends, the nabobs of Egyptian Jewry, getting drunk and jousting at poetry as he did when he was young! Besides the Nagid and his secretary, the company would probably have included Halfon ben Netanel; Halfon's brother Yehezkel, whom Halevi befriended in Fustat; Yitzhak ibn Ezra, and others.

By the norms of the times, there was nothing reprehensible about such a gathering, even if the age and standing of some of its participants might have caused a few tongues to wag. Yet after his reclusive conduct in Alexandria, Halevi's behavior calls for comment, especially in light of the poem he wrote for the contest he took part in. Natan had proposed, it would seem, that all present try their hand at a friendship poem for Aharon el-Ammani, to whom the conversation had fondly come around. Halevi did this in the form of a *qasida*. Like "The Earth's an Infant," written decades earlier to his patron Yitzhak ibn Yatom, this began as required with a preliminary overture unrelated to the main theme. For the subject of it, Halevi chose a musical performance he had attended in Fustat. The audience had been all male. Yet facing the garden the men sat in, with its fountains and its caged and strutting birds, was a latticed window through which women were allowed to look and listen. A crowd of them had formed, and Halevi found his gaze drawn more to it than to the performers. It was easier to let his eyes stray when the singers were silent and the musicians were playing by themselves, and his poem, reliving the moment, began with a playful appeal:

> Let's have more lutes
> For the lovely girls,
> You sweet singers!
> Give the instrumentalists their chance
> To serenade the secret sirens
> Looking through the lattice!
> Is it their fault,
> Unwitting archers that they are,

That their arrows have pierced hearts,
Though their bare arms
Never sought to lift a sword?
Well behaved they learned to be
From Laban's daughter at the well.*

The poet now turns his full attention to these "sirens":

So languidly they move
That you would think
They could barely raise an eyebrow,
Much less bear
The armor of their ankle bands and bracelets.
One look at the sun from them
And it would be sunburned!
"Let there be light," they say,
And it shines in their faces;
"Let it be dark"—
It's in their raven tresses.
Their tunics are bright
Like the splendors of friendship;
Their hair is as black
As the gloom of goodbyes.

The last two images anticipate the *qasida*'s main theme:
Halevi's friendship with Aharon el-Ammani and their parting. Yet like a musical motif sounded in advance of its full
development, this is quickly allowed to fade while the poet
continues wryly to describe the female beauty that, too old
to bid for its favors, he is nonetheless smitten by:

* The allusion is to the biblical Rachel, who, kissed by Jacob at the well,
runs like a proper young lady to tell her father about it.

They're so like stars
That I would be the sky
In which they orbited forever.
Full or delicate, luscious, lithe, or lanky—
I could fall for them all
And for their perilous red mouths,
Each perfect with two rows of pearly crystal.
Be gentle if you catch them making eyes
(At me, I hope),
Gentle with their wiles,
For they are burdened by
Silver bells of apples and of pomegranates,
And roses sprinkled with rare essences.
And what about that stately one back there,
Swaying like a palm tree in the wind?
Just count the hearts they've stolen!
I ask you:
Will they pay for them,
Or is it retribution
For the curls on their soft cheeks
Our eyes have poached on?

Only now, its first part completed, does the *qasida* turn to its main theme, elegantly pivoting on the conceit of a criminal trial for the heart stealers:

Ask a comrade!
Ask a rabbi!
Ask a judge
Who spans all knowledge with his wisdom's wings!
It's a clear case for Zion's son,
Who has God's statutes at his fingertips!

From here, Halevi launches into a catalog of Aharon el-Ammani's virtues and a lament for his absence. Then, as if suddenly reminded of the reason that he is in Egypt, he introduces a third theme, that of his journey to the Land of Israel, and glides gracefully to a finale:

> Can Egypt hold me
> When my soul's thoughts pull me
> To Zion's mount?
> On the day I take
> To her comforter's trail,
> My pilgrim's hair uncombed,
> My feet unshod,
> My heart's flame will scorch her stones,
> My eyes will flood her soil.
> Why, even as I write
> The tears pour down,
> Gusting before my sighs,
> As copious
> As all your many gifts,
> Each wrapped and tied—
> A bounty greater than these splendid girls,
> These fountains, strains of lutes, exotic birds.
> May our greetings to you, sire,
> Soar a hundred,
> A thousand,
> Ten thousand times higher!

The contest, it seems safe to say, was won by Halevi hands down. Yet when his poem was sent by messenger, along with its accompanying rhymed prose letter, to Aharon el-Ammani in Alexandria, it landed him in fresh trouble. By now El-Ammani had in his possession a small collection of Halevi's friendship poems, and he decided, as was his prerogative in an age that had no concept of an author's copyright, to circulate them publicly. An obvious act of self-promotion, this was nevertheless a perfectly acceptable thing to do. Friendship poems were written with the knowledge that they might be made public, and their possible benefit to their recipient's reputation was understood to be part of their worth.

Yet Alexandria's Jews were already angry at El-Ammani for having monopolized Halevi while he was among them; now, this additional flaunting of the two men's ties rubbed salt in their wounds. Worse yet, parts of the poems struck them as scandalous. How could the same man who had avoided all contact with them, as though fearing the pollution of social intercourse, now be reveling and writing lascivious verse in Fustat?

There was gossip. Halfon's shipping agent, Abu el-Ala, felt the need to let Halevi know. "If anyone," he wrote him, "were to read them [the poems written to El-Ammani] without reading the rest [of your poetry], he would ask: 'How can a man on a pilgrimage utter such rubbish?'" He hoped, Abu el-Ala added, requesting his letter be burned after it was read, that Halevi would not think him impertinent.

What Halevi thought of Abu el-Ala, we do not know. Halfon—to whom, far from burning it, Halevi gave the letter— thought him impertinent indeed. He must have sent a sharp rebuke, for in his next letter, Abu el-Ala apologized for his indiscretion and asked that his regrets be conveyed to Halevi.

Halfon knew the circumstances under which "Let's Have

More Lutes for the Lovely Girls" was written and could smile indulgently at them. But how are *we* to understand the poem? Now in his middle or late sixties, Halevi had not written anything of a sexual nature in years. What made him do so in Fustat? The seductive lushness of the Egyptian landscape? Old memories that, Andalusia gone forever, welled up incontinently within him? The reawakening of carnal desire by the need to bid it a last farewell before its obliteration by old age and death?

Perhaps all of these things. He does not, in any case, seem to have been troubled by them. His relations with Aharon el-Ammani remained close despite Abu el-Ala's letter, and there is no indication that he reproached the judge for the to-do he caused. Nor did he blame himself for it—or, for that matter, the Jews of Alexandria, whose reaction was perfectly, if narrow-mindedly, human. He was beyond all that now, in a realm where such things no longer mattered. His depression had lifted and he was feeling whole again, perhaps more than he had ever felt. Although his verse had dealt frequently over the years with the conflict between flesh and spirit, there is none of this in "Let's Have More Lutes for the Lovely Girls." We are not listening in this poem to two voices, one a body's that lusts and one a soul's embarrassed by its partner. A single speaker represents both, as if there were no longer any distinction between them.

In the verse and rhymed prose that he wrote while in Egypt, Halevi scolds himself often for lingering there but never for his responses to what he sees and feels. Of these, there is an almost joyous acceptance. The man who had given up everything had gotten some of it back. If desire's cessation, which frees the soul to contemplate beauty undisturbed by the body's wish to possess it, can be experienced as a blessing, its unexpected return, if only long enough for one final parting, comes as an even greater moment of grace. Having put the world behind him, Yehuda Halevi found that he was still in love with it. More than the Nile or the scenes from the Bible, this was Egypt's gift to him.

Halevi's rhymed prose letter to Natan ben Shmuel was written sometime in the late winter or spring of 1141. As usual, it was accompanied by a friendship poem, from which we learn that he was in the countryside at the time. Perhaps he had gone on an excursion with Halfon ben Netanel, with whom we know that he took at least one trip down the Nile. The wheat sprouting in November was almost ripe. Not far from him flowed the river. A bare-armed girl walked beside it. (Do the young ever have enough memories of their own to understand how many they evoke in the old?) At his back, where the watered valley yielded to the desert, were the cones of distant pyramids and the fronds of oases rising from the sands. A north wind blowing down the delta bent the stalks of wheat low. He was an old man about to set out on his last journey, and he was filled with a great thankfulness for everything. He wrote:

> Has time cast off its grim old clothes
> And dressed itself in its holiday best,
> And the earth put on an embroidered vest
> Festooned with patterns of checkered gold?
> The vale of the Nile is a blazon of fields,
> The land of Goshen an ocean of grain,
> Palm islands etched against the sky,
> The glint of far pyramids bright in the sun.

. . .

A girl by the banks of the river:
So like gazelles they are, but heavy-laden,
Heavy the bracelets on their arms,
The anklets circling their slim steps.
And the foolish heart forgets how old it is,
And remembers other boys and other girls,
Here, in this paradise of Egypt,
In these gardens, by the river, in these fields.
The yellow stalks are a rich brocade,
And when the sea breeze ripples through them,
They bow and pray in gratitude to God.

Several of Halevi's poems written in Fustat confirm that he had made up his mind to continue to Palestine via Sinai. One starts with the lines:

Lead me on past Tzo'an, the Red Sea, and Mount
Horev,
And let me make my way to Shiloh and the ruined
shrine's remains.

Tzo'an, the biblical name for the ancient Egyptian city of Tanis, was a synonym for Egypt in medieval Hebrew; Mount Horev, another name for Mount Sinai; and Shiloh, near Jerusalem, the home of the Holy Ark before the now "ruined shrine" of Solomon's temple was built.

This may not have been a practical itinerary. The traditional site of Mount Sinai lay in the far south of the Sinai peninsula; even the southernmost of Sinai's three main caravan routes, the celebrated "hajj road" taken by pilgrims to Mecca, passed well to the north on its way from Suez to Aqaba. And once in Aqaba, Halevi would have been left to his own devices, in need of further transportation to take him up the Arava Valley to the trading post of Zugar, the biblical Tso'ar, on the Dead Sea, and from there to Jericho and Jerusalem. The northern and central routes were better options.

In the end he did not take them, either. Perhaps he realized that the journey, with its many days of sitting on a swaying camel or walking by its side, would be too demanding for a man his age. Moreover, while most of Palestine was infested by bandits, its southwest—the country's entry point from Sinai—was a war zone as well. Fatimid garrisons continued to hold out in the port city of Ashkelon and to skirmish with Christian forces. Far safer was the sea route from Alexandria to Acre, the Crusaders' main harbor and the site of the country's largest Jewish community, numbering some two hundred souls.

Halevi's new acquaintances in Fustat would have told him this. Some went further and advised him against continuing to Palestine at all. It was unsafe. It was foolhardy. There would be nothing for him when he got there. Why live out the rest of his life among provincial Jews in uncouth Acre when he could spend it as a privileged guest in civilized Egypt? How could he cast all away for a country whose splendors existed only in his imagination?

He argued back, at times bitterly. A poem written in Fustat that begins "Let Egypt be first to be praised" ends with the biting riposte to his critics:

> Why do they make me their sport
> With their eloquent talk?
> If they believe in God's law,

> Let us meet in its court,
> And if not—
> Let it be nevermore!

It was the story of his friends in Spain all over again, with a new twist. Not only did the Jews of Egypt know better than those of Spain how inhospitable a place for an aging poet Palestine was, they could appeal to the same sacred history that Halevi did. Once Halfon ben Netanel had read his copy of *The Kuzari* and passed it on to others, or informed them of its contents, Halevi's whole argument could be turned against him. In a world imagined as a spiritual and geographical pyramid whose apex was occupied by the one people capable of prophecy and the one region where prophecy could exist, there was no need to go farther than Egypt, for prophecy had flourished there, too. Indeed, the greatest of all prophets, Moses, had been born in Egypt and never set foot in the Land of Israel at all! If the purpose of Halevi's journey was to scale the geographical ladder of Being, hadn't he already reached its top?

"Let Egypt Be First" argues back in the "court" of the Bible. While acknowledging Egypt's special status in biblical history, it refuses to equate it with the Land of Israel's. The temporary is not the same as the permanent. Egypt was a passing stage in the process of revelation. The Land of Israel is its eternal theater:

> God's presence here [in Egypt]
> Was like a traveler's,
> Resting in the shade beneath a tree.
> In Zion, it's at home and dwells
> Grandly, as all Scripture tells.

Besides feeling honored by his presence, Fustat's Jews were sincerely concerned for Halevi's welfare. They were also, however, put more psychologically on the defensive by him than were his acquaintances in Andalusia. Crusader Palestine might be hazardous, but it was not remote for them. While an ordinary Spanish Jew could not reasonably be called upon to visit the Holy Land, much less settle in it, Egyptian Jews did not have the excuse of distance. Yet they rarely traveled to Palestine, and Halevi's presence among them was also a reproach, which they reacted to by seeking to convince him that he was engaging in senseless heroics. Vindicating themselves meant keeping him in Egypt.

They stood no chance of succeeding. The man who could not be persuaded in Spain to forgo a journey not yet begun was not about to abandon one nearly concluded. Yet he did change his travel plans again, reverting to the sea route. It took him a while to decide. In the same scolding letter from Abu el-Ala, the shipping agent wrote that he was still waiting to hear from Halevi about booking passage for the spring season, whether "eastward" to Palestine or "westward" to Spain.

The westward tickets would have been for Yitzhak ibn Ezra and Shlomo ibn Gabbai. Abu el-Ala had every reason to suppose that Yitzhak wished to return to Andalusia as soon as possible. He had a wife and at least one child there, and he must have left them with the understanding that he would accompany his father-in-law as far as he could and sail for home. As much as Halevi would have welcomed Yitzhak's company, he can hardly be imagined agreeing to it had he suspected that his son-in-law would abandon his family.

But this is exactly what Yitzhak did. Toward the end of their stay in Fustat, he must have informed Halevi that he was not going back. The two men quarreled and a rupture took place, as can be seen from the fact that when, in the spring of 1141, Halevi sailed back down the Nile, Yitzhak remained in Fustat. Had they been on good terms, he would have at a minimum seen his father-in-law safely aboard ship in Alexandria and said goodbye there.

The son of an inveterate traveler (Avraham ibn Ezra lived at different times in North Africa, France, England, and Italy, where he was residing in 1140–41), Yitzhak may have inherited his father's roaming disposition. He had a mercurial temperament and a high opinion of himself, and disenchanted, it would seem, with married life, he resolved to start again in the East, where he expected to be received with open arms as a literary scion, an accomplished if somewhat stilted poet in his own right, and a representative of the prestigious Hebrew culture of Andalusia.

In this, he was mistaken. Though he was well educated and capable, his attempts to find a patron in Fustat after Yehuda Halevi's departure met, on the evidence of several angry poems of his, with failure. His falling-out with Halevi could not have enhanced his prospects.

From Egypt, Yitzhak traveled to Damascus. Obtaining no financial support there, either, he moved on to Baghdad. There, too, it would seem, the Jewish community denied him the recognition he thought he deserved, for before dying at a young age, he converted—so we are told by Al-Harizi's *Book of Tahkemoni*—to Islam. Three years after his death, his father Avraham wrote a moving elegy on the occasion of "bringing him home." If this means that his coffin was unearthed and shipped back to Spain for a Jewish burial, it would have been an unusual thing to do.

For Halevi, Yitzhak's desertion had to be a harsh blow—and the damning thing was that he himself was the cause of it. No matter how much he might tell himself that it was just as possible to forsake a wife and children while remaining in Spain, this would have been little comfort. His journey had cost the daughter and grandson he loved a husband and father.*

There was a bitter irony here. The king in *The Kuzari* becomes a Jew because he is told that mere intentions without actions are worthless, and Halevi's journey was predicated on this belief. Yet the king is never warned that actions, unlike mere intentions, can have unanticipated consequences. Now, Halevi had to sail back down the Nile to Alexandria with such a consequence weighing on his mind. Watching the great river uncoil from the deck of the boat carried along by the current, he wrote to Halfon ben Netanel's brother Yehezkel in Fustat: "Cursed be this serpent's crooked course that snakes / And takes me further with each bend, / And sets me on the wanderer's road again." His mood had turned once more and he was heavy-hearted.

The eight-day holiday of Passover began that year on March 26 and ended on April 2. Halevi probably spent it in Fustat and left soon afterwards for Alexandria, where Abu

* The reader interested in the debate over Yitzhak ibn Ezra's relationship to Yehuda Halevi is invited to consult Appendix E at this point.

el-Ala had reserved a berth for him on a ship sailing for Palestine in early May. By then the rainy season would have ended. True, Shavuot, the two-day Feast of Pentecost, was approaching, but Jewish law, which forbade travel on holidays, made an exception for sea voyages, and Halevi did not wish to delay his departure again. He had done so in September, and eight months later, he was still in Egypt.

He returned to Alexandria with Shlomo ibn Gabbai, whose devotion to him was great. It even earned Ibn Gabbai a bit of light verse that found its way into Halevi's Egyptian corpus:

> An ever eastward wanderer,
> Lone as a childless widower,
> I'm asked, "How could you get along
> Without the kindness of a helping hand?"
> "My luck," I say, "is that a righteous man
> Feeds me manna every day
> That tastes like sweets and choice viands."
> "Manna?" they say. "Don't you anachronize?"
> "Not," I reply, "when it's Ibn Gabbai's!"

The two men stayed with Aharon el-Ammani. Ibn Gabbai and El-Ammani were both at Halevi's side when, scant days before his embarkation, he found himself in yet another Alexandrian scrape—this time a serious one. Our knowledge of it comes from a letter written to Halfon ben Netanel by Abu Nasr ben Avraham and dated the third of the Hebrew month of Sivan—that is, May 11, 1141. After informing Halfon that he had received four newly arrived letters from Spain, two for Halevi, one for Yitzhak ibn Ezra, and one for Halfon himself, Abu Nasr wrote:

Nobody has had to go through what our master Yehuda [Halevi] has had to on account of that apostate dog Ben-Albasri, who filed a complaint with the police, saying: "There is a Jew among us with whom my brother sent thirty dinars for me. He is traveling to Palestine and says he will only give them to me if I go there with him and return to Judaism, even though I am a believing Muslim." The police then asked to see him [Halevi], and when he went, accompanied by the judge [Aharon el-Ammani], he was remanded to a Muslim religious court. . . . And so he [Ben-Albasri] went with him [Halevi] to the Qadi and demanded his thirty dinars, and when Master Yehuda denied [having the money], he was made to swear. But he [Ben-Albasri] kept hectoring and slandering him [Halevi] in public, and were it not for Master Yehudah's high standing in the city, the Muslims would have eaten him alive. But because of his [Halevi's] reputation, the Muslims wanted to kill the apostate. . . . Although we could easily have bought him [Ben-Albasri] off with some money, we didn't do it for fear that the Muslims might suspect Master Yehuda [of having sworn falsely]. Two days after this, his [Halevi's] traveling companion Suleiman ben Yosef [Shlomo ibn Gabbai] was also brought before the Qadi and asked for the money and made to swear [he didn't have it], which he couldn't do because it was in his possession. Then some third parties helped reach a compromise, and he [the Qadi] let him [Ibn Gabbai] go. I am indeed amazed at Your Grace. The man [Ben-Albasri] is known everywhere for his evil character and behavior. . . . How is it possible for such mental cases to drag strangers through the gutter without being prevented by you?

How Abu Nasr expected Halfon to have prevented this incident is unclear, especially since, however "evil" his character, Ben-Albasri was evidently telling the truth. Hoping that in Christian-ruled Palestine, where the apostate would be unknown, he could pass as an ordinary Jew and wipe away the stain of his conversion, his brother in Fustat had given Halevi the thirty dinars, with instructions precisely as charged. Halevi, loath to lie under oath, gave the money to Shlomo ibn Gabbai before appearing in court so that, technically speaking, he was telling the truth when he denied having it. As Abu Nasr ben Avraham observed, his high standing made him a believable witness.

None of this explains why Halevi agreed to be part of the scheme, in which his role was no mere passive accessory's. By approaching Ben-Albasri, he was running a great risk, since just as a convert to Islam who reverted to his former faith was punishable by death according to Muslim law, so were his accomplices. Although things turned out well, they could have ended badly.

Halevi could not simply have been doing a favor for a Fustat Jew whom he does not even appear to have known very well. Rather, endangering himself to reclaim a Jewish life must have seemed to him a defining act—on the same order, if not of the same magnitude, as his voyage to Palestine. Perhaps, too, his guilt over Yitzhak had made his own life, now nearing its culmination, seem forfeitable. He was in any case not acting by ordinary calculations; for if death is that after which no credible existence can be imagined, he had been traveling toward it all along. Had he not realized as much in Spain, he had surely grasped while in Egypt that, for a man like himself, Palestine would be a kind of afterlife.

Was he seeking martyrdom? It might be better to say that he was seeking completion. He was a poet and knew that there was always only one right word, and that, in the perfectly mono-rhymed Hispano-Hebrew poem, the same rhyme word was never repeated, so that, as line followed line, fewer rhymes were available until a poem's last line and last possible rhyme were reached together. Now, as he approached the end of the poem he had decided to make of his own life, it was clear what that had to be.

Halevi boarded the ship that was to take him to Palestine on May 7, 1141. We know this from another letter sent by Abu Nasr ben Avraham, also on May 11, to Abu Is'hak el-Na'ib, a business partner in Fustat. (El-Na'ib must have passed it on to Halfon, who dutifully filed it away.) Abu Nasr wrote:

> The ships from Andalusia, Mahdiyya [the port of the Tunisian city of Kairouan], Tripoli [in Libya], Sicily, and Byzantium have sailed with a good wind. Only one ship owned by the sultan of Mahdiyya hasn't set sail yet. Our master Yehuda, may God preserve him, has been waiting on board for the past four days, but the winds have been unfavorable. May God inscribe him for the best.

Presumably, Abu Nasr had gone to the harbor to bring Halevi the two letters that had arrived for him that same day. The Tunisian sultan's ship, having made the voyage from Kairouan to Alexandria, was now waiting for a west wind with which to continue to Palestine. An easterly had been blowing for several days, and ships returning to their home ports in Spain, North Africa, Sicily, and Constantinople had sailed with it.

Winds can change quickly. The ship was set to depart, its passengers warned not to stray far. The deckhands would have needed only a few minutes to pull in the gangplank, raise the anchor, cast off the mooring lines, and let their vessel be towed from the harbor by oarsmen, after which they would hoist the sails that were now folded and tied to their masts.

Halevi's state of mind was somber. Listening to the waves break against the seawall, he wrote a poem to Aharon el-Ammani in which he wished that he could pay him a last visit:

> Be still, you booming surf, enough to let
> A pupil go to kiss his master's cheek!
> (That's Master Aaron, whose unflagging rod
> The years have not made tremulous or weak.)
> A teacher who never says, "The lesson's done,"
> A giver who never fears to give too much,
> He makes me bless the east wind's wings today
> And curse tomorrow's gusts out of the west.
> How can a man who feels as though a scorpion
> Has stung him leave Gilead's balm behind?
> How trade the shade of a grand, leafy tree
> For winter's ice and summer's savagery,
> The shelter of a masterly mansion
> For the shriving of God's rain and sun?

Halevi had never spoken this way about his journey before. Calling himself the "pupil" of Aharon el-Ammani (his "unflagging rod" an allusion to his biblical namesake, Aaron) was the ordinary trappings of a friendship poem. But the remaining lines sound a new note. Always the west wind, carrying Halevi onward, had been his ally; the east wind, holding him back, his stubborn foe. Now their roles were reversed. Would that the wind keeping the sultan's ship at anchor would go on blowing! The "balm of Gilead" was no longer in the Land of Israel but in Egypt; the thought of Jerusalem, freezing in winter and broiling in summer, made Halevi yearn for El-Ammani's estate in Alexandria. Only recently he had compared God's presence in Egypt to a traveler beneath a tree, its real home Zion. Yet in "Be Still, You Booming Surf," the tree has become home, and Zion's rain and sun beat down on the homeless traveler.

He was afraid. He had always felt sure that arriving in the Land of Israel would be an exultant experience. Although he knew he would find a desolate country, he had felt confident of his imaginative ability to transform it into a higher reality. Now, about to encounter it at last, he had lost that certainty. He could no longer even be sure he had the moral right to do what he was doing. Intentions without actions were worthless—but might not the action that was called for be to give up his dream and return to his abandoned daughter?

"Be Still, You Booming Surf" need not have been given to Aharon el-Ammani in person. It might have been handed to Abu Nasr or Shlomo ibn Gabbai, Halevi's one other known visitor aboard ship. After he and Ibn Gabbai had said an emotional farewell, Halevi composed a poem, his last to come down to us, that is one of the simplest and most moving he ever wrote.

> At such a time, my eyes can't hold
> The tears back any more.
> They pour like hailstones,
> Hot from a storm-lit heart.
> To part from Yitzhak was the easy part,
> Even though the shock of it was rude.
> But now that Shlomo is gone, too,
> I'm left in solitude
> With no hope of seeing anyone again.
> And that's the last of all my friends from Spain!

He was utterly alone, more than he had been when setting out from Castile as a youth. Half a century had gone by since he had sat at a table surrounded by admirers, improvising a thank-you for a jug of wine. He was nobody then, although there must have been those who suspected that he would one day be a great Hebrew poet. Now he was that poet, the greatest of his age—and the age, though it adored him, could not boast a single soul ready to step with him into the unknown.

Why did not Shlomo ibn Gabbai travel with him to Palestine and help him get settled there? And what about Aharon el-Ammani? El-Ammani was an elderly man with a busy life and responsibilities, but he had five sons. Couldn't one of them have found the time to sail with their father's friend? Why did none of the Jews who had fought to wine and dine Halevi in Fustat and Alexandria volunteer to accompany him?

The only explanation is fear. Egyptian Jews were used to

traveling far on business. But the merchant who thought nothing of braving the seas to Spain and India was daunted by the short trip to Palestine. No matter where he voyaged within the House of Islam, he remained in a familiar world whose language he spoke and whose civilized customs he knew. Christian Europe was a crude and alien place, off the map of commercial travel, and the Crusaders—or "Franks," as they were known in the East—had a vicious reputation. Their burning alive of Jerusalem's Jews was still remembered. Entertaining Halevi in Egypt was one thing. Following him into a dragon's lair was something else.

Of the two letters that arrived for Halevi from Spain, the contents of one are unknown. Those of the other are revealed by a letter written by Abu Nasr to Halfon half a year later, in November 1141. Part of it reads:

> But as for the turban and coat that you say belong to our master Yehuda, Your Grace was not told the truth. When the letters from Andalusia were delivered by the letter carrier, and I brought them to him [Halevi] aboard ship, one was from Yehuda ben Ezra, who wrote that he could not remain [in Spain] any longer, and that he had made up his mind to come. He [Halevi] gave me a turban and said to me, "If Yehuda comes this year, let him sell it so that he can join me." He also wrote him a note, which is in my possession, telling him not to go to Fustat and to do whatever I told him. To which he [Halevi] added: "If he does not come this year, keep it [the turban] until you receive a letter

from me instructing you what items I need and buy them in exchange for it." . . . If the boy comes, he will get it, and if not, it will remain [with me] until someone comes who can rightfully claim it.

Coming at the last moment, this letter from Yehuda ibn Ezra must have electrified Halevi. Not only might he not have to be alone in Palestine, he now stood to have with him the grandson he loved, his parting from whom had "pierced his craw" a year earlier! Before he left Spain, it would seem, he and Yehuda had discussed the possibility of the boy's following him and had agreed that Yehuda would wait for him to reach his destination and see what conditions there were like. But Halevi had lingered in Egypt longer than planned, and Yehuda had impatiently decided to set out. The knowledge that his grandson wished to join him must have been immensely gratifying.

But Halevi's joy would have been clouded by new worry. Yehuda was his mother's firstborn, a boy who might not even have reached bar mitzvah age, younger than Halevi himself had been when he first left Christian Spain. His mother's double loss now stood to be a triple one. Did her father have the right to do this to her?

And what about Yehuda himself? With his education and family connections, his future in Andalusia was assured. Was it fair to take him away from an urbane and comfortable world for a primitive Frankish satrapy in which he would be saddled with an aging grandfather? While in Egypt, moreover, he would want to see his father in Fustat; what guarantee was there that Yitzhak would not talk the boy into staying with him? Surely it was Halevi's duty to write to

Yehuda, thank him for his loyalty, praise his spirit of adventure, and tell him to remain with his mother.

Yet it might already be too late for that. Such a letter would not reach Spain before midsummer, and by then Yehuda might have started out. And how could Halevi order his own grandson not to travel to the Land of Israel? If life in Palestine was a fate he wished to spare the boy, how could he demand it of other Jews? Of course, there were special circumstances in Yehuda's case—but so were there in every case. Suddenly, as if his entire voyage had until now proved nothing, the coherence of Halevi's thought hung again in the balance.

A conscience wrestling with itself is not like a conscience wrestling with temptation, because now conscience *is* the temptation. In the end, Halevi acquiesced in Yehuda's coming. Perhaps he justified his decision by reflecting that the boy could always return to Andalusia if his mother needed him or if life in Palestine did not agree with him. The thing Halevi feared most was Yehuda's traveling to Fustat to see his father, and he wrote a note forbidding it. It is an indication of how bitter the rift with Yitzhak was that he felt compelled to do this—and of how strong was the bond with Yehuda that he expected to be obeyed.

There remains the puzzling detail of the turban and coat. Halevi was no doubt traveling with a sizable amount of money. Why leave Yehuda items of clothing to sell instead of cash?

The date of the sultan's ship's departure answers the question. We know what it was from a brief letter sent by Abu Nasr to Halfon on May 19. In it he wrote that "our master Yehuda Halevi, may a thousand farewells go with him, sailed last Wednesday, the first day of Shavuot."

The first day of Shavuot in 1141 was May 14. When Abu Nasr, it can be conjectured, came to the port to see Halevi that morning after attending services in synagogue, the east wind had dropped, and the two men realized it was their last meeting. Halevi informed Abu Nasr of his decision regarding Yehuda, gave him a note for the boy that he had written in advance, and stated that he wished to pay for his grandson's passage from Alexandria to Acre. However, it was a holiday; the same rabbinic laws that permitted sea travel forbade the handling of money. Abu Nasr, needless to say, would have gladly lent Yehuda what he needed. But Halevi was adamant: he would pay for his grandson himself. He went below deck, fetched an expensive turban and coat from his traveling trunk, and told Abu Nasr to sell them when Yehuda arrived. Then the two men said goodbye.

When a wind shifts slightly, say from east to northeast, it goes on blowing steadily. But when it changes by 180 degrees, there is an intervening calm. Ships stop rocking at anchor. Telltales droop on their shrouds. The familiar sounds of a port—the creak of timbers, the flapping of canvas, the knocking of masts and spars—fall still.

The air holds its breath. When it lets it out again, it does so in a barely perceptible sigh. Then this becomes a soft whisper. If he had not already noticed, Yehuda Halevi would have been alerted by the activity on deck: a towline being secured to a prow belaying pin, the last visitors and vendors shooed ashore. The telltales trailed eastward.

There is a poem of Halevi's that once was thought to have been written at this moment. Today we know it could not have been, since writing, too, was an act forbidden on the holiday. Yet though it must have been composed earlier, there is nothing to keep us from imagining with Raymond Scheindlin that it "could well have come to Halevi's mind" as the sultan's ship hoisted its sails. Did his heart rebound as they went up, his doubts and fears drop away like the stage fright of an actor when the curtain rises?

Spikenard-and-apple-tinged,
Winged from the west,
You, wind,
Come not from the Cavern of Winds,
But from the storerooms of a spice merchant:
Scented like incense,
Swift as a bird,
Bearing my freedom.

How you were longed for
By those who rode
The sea's back this far
While they bestrode
The deck of a bark!

Stay not your hand from us now.
Fill our sails, long becalmed.
Stamp flat the depths.
Part the water in two.
Rest not till you reach the most sacred of mounts.
Rebuff the easterlies that stir the sea like a bubbling
                                                    stew!

Now leashed, now loosed—
What could a Lord-lashed prisoner do

But trust in Him,
Maker of mountains and winds,
To send you?

He was at last where he had always wanted to be: entirely in the hands of God.

7

Three letters of the Hebrew alphabet have been left out of our story. They occur in Abu Nasr ben Avraham's letter of November 12, 1141 to Halfon ben Netanel. What Abu Nasr actually wrote was: "But as for the turban and the coat that you say belong to our master Yehuda, *zayin, tsadi, lamed,* Your Grace was not told the truth." *Zayin, tsadi,* and *lamed* stand for the words *zekher tsaddik livrakhah,* "may the memory of the righteous man be a blessing," and they tell us that Yehuda Halevi was no longer alive when they were written.

Abu Nasr did not end there. He continued:

Also, a ship has arrived from Mahdiyya with the nephew of Ibrahim ben Mukleh of Almería. . . . He related that our master Yosef ben Alshami died in Nisan and that our master Rabbi Yosef ben Megas died in Sivan. See how three most excellent men have passed away within five months!

Yehuda Halevi's friend Yosef ibn Megas was head of the Lucena yeshiva, while Yosef ben Alshami was a prominent Andalusian Jew to whom Halevi once addressed a poem; the third "excellent" man was clearly Halevi himself. Since in 1141 the Hebrew month of Nisan began on March 13, followed by Iyar, Sivan, Tammuz, and Av, which ended on August 7, Halevi must have died in July or early August, less than three months after arriving in Palestine. His premonition that his end was near had been accurate.

There is no account of his death in the writings of his contemporaries or of the generations that followed. The earliest is found in a Hebrew miscellany entitled *Shalshelet ha-Kabbalah*, "The Chain of Tradition," published in Venice in 1586 by the Italian Jew Gedalia ibn Yahya. In this book is a fanciful tale about the marriage of Yehuda Halevi's daughter to Avraham [!] ibn Ezra.* In Halevi's old age, Ibn Yahya adds, he journeyed to the Land of Israel, where,

> reaching the gates of Jerusalem, he rent his clothes, trod the earth with bare feet—it being written [in Psalms], "For thy servants take pleasure in her stones and favor the earth thereof"—and recited his lament "Zion, Do You Wonder." An Arab horseman stricken with envy of his religious passion charged at him and trampled him to death.

Shalshelet ha-Kabbalah was a popular work that was reprinted dozens of times and Ibn Yahya's account of Halevi's death, though it did not state its sources, was quickly accepted at face value. It answered a long-puzzling question. Last placed by his poems in Egypt, Halevi had then vanished without a trace. Uncertainty over his fate probably set in soon after his lifetime. Some lines about him in Alharizi's *Book of Tahkemoni* may imply as much:

> Many ran after him and gave up
> All hope they might ever find him.

---

* See Appendix E.

> Alone he stole into the storehouse of verse,
> And crept out and sealed it behind him.

This can be read as a simple tribute to Halevi's peerlessness as a poet. It might also, however, be an allusion to a life that took with it the clues to its own ending.

Ibn Yahya's story had a romantic appeal. It described, if not how Halevi had died, how he should have died: within sight of Jerusalem, murmuring the greatest of his songs of Zion, his mouth in the dirt he had dreamed would taste like honey. It had the right proportions of fatedness and accident, fulfillment granted and denied: he had reached Zion but had not entered it, had met a sudden end that seemed chosen for him in advance, had been dealt the most meaningful of deaths by someone to whom he meant nothing. Who could doubt the truth of it?

Modern scholars could, of course—and did. Precisely the poetic justice of Ibn Yahya's account led them to conclude it was a literary fiction. Yet they appraised it in different ways. Agreeing with Luzzatto, Heinrich Graetz, the dean of nineteenth-century Jewish historians, considered it a pure legend and was not convinced that Halevi had ever reached Palestine at all. His early-twentieth-century counterpart Simon Dubnow, on the other hand, disagreed and thought the story had a kernel of truth despite its obvious embellishments and its substitution of a Muslim assassin for a more probable Crusader one.

Dubnow's contemporary Israel Zinberg, the author of a multivolume history of Hebrew and Yiddish literature, had his own theory. Halevi, he believed, had indeed reached Palestine and been so devastated by his experience there that he returned to Spain a shattered man. Zinberg based this surmise on a remark by the Hispano-Hebrew grammarian Shlomo ibn Parhon, who, in the foreward to his biblical dictionary *Maḥberet he-Arukh*, completed in 1160, claimed to have had a conversation with Halevi "before his death" in which he "penitently pledged never to write any more poetry." Since Halevi, Zinberg argued, composed verse continually in the years preceding his journey, as well as at sea and in Egypt, this pledge could only have been made after visiting Palestine. If no poems from the period of the visit exist, this must be because he fell silent at its outset.

On the whole, Graetz's judgment prevailed. Published in the 1950s, in the same years that Goitein was burrowing through Halfon ben Netanel's correspondence in the Cairo Geniza, a lengthy entry in the monumental thirty-two-volume Israeli *Encyclopaedia Hebraica* began: "Yehuda ben Shmuel Halevi (b. before 1075 in Tudela, northern Spain–d. 1141 in Egypt)."

Because of Goitein, we now know this is not so. Indeed, another Geniza document, dating to the year of Halevi's death, suggests that Dubnow may have been right. This is a copy of a letter sent by Natan ben Shmuel, Shmuel ben Hananiah's secretary, to Avraham ben Mazhir, a prominent rabbi in Damascus. Written in an ornate and cryptic Hebrew in the month of Heshvan, which commenced on October 6, it mentions Halevi in a passage of which key parts are no longer legible.

What remains, though, is doubly tantalizing. First, in speaking admiringly of Halevi, Natan appends to his name not *zayin, tsadi, lamed,* but *zayin, kuf, lamed,* that is, *zekher kadosh livrakhah*—"may the memory of the saint be a blessing." The word *kadosh*, "saint" or "holy man," also means "martyr" in rabbinic Hebrew, and such a formula often refers to a martyr's death.

Second, in a largely undecipherable section of the letter a few lines further on, appears the phrase "at the gates of Jerusalem."

In itself this proves nothing. Natan might have considered the death of any Jew traveling to Crusader Palestine a form of martyrdom, while "at the gates of Jerusalem" could refer to someone or something else entirely. Yet it is also possible that Natan was alluding to a death like that described by Gedalia ibn Yahya over four centuries later. Ibn Yahya, though he had a reputation for tall tales, did not make them up from whole cloth; his identification of Avraham ibn Ezra as Halevi's son-in-law, for example, derives from an older tradition that appears in fifteenth-century texts.* Might he not also have come across an old story about Halevi's death? It is noteworthy that the last years of his life, in which *Shalshelet ha-Kabbalah* was written, were spent in Alexandria, where he moved from Italy in 1575, and that the section on Halevi begins with the statement, "I have heard tell that Rabbi Yehuda Halevi, the author of *The Kuzari*, was a very rich man with an only, beautiful daughter." Conceivably, he was privy to some local Alexandrian lore that had been handed down, "not denied by father nor by son," from the time of Aharon el-Ammani and Avraham Abu Nasr.

One is free to speculate. The ninth day of the month of Av marks the fast of Tisha b'Av that commemorates the destruction of the Temple. On it, as they still do today, Jews gathered in medieval times at the Wailing or Western Wall in

* See Appendix E.

Jerusalem to pray and recite lamentations. "Thither," wrote Benjamin of Tudela, who visited Palestine less than thirty years after Halevi's death, "come all the Jews to pray before the wall of the court of the Temple."

In 1141 Tisha b'Av fell on July 18. Halevi's ship would have reached Acre in late May. After a few days' rest, he might have proceeded directly to Jerusalem. Yet as there were other sights he wished to see—"I would cross Gilead and Carmel's woods," he had written, "and stop to marvel at [the] lofty peaks across the Jordan"—he might have decided to put off his visit to the holy city until the fast. (Benjamin of Tudela, who arrived in Palestine by the land route from Syria, took time to visit Galilee, Capernaum, Mount Gilboa, Caeasaria, Lydda, and Nablus before coming to Jerusalem.) One way or another, Halevi would have wanted to be at the Western Wall on Tisha b'Av. He might have been killed before the fast as he approached the city's gates.

On the other hand, Benjamin of Tudela reported having seen Halevi's grave in Tiberias, by the shore of the Sea of Galilee. Most modern Jewish historians have doubted this claim, in part because no such grave is mentioned by subsequent Jewish travelers; in part because graves and tombs are notorious for being associated with historical figures never buried in them; and in part because some medieval manuscripts of Benjamin's *Travels* say "Yonatan ben Levi" instead of "Yehuda Halevi." But the oldest manuscripts say "Yehuda"; authentic sites can be forgotten just as inauthentic ones can be celebrated; and a false tradition regarding a tomb's occupant is unlikely to spring up so soon after his death. In light of current knowledge, Benjamin's testimony must be taken seriously.

Perhaps, then, Yehuda Halevi died of illness or some

other cause in or near Tiberias (a city having, according to Benjamin, some fifty Jewish inhabitants at the time), and the place and manner of his death were transferred by legend to Jerusalem. This need not mean that Gedalia ibn Yahya was the legend's author. In a sense, it had started with Halevi himself. He had longed to embrace the earth and stones of Zion. Pounded into them by the hooves of a horse, he would have had his wish starkly granted.

Yehuda Halevi lived at the end of the Andalusian "golden age," which was effectively terminated by the Almohads' invasion and conquest of southern Spain in 1146. (This followed the completion of their takeover of Morocco in 1140.) More persistent in their zeal than the Almoravids, the Almohads enacted long-lasting anti-Jewish and anti-Christian measures that included episodes of forced conversion to Islam. Thousands of Jews, especially from the wealthier and more educated classes, fled northward to Christian Spain; others migrated elsewhere, such as the family of Maimonides, who ended up settling in Fustat. Few returned to Andalusia. Its days of glory as a center of Jewish culture were over.

Hebrew poetry found new homes. It prospered in northern Spain, in southern France, and in Italy. Yet never again did it mean as much for an entire society as it had meant in Andalusia, and never again until the twentieth century did it shine as it had shone there, where five of its brightest stars—Shmuel ha-Nagid, Shlomo ibn Gabirol, Moshe ibn Ezra, Yehuda Halevi, and Avraham ibn Ezra—lived overlapping lives. While formally rigorous verse open to universally human themes continued to be written in Hebrew, it failed to spread from Andalusia to other Muslim lands or to the Ashkenazi communities of Central and Eastern Europe. Gradually, it was pushed to the margins of Jewish consciousness.

Most of Yehuda Halevi's poetry was forgotten. Though his secular poems continued to be read for a while ("his coal-bright love songs burn through the years," wrote Alharizi), they gradually dropped out of circulation. Best remembered were his *piyyutim*, especially those that were incorporated into the Sephardic liturgy. His single most celebrated poem, however, was introduced to the synagogue by Ashkenazim. This was "Zion! Do You Wonder?," which was adopted by the Ashkenazi book of lamentations for Tisha b'Av and inspired numerous imitations. Two early ones—Avraham ha-Hozeh's "Zion! All Gilead's Balm Could Not Assuage Your Dolors" and Elazar of Würzburg's "Zion! Crown of Beauty Joyed in by Your Masses"—were composed within decades of Halevi's death. They borrowed his mono-rhyme of *-ayikh*, duplicated his Arabic-style meter, and fell far short of their model.

As for *The Kuzari*, it had to be rendered into Hebrew before it could be read by non-Arabic-speaking Jews. This was done in 1167 by Yehuda ibn Tibbon, the Andalusian-born founder of a dynasty of noted translators in Provence. Had Halevi lived to see Ibn Tibbon's translation, with its heavily Arabized phrasing and syntax, one suspects he would have felt compelled to redo it; to this day it seems unfair that one of the great masters of the Hebrew language had to be known to posterity in such awkward Hebrew prose. (Ibn Tibbon, it must be said, was keenly aware of his stylistic shortcomings, which he justified by the need for fidelity. "I realize," he wrote in a preface to his translation of Bahya ibn Pekuda's *Duties of the Heart*, "that I have taken my life in my hands, and bared my back to lashes, and made myself a target for the arrows of my betters, but I have tried my best to change nothing that the author wrote and to translate wherever possible word for word, however inelegantly." He would have said the same of his *Kuzari*.)

It was in Ibn Tibbon's translation, in any event, that *The Kuzari* entered the Jewish canon. References to it in rabbinical literature can already be found in the writings of the Talmudic authority Abraham ben David of Posquiéres (1125–1198). It was cited frequently by the prominent Catalonian scholar, theologian, and biblical commentator Moshe ben Nachman or Nachmanides (1194–1270) and his students, and—although rarely mentioned by them by name—was apparently highly regarded by many of the early kabbalists of the thirteenth century who were active in Catalonia and Provence. Indeed, the argument has been made that certain important concepts of early Kabbalah, such as the theurgic nature of the "commandments of obedience," were influenced by *The Kuzari*. In several places in the *Zohar*, the great kabbalistic work written toward the end of the thirteenth century by the Catalonian mystic Moshe de León (c. 1240–1305), appear key images that almost certainly derive from Halevi's book, such as the comparison of the Jewish people amid the nations to the heart in the human body. The *Zohar* proceeds to follow Halevi's metaphor even more closely by observing, as does the rabbi to the Khazar king, that as the heart is the most susceptible of all organs to illness, so Israel is more degradable than other peoples by misfortune.

Both early Kabbalah and the writings of Nachmanides form part of the thirteenth-century reaction to the Aristotelian rationalism of Maimonides' *The Guide for the Perplexed*. Completed in 1190, *The Guide* quickly became one of the most influential and controversial books in Jewish history, one that was read in its own day—and can still be read—in one of two ways: either as the comprehensive attempt its author claimed it was to demonstrate the compatibility of Judaism with philosophy, or as the cleverly concealed replacement of Judaism by philosophy that it was accused of being by its critics. Although Maimonides' immense reputation as a Talmudic scholar and halakhic authority made it difficult to accuse him of religious unbelief, there were rabbis of his age who did not flinch from doing so.

The Maimonidean controversy, which reached its height in the public burning of *The Guide for the Perplexed* in a number of Jewish communities in southern France, divided the rabbinic world. The main issue was whether human reason was a sufficient tool for understanding the universe and God's role in it, or whether there were fundamental truths graspable only with the help of Scripture and the prophetic imagination. The debate resembled our own contemporary one over the ability of science to account adequately for a cosmos whose deepest mysteries, the skeptics assert, can never be explained by any amount of scientific progress.

The Kuzari occupies an anomalous place in this controversy. In a strict sense, it is not part of it at all, since it was written before *The Guide for the Perplexed* and is not referred to in *The Guide*'s pages. Moreover, its critique of philosophy is aimed more at the Islamic Neoplatonism of Al-Farabi and Avicenna than at the Aristotelianism espoused by Maimonides that came into fashion in the mid-twelfth century, and it is by no means rigorous or systematic by philosophical standards. As such, it was of relatively little use to later Jewish thinkers who sought to refute Maimonides on philosophical grounds.

In another sense, however, *The Kuzari* seems almost to have been written with *The Guide for the Perplexed* in mind. Inasmuch as it aimed to challenge the relevance to Judaism, not of this or that philosophical school but of philosophy itself, the specific philosophical doctrines addressed by it hardly matter. The more reputable the philosopher, the better a target he would have made—and no philosopher's reputation has ever rivaled Maimonides' among Jews. Though preceding *The Guide* by fifty years, *The Kuzari* can thus be read as a response to it, the most artful ever written.

It is true that, as the University of Pittsburgh scholar Adam Shear has pointed out at length in his recent book *The Kuzari and the Shaping of Jewish Identity: 1167–1900*, Jewish intellectual tradition over the ages preferred attempting to harmonize the thought of Yehuda Halevi and Maimonides to contrasting it. Although there were always anti-Maimonideans willing to enlist Halevi in their cause, such as the Spanish kabbalist and critic of philosophy Shem Tov ibn Shem Tov (1380–1441), who declared Halevi's opinions to be the total "opposite of the opinions of the man who wrote *The Guide for the Perplexed*," most rabbinical writers, especially once the Maimonidean controversy died down and *The Guide*'s canonicity became widely accepted, were reluctant to stress the differences between two figures of such stature. It was not until the twentieth century, starting with the publication in 1912 of an influential essay by the young historian of medieval philosophy Harry Wolfson, "Maimonides and Halevi: A Study in Typical Jewish Attitudes Towards Greek Philosophy in the Middle Ages," that the dichotomy began to be regularly stressed.

Still, it is a dichotomy that, to modern eyes, is striking.

It has been said that every intellectual is by inclination either an Aristotelian or a Platonist. In the same vein, every Jewish intellectual might be called a Maimonidean or a Halevian. He either believes that Judaism can and needs to be harmonized with the advanced thought of his age, or he doesn't. He considers the highest level of Jewish self-realization to lie either in the inward or in the outward life. He regards the notion that one can be born with a Jewish soul as either fanciful nonsense or an intuitive truth. He thinks of himself as belonging first to the species of Jew and then to the genus of man or vice versa.

Of course, such antitheses are simplistic. The same person may harbor both Maimonidean and Halevian leanings and form his opinions by the tug-of-war between them. (There was even, it can be said, a Halevi in Maimonides and a Maimonides in Halevi.) Still, whoever reads both *The Kuzari* and *The Guide for the Perplexed* will tend to feel instinctively more drawn to one or the other. The reader attracted to Maimonides will find *The Kuzari* irrational in its assumptions, careless in its logic, dismissive of scientific thinking, presumptuously ethnocentric. The reader attracted to Halevi will object to *The Guide*'s cerebralism, its neglect of the emotional dimension, its reduction of God to an intellectual abstraction, its disinterest in the ordinary Jew who cannot rise to philosophy's heights.

What *The Guide* lacks most from a Halevian point of view

is a sense of the everyday drama of things. Its philosophical Jew aspires to an empyrean detachment. He would comprehend all and thus lack nothing, like a microcosmic version of his God, whose perfection would be marred by needs or desires. Although his ideal is not, as in Buddhism or Sufism, the extinction of the self in God, it is not entirely dissimilar, for he would refine his intellect to the point that, having grasped the laws of the universe, its contents are indistinguishable from them. Such is Maimonides' paradoxical notion of immortality: the philosopher lives forever with that part of his mind that is no longer himself. This is, as *The Guide* puts it, the "true perfection of man," next to which all else is "only a preparation," for if you "imagine a person being alone, and having no relationship with any other person whatsoever, all his good moral principles are at rest; they are not required and give man no perfection at all." Not that Maimonides is indifferent to human relationships, which a high proportion of the Torah's commandments are about, but they are not his ultimate concern.

The Kuzari deals with wholeness but not with perfection. Its model is the *ḥasid*, the well-balanced Jew who lives in the world of human interaction, of which the book's dialogue form is an expression; whoever, the rabbi tells the king, wishes, like Maimonides' philosopher, "to retire into ascetic solitude only courts distress and sickness for soul and body." Action is necessarily *im*perfect, since it seeks either to obtain what is missing or to prevent the loss of what exists. A right thought cannot be unthought; having arrived at it, the philosopher is in no danger of regressing to a wrong thought on the same subject. But not only does a right thought not guarantee a right act, a right act has no power over the future; it can be undone at any time by a wrong act. Although all philosophers' minds, therefore, may be ideally the same, the ideal life is always unique. Hence, Halevi's conception of immortality is conventional. *The Kuzari* illustrates it by means of the biblical story of the ghost of Samuel, which prophesies to Saul after Samuel's death just as Samuel did when alive because he has remained the same person. We will forever be who our lives have made us—or, more precisely, what we have made of them. This is what makes *The Kuzari* a morally engaged book in a way that *The Guide for the Perplexed* is not.

A part from the case of Yehuda ibn Ezra, from whom we hear no more after the delivery of his letter to his grandfather aboard ship in Alexandria, we have only circumstantial evidence that some medieval Jews may have journeyed to the Land of Israel because of Yehuda Halevi. History tells us that the first organized immigration to Palestine of non-Karaite Jews from the Diaspora took place seventy years after Halevi's death. This was "the *aliyah* of the three hundred," a group of French and English rabbis and their followers who settled with their families in Acre and Jerusalem in 1209–1211. One of their leaders, Yehonatan Hacohen of Lunel, hailed from the same town in Provence in which Yehuda ibn Tibbon lived while translating *The Kuzari*. Yehonatan knew Ibn Tibbon and his work well and even commissioned a translation of *The Guide for the Perplexed* from Ibn Tibbon's son Shmuel. Another of the three hundred was Yosef ben Baruch of Clisson, who commissioned a second Hebrew translation of *The Kuzari*, which has survived in fragmentary form, from the Provençal scholar Yehuda ben Kardinal. Was *The Kuzari* an influence on the group's decision? It certainly may have been.

"The *aliyah* of the three hundred," though limited in numbers, commenced a new Jewish discourse about the Land of Israel. By transforming the duty or desirability of living there from a theoretical to a practical issue, it touched off a debate in rabbinic literature that continued until modern times, when it merged with the more historically monumental controversy over Zionism. On one side of the argument were rabbis who vehemently opposed any resettlement of Palestine. The same Elazar of Würzburg who modeled a lamentation on "Zion! Do You Wonder?" was undoubtedly alluding to "the *aliyah* of the three hundred," which took place during his lifetime, when, in commenting on the verse in Exodus, "Go not up unto the mount [of Sinai] or touch the border of it: whosoever toucheth the mount shall surely die," he wrote grimly:

> The mount is the Land of Israel: whoever makes haste to settle in it will die. . . . [This is true of] whoever settles there before the [messianic] End, because, while the Exile exists, there can be no freedom from it. When will Israel depart the Exile for its land? When the ram's horn [of the Messiah] is sounded.

Elazar was the first of a long line of rabbinical authorities to articulate a position that, by the inception of political Zionism in the late nineteenth century, had come to represent the mainstream of religious Orthodoxy. Its major premise was that, exile being God's punishment for Israel's sins, any pre-messianic return to the Land of Israel was a

defiance of God's will. To this some added the theologically more radical contention that when the Jewish people
were driven from their land, the Shekhinah departed from
it, too; shorn of God's presence, Palestine was therefore a
country like any other, the danger and hardship of living
in which had no religious justification. Indeed, in the opinion of the Catalonian kabbalist Azriel of Gerona, a contemporary of Elazar of Würzburg and Yehonatan of Lunel, it
was not even a country like any other, since the Shekhinah
now dwelled exclusively in the Diaspora. Wherever, Azriel
wrote,

> the people of Israel is in exile, holiness resides with them
> and is in that place. Hence, I must not approach . . . the
> earthly Jerusalem until the time of the End, when
> the people of Israel returns [to the Land of Israel] and
> the Shekhinah returns with it.

As a kabbalist, Azriel was far removed from Maimonides,
for whom holiness was a strictly behavioral attribute,
belonging to whatever human beings or communities mer-
ited its ascription by their conduct. Yet regarding the Land
of Israel, there was a convergence between the two. Neither
thought it was naturally endowed with spiritual qualities;
these were bestowed on it by sacred history, which had been
absent from it since the destruction of the Temple. Maimonides, who resided in Acre for several months in 1165
before continuing from there to Egypt, does not seem to
have regarded the experience as particularly memorable. In
his *Epistle to Yemen*, a letter encouraging that country's Jews
to remain steadfast in the face of Muslim persecution, he
warned them, in an allegorical reading of the Song of Songs,

the biblical love poem ascribed to Solomon, against escaping their predicament by a return to Palestine:

> Solomon, of blessed memory, inspired by the Holy Spirit, foresaw that the prolonged duration of the Exile would incite some of our people to seek to terminate it before the appointed time, and as a consequence they would perish or meet with disaster. Therefore he admonished them and adjured them in metaphorical language to desist, as we read: "I adjure you, O maidens of Jerusalem, by gazelles or by hinds of the field: do not wake or rouse love until it please." Now, brethren and friends, abide by the oath, and stir not up love until it pleases!

Yehuda Halevi stood at the opposite pole. For him, the Land of Israel was holy in itself, and the punishment of exile was as much self-inflicted as God's. No one before him had ever stated such views so clearly—nor, in the centuries after him, did many rabbis state them again. Yet there was a minority who did, forming a counter-tradition that ran through medieval and post-medieval times. Its first major representative was Nachmanides, who himself settled in Palestine in 1267 and wrote that the commandment to do so was "incumbent on every single one of us, even in a time of exile." A similar opinion was held by Shlomo Alkabetz (1505–1584), one of the sixteenth-century kabbalists who clustered around the charismatic figure of Yitzhak Ashkenazi Luria, the "holy lion of Safed" in the Galilee. In his book *B'rit ha-Levi*, Alkabetz cited *The Kuzari* in stating:

> Many have thought that the special virtue of the Land of Israel can be ascribed to the people of Israel's

dwelling in it and that it loses this virtue in their absence. This is a consequence of thinking that [the land's] uniqueness comes from observing the commandments that can only be kept within its borders and not that these commandments are unique because of it. But this is a great mistake! You should know that the perfection of the Land of Israel derives from its inherent nature, it having been the starting point of Creation. . . . All this was explained by the rabbi to the king of the Khazars. It is why the biblical patriarchs longed for the land even when it was polluted with idol worship, thus demonstrating how unsullied it was in itself.

There was hardly a generation in which such a point of view was not expressed, down to early Zionist rabbis like Yehuda Alkali (1798–1878) and Tsvi Hirsh Kalisher (1795–1874). Its two strands of mystical geography and practical settlement, however, were not always closely intertwined. Men like Alkali and Kalisher were primarily concerned with encouraging Jewish immigration to Palestine. In the writings of a figure like Yehuda Liva (better known as the Maharal) of Prague (c. 1512–1609), on the other hand, the legendary creator (and destroyer) of the famed Golem of Jewish folklore, the intrinsic holiness of the Land and people of Israel is emphasized to an extreme degree, while any pre-messianic movement back to the land is frowned upon. A full synthesis of both elements had to wait for Avraham Yitzhak Hacohen Kook (1865–1935), the chief rabbi of British Mandate Palestine, whose writings proved crucial for the evolution of religious Zionism in the state of Israel.

It is not possible to spell out precisely what Yehuda Halevi's influence on any of these men was. He was not always mentioned by them, and once an intellectual tradition is established, anyone belonging to it may have been affected by anyone preceding him. *The Kuzari* was the chain's first link; Kook, a great admirer of Halevi's, its last. The story is told that, while in London in the 1920s, he awoke one night in his hotel room, could not fall asleep again, took a notebook, and copied from memory a *piyyut* of Halevi's that begins:

> Roused by my thoughts and driven to profess
> God's praise in song and plead my neediness,
> I from my eyes brush midnight's sleepiness
> To seek the pleasance of the Lord's palace.

Once back in Jerusalem, Kook is said to have set these words to music and to have sung them every year with his pupils on Simhat Torah, the holiday of the Rejoicing of the Law. The truth of the story is borne out by the fact that his memory, phenomenal though it was, betrayed him that night in London and turned the line "To seek the pleasance of the Lord's palace," which occurs only once in Halevi's poem, into the refrain of each of its four stanzas. It clearly had great meaning for him, perhaps because of its use of the word *hekhal*, "temple" or "palace"—an allusion both to the Temple in Jerusalem and to the ancient Jewish school of Hekhalot mysticism, in which the adept rises through the heavens from one "palace" of God's to the next. For Kook, as for Halevi, one not only ascended to Zion, one continued to ascend from it.

Although *The Kuzari* is a critique of philosophy, it was not always considered one. Indeed, as Adam Shear shows, it was traditionally taken by many of its readers to be foremost a demonstration, less threatening to the beliefs of Judaism than was *The Guide for the Perplexed*, that these beliefs were consistent with philosophical thought. Such a point of view became particularly prevalent in sixteenth- and seventeenth-century Italy, where the influence of the Renaissance on Jewish intellectuals was great, and carried over to the early period of the Haskalah, the Central and Eastern European Jewish version of the Enlightenment. Two of its proponents, Yisra'el Zamosc (c. 1700–1772) and Yitzhak Satanov (1732–1804), wrote commentaries on *The Kuzari*, and Zamosc's pupil Moses Mendelssohn (1729–1786), the early Haskalah's most prominent thinker, held the book in high esteem.

As both religiously observant Jews and European intellectuals, men like Zamosc, Satanov, and Mendelssohn were fighting on two fronts: against a rabbinical establishment they considered ossified, which opposed all rationalistic defenses of Judaism as subverting the need for faith in Revelation, and against the European Enlightenment they identified with, which scorned revealed religion in general and Judaism even more. *The Kuzari* was enlisted in both battles. Unlike *The Guide*, it had never been regarded with distrust in Orthodox circles or suspected of heterodox tendencies (the eighteenth-century Gaon of Vilna even called it "a holy of holies"); hence, its use of reason to challenge an overreliance on reason could be cited as proof that Judaism might safely philosophize at no risk to itself. And at the same time, its authority could be invoked as an argument that Judaism, not being a faith-based religion like Christianity, was immune to the attacks made on the latter by *philosophes* like Voltaire and Diderot.

For the eighteenth century, Yehuda Halevi was the model Jewish *philosophe*. In the nineteenth, he became the great Jewish romantic poet.

True, by the time Luzzatto published *B'tulat bat Yehuda* in 1840, with its previously unknown poems that showed Halevi to be more than just a writer of *piyyutim*, European romanticism was past its heyday. Yet Hebrew literature lagged behind the rest of Europe; its own romantic period only began in the 1840s with the verse of Micha Yosef Lebensohn, who died in 1852, a not fully developed talent, at the age of twenty-four. Lebensohn had read *B'tulat bat Yehuda* and been impressed by it. He was also familiar with Gedalia ibn Yahya's account of Halevi's death, and in 1849–50 he wrote a ballad that was Hebrew literature's first treatment of the Halevi legend. In it, Halevi is depicted on his way to the Land of Israel, intrepidly defying the elements as he composes one of the sea poems in Luzzatto's volume:

Grim thunder and lightning dueled in the sky,
But he stood on the deck of the ship without fear;
Even while looking death in the eye,
He thought of his land and was filled with good cheer.

Then he summoned his muse and notes flew from her
lyre,
And over the waves rang the song of the bard.
All the sea's sirens fell silent as higher
Rose the voice of the water-borne prophet of God.

Yet arriving in Palestine, Lebensohn's Halevi is so crushed by the desolation he sees everywhere that his muse deserts him and he can write no more poetry. He wanders dejectedly through the land and finally reaches the mighty cedars of Lebanon. There he lies down, falls asleep, and dreams that he is surrounded by a horde of maimed and bloodied dead, the murdered martyrs of the Jewish people, who clutch at him to claim him for themselves. (This scene was probably inspired by the underworld episode in Virgil's *Aeneid*, a section of which Lebensohn had translated into Hebrew.) Then:

> As the hands of the dead went on holding him tight,
> And the dread of his dream caused his spirits to reel,
> All of a sudden—ah mercy, the fright!—
> A live hand ran him through with the coldness of
>   steel.

> A cold, cruel sword in his dreaming heart
> That gushed like a mountain stream as it bled!
> Thereupon did his soul depart.
> "You are one of us now!" exclaimed the dead.

> Not fear of the grave, but a languorous smile,
> The glow of God's glory, came over him then.
> So ended a dream more bitter than bile.
> The poet's eyes never opened again.

Stricken with tuberculosis, Lebensohn was projecting his own psychological and emotional state onto the Halevi of legend: he, too, felt doomed to die "at the gates of Zion," his life cut short and his voice prematurely silenced. His Halevi, anticipating Israel Zinberg's, is a tragic figure, a divine seer whose vision turns into a nightmare. Yet in the final epiphany that comes as life drains from him, the God who has deceived him and his people with an illusory hope of redemption is revealed to be an illusion himself, a man-made specter unlike the comfortingly luminous presence into which the poet is ushered by death.

Heine, that great anti-romantic romantic, wrote his own ballad about Yehuda Halevi close to the time when Lebensohn wrote his. Like Lebensohn, he owed his interest in Halevi to Luzzatto, some of the songs of Zion made available by whom, such as "My Heart Is in the East," "O Fair of View! World's Joy" and "Has a New Flood Drowned the Land," were translated into German by Michael Jehiel Sachs. Sachs' volume also included verse by Ibn Gabirol, Moshe and Avraham ibn Ezra, and other Hispano-Hebrew poets, accompanied by a critical essay on each.) Like Lebensohn, too, Heine was fatally ill when he wrote his ballad, a bedridden invalid. Yet it would be hard to imagine two more different treatments of their subject: Lebensohn's all earnest pathos, the frightened cry of someone too young to die, Heine's wry and teasing, the musings of a man who has seen and suffered too much to wish to cling any longer to life.

On the face of it, Heine's Halevi is every bit as romanticized as Lebensohn's. At the end of an opening section in which he is described growing up as a child prodigy in Toledo, studying the great books of Judaism while "lullabied by the golden Tajo," we are told:

> But Jehuda ben Halevy
> Was no mere outstanding student.

He became a master poet,
Indeed, among the very greatest—

Yes, of poesy a master,
Star and beacon of his epoch,
Lamp and lantern of his people,
Great and wondrous like a column

Of song-incandescent fire,
Guiding through the midnight's darkness,
Through the wilderness of Exile,
The doleful caravan of Israel.

Pure and truthful, without blemish.
Was his verse, just as his soul was—
For when the Creator made it,
So pleased was He with His creation

And its beauty that He kissed it,
And the sweet reverberation
Echoed on in every poem,
Consecrated by that grace note.

For as in life, so in a poem,
Grace's gift is all that matters.
He who has it never blunders,
Not in prose and not in meter.

By the grace of God a poet,
Such a man is called a genius,
Absolute monarch of thought's kingdom,
Answerable to himself only.

Heine was projecting, too, of course: the genius was also himself, the leading German poet of his time. But his identification with Halevi was with a cultural ideal as well. It was one he had believed in as a young man in the 1820s, when he had belonged, together with such German Jewish intellectuals as Leopold Zunz, Eduard Gans, and Moses Moser, to the newly founded *Verein für Kultur und Wissenschaft der Juden*, the Society for the Culture and Study of the Jews. As a Haskalah thinker like Mendelssohn had hoped it would, German society, with all its opportunities, was finally opening up to young Jews—but only if they passed through its doors as Christians. By the early nineteenth century, droves of them, unaware of a heritage that their stunted Jewish educations had failed to transmit, were abandoning a parental religion deemed irrelevant for what seemed the mere formality of baptism. The goal of the *Verein* was to stem this tide by educating a new type of German Jew, one who, versed in the best of his people's culture, felt as proudly at home in it as he did in that of nineteenth-century Europe. For this, no period of Jewish history offered a better model than that of the *convivencia*.

And yet without a good knowledge of Hebrew, the major texts of this period could not be read, thus rendering them inaccessible not only to Heine but to the entire population the *Verein* hoped to reach. As an idea, the *Verein* was a seed that was eventually to germinate; as an organization, it soon fell apart, and in 1825 Heine went to the baptismal font himself. Now, two decades later, remorseful over what he had come to regard as an act of self-betrayal, he was introduced by Sachs' anthology to Hispano-Hebrew verse for the first time. "Jehuda ben Halevy" was his enthusiastic reaction, one in which he conferred on the Jewish experience in pre-

reconquista Spain the epithet of a *Goldzeitalter,* a historical "golden age," that has stuck to it to this day.

It is a typically Heine-esque poem. Partway through its more than two hundred leisurely stanzas, it brings the story of Yehuda Halevi to a climax with his murder by an Arab horseman—in reality, the reader is told, an angel in disguise, sent to fetch the poet's soul to heaven, where he is greeted by a seraphic choir singing his immortal Sabbath hymn *Lekha Dodi.* (Here, Heine stumbled: *Lekha Dodi* was written centuries later by Shlomo Alkabetz.) This sentimental tinsel, as any knowledgeable reader of Heine would have guessed, could only portend the ironic anticlimax to come. And come it does in the form of a long comic digression on the origins of the German-Jewish word *schlemihl,* traced to the minor figure of Shlumiel ben Tsurishaddai in the Book of Numbers—who, the poem informs us, citing a folk exegesis passed on to Heine by a friend in Berlin, haplessly got in the way of a spear meant by the avenging zealot Pinhas for the whoring sinner Zimri. Shlumiel's death is thus linked to Halevi, also absurdly killed by an assassin ignorant of his identity, and thence to Ibn Gabirol and Ibn Ezra— both, according to legends related by Sachs, butts of similarly cruel pranks of fate. And, Heine declares, speaking for all true poets:

> The years have come and they have vanished,
> All in all, a round three thousand
> Since the death of our first father,
> Herr Schlemiel ben Zurishaddai.

> Pinhas, too, is long since gone—
> And yet still his spear is brandished

And we hear it as it whistles,
Whirring through the air above us.

The best hearts are those it strikes at,
Like Jehuda ben Halevy's,
Or like Moses Ibn Ezra's,
Or like Solomon Gabirol's.

Or like Heinrich Heine's, dying in lonely exile in Paris, a victim of political tyrants and philistine readers. Of the ballad's two versions of Halevi's death—a heaven-orchestrated pageant and the senseless mishap of a dreamer who should have kept his head up and on the lookout for danger rather than pressed to the earth of Jerusalem—the second is clearly the "real" one. Heine's Halevi is a schlemiel because the journey that takes him to his death is a *beau geste*, a beautiful but pointless gesture.

But the anticlimax of Heine's poem is not its final resting place, either. Although his Yehuda Halevi could not have been welcomed by angels to a heaven that does not exist, he would have been if it did. Poetry, too, is a *beau geste*. It is the impractical putting together of beautiful words for their own sake, and those who dedicate themselves to it, though perhaps fools in the eyes of men, are heroes in the eyes of the angels imagined by men. Heine's identification with Halevi was genuine, even though, while turning out to be more attached to his Jewishness than he had thought he was when abandoning it, he did not think it was anything worth dying for.

There were, however, westernized Jewish intellectuals of the age who thought the Jewish people had more of a future than Heine granted it. For some, stirred by the spirit of nineteenth-century nationalism that Heine disdained and hoping it might be the answer to Jewish assimilation, Yehuda Halevi now became the national poet as well.

Graetz, who died in 1891, five years before the publication of Theodor Herzl's *The Jewish State*, is a case in point. Precisely because his Jewish nationalism was of a hesitant, pre-Zionist variety, one is struck by his attitude toward Halevi—that "God-kissed lyrical poet," as he called him, echoing Heine, "whose magical verse overshadows anything created in the Hebrew language since the cessation of prophecy among Jews." Yet although Graetz was a secular Jew, it was not the great secular poems like "Why, My Darling Have You Barred All News?" or "Wander-life, You Are an Old Friend" that were taken by him to be the high point of Halevi's career. Nor was it Halevi's sacred poetry, "which does not convey the full splendor of his poetic genius and sublimity." Rather, Graetz wrote, Halevi's full stature was revealed only in the "national religious verse" of his songs of Zion. Here alone were the thinker and poet united, "Jewish national feeling" (*das jüdischer Nationalgefühl*) and "Jewish national thought" (*der nationaler Gedanke von Judentum*). Halevi was for Graetz "the first to grasp the significance of Judaism as an independent historical manifestation" because he was the first to regard Jewish nationhood as a historical force in its own right, so much part of the created order of things that it could, in the nineteenth century, be emancipated even from its Creator.

Of course, to view Halevi in such a light, one had to consider desirable a people-centered rather than a God-centered Judaism. No less than Lebensohn and Heine, Graetz was also projecting.

On May 15, 1967, the nineteenth Independence Day of the state of Israel, Egyptian forces entered Sinai in large numbers after weeks of growing military tension. That evening, in celebration of the holiday, a song festival attended by prime minister Levi Eshkol and army chief of staff Yitzhak Rabin was held in Jerusalem's National Auditorium. The hit of the evening was a lyric called "Jerusalem of Gold," written for the occasion by the librettist and composer Naomi Shemer and sung to a haunting minor-key melody by a wispy-voiced vocalist named Shuli Natan. The second line of its refrain of "Jerusalem of gold, of copper, and of light, / To all your songs I am a lute" was taken from Yehuda Halevi's "Zion! Do You Wonder?"

Three weeks later, the Six Day War broke out. On its third day, the old walled city of Jerusalem, with its golden Dome of the Rock and Temple Mount, fell to Israeli troops. Wet-eyed paratroopers sang "Jerusalem of Gold" at the Western Wall. The war's unofficial anthem and one of the most popular Israeli songs ever written, it marked the moment, one might say, at which Yehuda Halevi went from being a national poet to a fully nationalized one.

On the whole, though, twentieth-century Zionism's appropriation of Halevi took place in a more scholarly environment. It belonged to what cultural historian David Myers, in his *Re-Inventing the Jewish Past: European Jewish Intellectuals and the Zionist Return to History*, has called "a radical paradigm shift . . . the transition from faith to *Volk* as the source of Jewish identity and historical inquiry"—an enterprise, tentatively begun by Graetz, that was largely associated with a school of historians active at the Hebrew

University of Jerusalem after the latter's establishment in 1924. Of its three most prominent members, two—Yitzhak Baer and Ben-Zion Dinur—wrote on Halevi at length.

In 1935 Dinur published an essay entitled "Yehuda Halevi's Aliyah to the Land of Israel and the Messianic Ferment of His Age," in which he argued that Halevi's journey to Palestine represented a fundamental turning point in Jewish history. In doing so, he took issue with the German-Jewish scholar David Kaufmann, whose 1877 biography of Halevi maintained that the poet set out on his voyage for strictly personal reasons—principally, the desire to atone for the sinful years of his youth. Halevi, Kaufmann believed, was guilt-ridden for having once been attracted to philosophical positions that led him to doubt the verities of Judaism and now sought to make spiritual amends.

Not so, argued Dinur. Halevi's journey was not a private act but a public manifesto, a call for action and emulation. It needed to be seen against the background of the age, one of messianic expectations fueled by the deteriorating Jewish situation in Muslim and Christian lands. Having witnessed several messianic fiascos in his lifetime, Halevi developed, Dinur held, a new conception that stood traditional Jewish messianism on its head; for whereas in the classical formulation, the Messiah would arrive and lead a redeemed people of Israel back to their land, in Halevi's reworking of it, the return to the land would come first. The Land of Israel's re-inhabiting was a precondition for redemption, not its consequence. "I would say," wrote Dinur,

that Yehuda Halevi's projected path of redemption was a serious attempt, if not to found a new type of messianic movement, at least to blaze a new trail for a messianism that would engage less in calculating the awaited end than in hastening it . . . and that would demand of Jews that they settle in Palestine of their own accord rather than wait to be magically transported there.

Baer concurred. Published the same year, his "The Political Situation of Spanish Jewry in the Age of Yehuda Halevi" sought to make the case for Halevi as a political thinker. Living at a time that saw large numbers of Jews leave the Muslim south of Spain for the Christian north, Halevi, Baer wrote, had the prescience to foresee that Christian rule would end badly, too, and that the age-old Jewish strategy of cultivating the powers that be was doomed to perpetual failure. "The greatest realist of all Jewish poets and intellectuals prior to modern times," Halevi understood that Gentile oppression was the inevitable result of exilic existence rather than merely one of its hazards, so that, in calling upon Jews to end their exile by their own efforts, he was urging them to cast oppression permanently off. It remained for Zionism, centuries later, to do so.

Secular Zionism's keenness to claim Halevi as a precursor fit into its overall project of "Zionizing" Jewish history, regarded by it as the long march of a people back to their land—a roundabout, two-thousand-year-old trek whose greatest heroes were men able, like Halevi, to discern its true destination through the fog of messianic symbolism surrounding it. And yet while Halevi could be claimed for Zionism, he could hardly be claimed for secularism. His real influence was on religious Zionism—and then, too, mostly mediated by the thought of others, especially of Avraham

Yitzhak Hacohen Kook and his son Tsvi Yehuda Kook (1891–1992).

Although better known in his lifetime as a public figure, Kook the father was a theologian of some originality. The late-nineteenth-century religious Zionism he emerged from had been forced to defend itself against a largely hostile Orthodox rabbinical establishment that considered the Zionist movement to be but the latest—and historically, the most dangerous—form of false messianism. Pro-Zionist rabbis had tried to rebut this criticism. Zionism, they contended, was strictly limited in its goals, which were to improve the material and spiritual lot of the Jewish people by reestablishing a portion of it in its land. Since so modest a project was not meant to "force the end" of God's redemption, there was nothing religiously impermissible about it.

Facilitating this argument was the fact that early Zionist settlement in Palestine, even after Herzl's meteoric appearance in the 1890s, was mostly Orthodox in character. Yet the young socialist pioneers who began arriving in the country in the early twentieth century and quickly established their political dominance were aggressively anti-religious as Herzl never was. Their vision of a secular, revolutionary Jewish society was anathema in Orthodox eyes. How could collaboration with them be justified?

Kook's writings took off from this point—with a running start going back to Halevi. The religious anti-Zionists, he proclaimed, were right: religious Zionism *was* redemptive in its goals. What neither religious Zionists nor anti-Zionists understood, however, was that Redemption was a dialectical process in which opposites furthered each other until united in a final outcome. Because the people and Land of Israel were intrinsically holy, all secular Jewish endeavor in the land was holy, too. The pioneers laboring to till Palestine's soil and establish a society based on equality and justice were unwittingly doing God's work by accomplishing what a stagnant Orthodoxy forgetful of prophetic ideals was incapable of. One day they would understand this themselves and embrace a Judaism purged and renewed by its contact with them. Then God's word would go forth from Zion in the form of a perfected religion to which a world weary of exploitation and violence would turn for inspiration, and the messianic age would blossom.

It was only after the 1967 war that Kook's thought came into its own in Israel's "national religious" community—the common term, using adjectives first conjoined by Graetz, for the country's modern Orthodox, Zionist population as distinguished from its non- or anti-Zionist ultra-Orthodox. Until then this community had taken a backseat to secular Zionism, which set and carried out the national agenda. Now, though, especially once the euphoria of the 1967 victory yielded to the national depression that followed the heavy losses of the 1973 Yom Kippur War, the baton passed to it. In the face of temporary reversals, it alone understood, so it believed, the divine miracle of the Six Day War's conquest of the Temple Mount, the Western Wall, Rachel's Tomb in Bethlehem, the Cave of the Patriarchs in Hebron, the mountains of Judea and Samaria, and other biblical sites. And yet this miracle, which most secular Israelis were blind to, had been wrought by the secular army of a secular state, whose might was needed to settle and retain what God had restored to His people. How explain and exploit this paradox?

As interpreted by his son Tsvi Yehuda, Kook's theology answered the question. The secular state of Israel was itself the instrument of God's redemption! It made no difference that its leaders had no inkling of this. Who they were or what they thought they were doing was not the reality. The reality was objective, ontological. All the rest, Tsvi Yehuda Kook declared, was composed of

> mere detail, smaller or larger impediments, problems and complications; none of it can detract in any way from the holiness of the state [of Israel]. The inner value of the state has nothing to do with whether its citizens are religiously observant. Naturally, we would like the entire nation to live a life of Torah and its commandments, but the state is holy in any case!

Tsvi Yehuda Kook was the spiritual mentor of Gush Emunim or the "Bloc of the Faithful," the activist organization founded in 1974 that spearheaded the religious settlement movement in the occupied territories and brought tens of thousands of Jews to live in their more remote areas. Although ostensibly, the son was inhabiting the conceptual world of his father, the concepts had changed. Instead of pioneers, a state; instead of the Land of Israel as a platform for a perfect society, an imperfect society as a platform for the Land of Israel; instead of a redemptive process carried forward by revolutionary lives, one leaning on institutionalized power. Never indeed had secular Israel, swept by the first waves of hedonism and consumerism that reached its shores from Europe and America in the 1970s, been so far from Kook the father's ideals. But if secular Israel was holy without knowing it, what did any of that matter?

Ein Liebling aller Menschen, "everyone's darling," Heine called Halevi, and there is something about the man—a bonhomie and sweetness of temper—that is ingratiating. Maimonides has been revered by Jews; Halevi has been loved by them. It must therefore have come as a shock to the audience when, at a symposium held in Jerusalem in 1977, the religious thinker Yeshayahu Leibowitz turned on Halevi in terms never heard in public before.

Leibowitz, a maverick in Israel's "national religious" community for his denunciations of military rule and Jewish settlement in the occupied territories, had not planned his remark. He had been explaining why, in his opinion, no state, including a Jewish one, could have "intrinsic value," much less holiness, the ascription of which to "men, nations, objects, or countries" was "idolatry," when a voice called from the audience: "But Yehuda Halevi attributes holiness to the Jewish people!" To which Leibowitz replied:

"Yehuda Halevi was a divine poet, but as author of *The Kuzari,* he stumbled into nationalist and racist chauvinism! The Maharal [of Prague] and Rabbi Kook followed in his footsteps."

Such a remark would not, one imagines, have been made a decade earlier. But aspects of *The Kuzari* that might have seemed harmless in 1966 no longer seemed so in 1977. Halevi, Leibowitz wrote elsewhere, was guilty of introducing "the notion that Jewish man is endowed with characteristics that non-Jews lack," a conception in which "religious faith and national arrogance fused." Just as the attribution of intrinsic holiness to the Land of Israel fetishized the territories and made their relinquishment impossible, so its attribution to the Jewish people served to justify Israeli domination of the Palestinians. "The concept of Jewish uniqueness," Leibowitz declared,

> requires us to choose between two traditions of interpretation. One is represented by Yehuda Halevi . . . some centuries later by the Maharal, and in our times, by Rabbi Kook and Ben-Gurion [who symbolized for Leibowitz secular Zionism's appropriation of Judaism for political ends]. The other tradition has descended from Moses, via Maimonides, to the *Shulḥan Arukh* [the great authoritative sixteenth-century Jewish code of law]. The uniqueness of the Jewish people is not a *fact;* it is an endeavor. The holiness of Israel is not a reality but a task. "Holy" is an attribute that applies exclusively to God. It is therefore inapplicable to anything in the natural or historical domain. He who does so apply it . . . exalts something natural or human to the level of the divine.

It was precisely *The Kuzari*'s canonical status among "national religious" Jews that motivated Leibowitz's attack on it. Although a secular Jew could comfortably blame right-wing religious nationalism on Judaism itself, an observant Jew on the political Left could not. And if such nationalism was a distortion of Judaism, it had to be asked: where did Judaism go wrong?

For Leibowitz, the answer was: with Halevi. So it is, too, for Avraham Burg. Burg, son of onetime National Religious Party leader Yosef Burg and former director of the Jewish Agency and speaker of the Knesset, abandoned his political career after narrowly losing a primary campaign to head the Labor Party in 2003. In 2007 he published a book, translated into English as *The Holocaust Is Over*, that caused a furor in Israel, accused in it of anti-Arab bigotry, endemic xenophobia, and a paranoiac clinging to the trauma of the Holocaust.

Once again Yehuda Halevi was singled out as a seminal culprit, his strident Jewish particularism contrasted with the universalism of Maimonides. Against the background of its times, Burg wrote, Halevi's wish to assure a humbled people that it was "still the best" was understandable. Yet what may be a functional compensatory fantasy in a state of powerlessness can become a dysfunctional pathology when "the template is turned around and the slave becomes the master." The state of Israel, wrote Burg, had become like the abused child who grows up to be an abusing adult, "a humiliated and persecuted people that has turned into a replica of the worst of its enemies"—and the earliest warning signs were in *The Kuzari*.

Yet another discussion of post-1967 Israel in terms of the Maimonides-Halevi polarity was undertaken by David Hartman, an American Orthodox rabbi, scholar, and educator who settled in Jerusalem in 1971. Thirty years later, in his *Israelis and the Jewish Tradition*, Hartman opposed Yehuda Halevi's "God of history" to Maimonides' "cosmic God" and argued that "Maimonides and Halevi offer two distinct religious sensibilities that can shed light on the conflict between traditional Judaism and modern democratic values." The difference between them, wrote Hartman, is not only that *The Kuzari* emphasizes the unique holiness of Israel while *The Guide for the Perplexed* stresses "the common humanity shared by Israel and the rest of the world." *The*

Kuzari's "event-based theology" also ascribes holiness to history, which it views as an ongoing arena for divine intervention, whereas *The Guide* rejects "a dependence on events as manifestations of God's love." "It is no accident," Hartman declared,

> that some of the major topics of *The Kuzari* are absent from *The Guide*, for example, the meaning of Jewish exile, a theology of history, and a polemical confrontation with Christianity and Islam. In the whole of *The Guide*, Maimonides never once introduces the idea of a redemptive scheme for history. . . . Whereas *The Kuzari* is concerned with the historical need to revitalize the Jewish people, *The Guide* openly expresses its preference for the single individual over "a thousand ignoramuses."

But this, Hartman writes, is all the more reason for preferring Maimonides and his "neutralization of history as the framework of faith in the living God of Judaism." Although he decided to settle in Israel under the impact of the Six Day War, Hartman's subsequent life there convinced him of the "devastating psychological effects" of detecting God's hidden hand in historical developments, the "manic-depressive consequences" of which lead from the euphoria of messianic anticipation to the dejection of messianic disappointment and back again. Maimonides, by denying God political intentions, forces us to think politically for ourselves. Halevi, by encouraging us to identify our politics with God's, excuses us from examining them rationally.

Although the post-1967 counterreaction to Halevi started in Orthodox Jewish circles, it has not been confined to them. In a postmodern world in which nationalism has been discredited and multiculturalism is the new standard, and in which unitary thinking is out of fashion and multiple perspectives are in vogue, Halevi was bound to draw fire from other quarters as well. A notable example is Yale professor María Rosa Menocal in her highly praised *The Ornament of the World: How Muslims, Jews, and Christians Created a Culture of Tolerance in Medieval Spain.*

Menocal's 2002 book is a paean to a place and period—tenth-through-fourteenth-century Spain—in which "Jews, Muslims, and Christians lived side by side . . . in the cultivation of the complexities, charms, and challenges of contradictions." The Spanish *convivencia* represents for her, as it has done for many historians, a high-water mark in the history of human collaboration, an epoch of intense creativity and cross-fertilization in which, despite its strains and tensions, followers of the three monotheistic faiths coexisted in harmony.

But *The Ornament of the World*, whose postscript was composed in the immediate aftermath of September 11, 2001, is also a lament for *convivencia*'s collapse and repudiation in the Christian *reconquista*, the Inquisition, and the ultimate expulsion of Spain's Jews and Muslims. "What happened?" Menocal asks, writing in the shadow of the "unimaginable violence" that came "quite literally flying out of the blue" into American life. "How and why does a culture of tolerance fall apart?" Her answer has its ecumenical heroes and exclusionist villains. The heroes include statesmen like Abdel-Rahman III, Hasdai ibn Shaprut, and Alfonso VI, poets like Ibn Hazm and Shmuel Hanagid, and philosophers like Averroes and Maimonides. High on the list of the villains is Yehuda Halevi.

What bothers Menocal about Halevi so much? To begin with, the same ethnocentrism that bothered Leibowitz, Burg, and Hartman. Written in the early stages of the *reconquista*, *The Kuzari* is read by Menocal as a first unraveling of the Muslim-Jewish-Christian symbiosis—"an omen from the inside," as she puts it, "of things to come." The Almoravids' assault on *convivencia* had been political; Halevi's was intellectual and so pierced deeper. Its main vehicle, the rejection of philosophy, was a blow to *convivencia*'s very essence, it having been the philosophical assumption of a universal rational faculty in which all minds could meet that had sustained Spain's interfaith dialogue. In rejecting "the very premise of the commensurability of philosophy and religion," Halevi was undermining "the bedrock of Andalusian Jewish culture for hundreds of years . . . the premise that genuine Jewish culture and devout faith in Judaism were not at destructive odds with the whole complex of secular activities" that Jews, Christians, and Muslims shared.

But this was still not Halevi's worst betrayal. That, in Menocal's eyes, was the voyage with which his life ended. "He chose to leave it all, to abandon the culture that had made his poetry possible!" she writes aggrievedly. "He repented not merely for himself; he also denounced a culture, his culture, which he saw as decadent." It is almost as if Halevi, in forsaking Spain, had walked out on Menocal personally, leaving her with terrorism and 9/11—and in a sense, this is exactly what he did, for "the Andalusian moral is that there are Judah Halevis within each of us, and thus within our communities." Instead of dealing with "the accommodation of contradictions," Halevi took "the easy way out" by insisting on "the strict harmony of cultural identity." In his advocacy of "deadly simplicities," he was the opposite of Maimonides, who resisted "any sort of imposed unity or trivial consistency in the life or the intellect."

For Menocal, Halevi's voyage was a defection. For the American-Israeli literary critic Sidra deKoven Ezrahi, it was a perilous rendezvous with "the danger of literalization." For centuries before Halevi's time, Ezrahi wrote in 2000 in her *Booking Passage: Exile and Homecoming in the Modern Jewish Imagination*, Jews, in their longing, had constructed a legendary Zion, an idealized country where messianic dreams would come true. Yet such a Zion could only exist as long as it was not returned to, for "a myth of perfection" is "effectively annihilated" when one seeks to live it.

One can only long for what is not possessed. Can it be, Ezrahi asks in her opening chapter, "The Poetics of Pilgrimage: Yehuda Halevi and the Uncompleted Journey," that arrival in the Land of Israel was therefore not only Halevi's greatest wish but also his greatest fear, the real reason he postponed his departure from Spain for so many years while increasingly aggravated with himself for doing so? Might this not explain why, after arriving in Egypt, he waited another year before setting out for Palestine, driven by "the psychological and poetic as well as the theological function of deferral"? For the romantic poet, as for the romantic lover, the secret of success is failure. He must never obtain the object of his desire, which is why marriage is not a theme of romantic poetry. What then happens to Yehuda Halevi when he attempts, as it were, to take the Land of Israel as his bride?

We know the answer, of course. He dies, whether of illness or because he is fortuitously killed. But for Ezrahi, Halevi's fate cannot be viewed as fortuitous. It is the logical—one might say the sole possible—outcome of his journey, the "inevitable consequence of union with the loved one." Once romantic love is consummated, there is no other way to avoid losing it. "Jerusalem as a ruin welcomes the poet into her rubble and lures him to his death."

Ezrahi objects to treating Halevi's writings as though they were a "proto-Zionist manifesto." Yet at the same time, she does not hesitate to draw an imaginative parallel between his voyage to Palestine and the Zionist establishment of a Jewish state there. Arrival in the Land of Israel, whether a poet's or a people's, "necessarily brings disenchantment." Because "the long, rich life of the Jewish imagination in fictional landscapes" can only be led in exile and "the symbolic and the material dimensions" must be "severed" for "dreamscapes" to be preserved, the Zionist attempt to fit Jewish dreams "into specific geopolitical boundaries" has been a "Pyrrhic victory."

Ezrahi does not despair of Israel's ability to extricate itself from its predicament. Dreams that have been falsified by coming true can be given up, however painfully. Only when they continue to be clung to in the face of reality do they turn lethal. Thinking of the Israeli-Palestinian and Israeli-Arab conflicts and of Jewish nationalist claims to all of Palestine, Ezrahi writes in her concluding chapter:

> The insistence that endings must reconnect with beginnings—that what has traveled through space as a symbol, when finally (re)grounded in sacred soil, stakes an incontrovertible, inalienable, and *total* claim—reveals

the seduction of an *aesthetics of the whole*. The whole holy land. Undivided Jerusalem. The aesthetics and politics of wholeness are built on sacrifice and exclusivity, on a messianic perfection of the form that can be fully realized only in death. The eternity of Jerusalem is privileged over the ephemeral lives of its inhabitants, fulfillment over deferral, original and indivisible space over all forms of partiality, imitation, fragmentation, or duplication. Death celebrated as glorious, as sacrificial or heroic, preserves the image of the integrity of the body, unsullied by the ravages of the battlefield.

In the end, then, Ezrahi, too, reconnects her ending with her beginning by treating the death of Yehuda Halevi at the gates of Jerusalem as a trope for the possible downfall of a Jewish state. Her Halevi, it would seem, is a type of proto-Zionist after all.

He is definitely not one for Raymond Scheindlin, whose *The Song of the Distant Dove: Judah Halevi's Pilgrimage*, published in 2008, is a study of the final year of Halevi's life. Making full use of the published Cairo Geniza documents as edited and commented on by Gil and Fleischer, Scheindlin has written a close account of Halevi's voyage to Palestine, from his departure from Spain in the summer of 1140 to his death in the summer of 1141. A careful synthesis of all that is now known about the subject, the book has its own paradoxical perspective—namely, the thoroughly Islamic nature of Halevi's quest to purge himself of non-Jewish adulteration.

Like many scholars before him, Scheindlin observes that

Halevi must be viewed in the context of the Islamic culture of Spain. He is the first to point out, however, that this also pertains to Halevi's decision to leave Spain. Halevi's turning away late in life from society, his yearning for a secluded religious existence, his setting out on an uncertain and dangerous journey—all these things, Scheindlin maintains, have their parallels in Muslim lives of the period. Starting with the ninth century, Islamic religious literature developed a genre of "*zuhd* verse," ascetically inclined poetry in which the middle-aged poet or reader is called upon to "take charge of his soul . . . before it is too late." This literature, Scheindlin writes,

> is replete with characters who took this advice seriously, not merely by doing penance for particular sins, nor by merely repenting inwardly, but by changing their lives . . . often accompanying the change by a dramatic gesture: becoming a wandering mendicant, retreating to a Sufi community, going on jihad, or settling in Mecca to become a "neighbor of God." Whole treatises were devoted to anecdotes about people in high positions who abandoned their wealth and embraced asceticism. . . . We see the reflection of this attitude in Halevi's story as well.

The most famous case of this in Halevi's age was that of Al-Ghazali,

> an academic celebrity until, at age thirty-seven, a religious crisis induced him to resign his professorship and abandon Baghdad. Traveling first to Damascus, he went to Jerusalem and spent some time there. At last,

he made the pilgrimage to Mecca and Medina by way of Hebron and returned to his hometown of Tus. There he lived in ascetic seclusion until, under government pressure, he resumed his post in Baghdad and taught there until his final retirement.

Accompanying the concept of *zuhd* was that of *tawakkul*, "trust." As Scheindlin puts it, *tawakkul* "was understood to mean that a person should accept whatever befalls as God's will and be satisfied with whatever God decrees for him." He who lived by it was a *mutawakkil*, and Halevi's setting out for Palestine against the advice and urging of his friends exhibits the determination to follow the *mutawakkil's* path. As much as he may have believed that he was casting off the foreign influences of exile, his journey was steeped in Islamic patterns of thought.

Such a Halevi had no grand national or messianic aspirations. True, the rabbi in *The Kuzari* sometimes speaks in such terms, but this is

no more a call for a mass movement to Zion than is the rabbi's solitary departure at *The Kuzari*'s end. If we are to read Halevi's pilgrimage in the light of *The Kuzari*, all we can say is that it was the act of a man who had given up on the masses and the leaders of his people and on the idea of an imminent redemption altogether, but who believed that there were steps that a person could take who wanted to come as close as possible to the divine presence. He would do God's will the best he could, even at the cost of giving up his comfortable religious life. . . . Not messianism, but solitary devotion, is the constant theme of [his] poems.

We are back to the Halevi of David Kaufmann, whose early study Scheindlin praises as "astute" while criticizing Fleischer and Gil's Zionist interpretation of Halevi's journey as "a perversely modernizing reading" that imposes a twentieth-century "ism" on a medieval literary figure. Scheindlin's Halevi is a historical personage rescued by scrupulous scholarship from the Jewish debates of our age and restored to the safekeeping of his own time and place, where he is protected from ideological marauders. Though still a great poet and an impressive human being, he is not the doomed romantic of Lebensohn and Heine, the anti-Diaspora trailblazer of Baer and Dinur, or María Rosa Menocal's renegade slamming the door on *convivencia*. No longer, as he sees the Spanish coast recede or waits for the wind to change in Alexandria, does he have the burden or the comfort of believing that he is acting on behalf of a people. His journey to Palestine is "a supreme act of self-consuming personal piety" and no more. The national poet, in the spirit of the first years of the twenty-first century, has been privatized.

8

This book began with another book.

In 1975, when I was still a fairly new immigrant in Israel, to which my wife and I moved from New York in 1970, I was asked to write a book—my first—by Meir Deshell, then editor in chief of the Jewish Publication Society of America, or the JPS, as it is known. Meir wanted me to write about Israel and the Diaspora, and I chose to do this in the form of six long letters addressed to an imaginary American Jewish friend. In them I tried convincing my friend that if he was serious about being Jewish, the only honest place to be it in was Israel. It wasn't a totally one-sided argument, because I had him answer back in letters of his own and quoted extensively from them. I even gave him a few good lines at my expense, although I kept the best ones for myself.

At the time of its completion, the book had no name. In my contract with the JPS, it was referred to as "Letters To An American Jewish Friend," but this was understood to be merely a working title until something better came along. Yet the weeks went by, the book went from manuscript to page proofs and from page proofs to bound galleys, and nothing better occurred to anyone. Time was running out. And then one evening, as I was reading, for the first time, Yehuda Halevi's *Kuzari* in Shmuel ibn Tibbon's Hebrew translation, I came across the passage in which, confronted by the king's accusation that Jews pray daily for their return to Zion but do nothing about it, the rabbi replies that, alas, the king is right. All the Jews' talk about the Land of Israel is no better than "the starling's caw."

I put down *The Kuzari*, dialed the JPS in Philadelphia, and asked to speak to Meir. "I've got it!" I said.

"Got what?"

"Our book's title. We'll call it 'The Starling's Caw.'"

I described the passage in *The Kuzari*.

There was silence. Then Meir said:

"Over my dead body will we do that."

"But why not?" I asked.

"Because people will think you've written a guidebook to birdcalls," he said.

I protested, but it did no good. Perhaps Meir might have relented had he known there would one day be a book about Halevi called *The Song of the Distant Dove*, but I doubt it. Caws aren't coos. More days went by, the final buzzer sounded, and *Letters to an American Jewish Friend* became my book's lackluster title by default.

I was annoyed. For several months Meir and I didn't speak. Then, as the publication date was nearing, I received a long-distance call from him. He lived in a town house in Philadelphia. "You'll never guess what happened," he said.

"What?" He sounded shaken.

"I was in New York for the weekend. When I came home last night, I nearly fainted. My Chinese vase was in pieces on the floor, a lamp was smashed, and there was a dead bird on the carpet."

"I'm sorry to hear that," I said. "How did it get in?" I didn't understand why he was telling me all this.

"It must have flown down the fireplace chimney. It panicked and crashed into things. I have a neighbor who knows about birds. He identified it."

"And?"

"It's a starling."

Perhaps, then, *Letters to an American Jewish Friend* should have been called "The Starling's Revenge."

The Kuzari was not my earliest encounter with Halevi. That was with his poetry, which I first read in a beautifully bound and printed edition of Chaim Brody's *Anthologia Hebraica* published in Leipzig in 1922. I bought it in 1964 in Israel, where I had gone to take time-out from a girlfriend in New York. Halevi dazzled me. I hadn't known you could write like that in medieval Hebrew, that you could say things like:

> O swear by Love that you remember days of embraces
> As I remember nights crammed with your kisses,
> And that, as through my dreams your likeness passes,
> So does mine through yours!

Not that I had any proprietary right to such lines, because it was my girlfriend who was the abandoned lover and I who had left her for my travels, but I missed her and Halevi had the words for it.

I wasn't just trying to decide about a girl in America. I was trying to decide about America itself. I had come to Israel with the vague plan of staying for a while—or for longer—or forever. I needed to sort myself out. Born and raised in the 1940s and '50s in an enlightened Orthodox Jewish home in New York, I had attended a religious day school, gone as a boy to Hebrew-speaking summer camps, studied at a New York public high school, graduated from Columbia College, spent a year on a fellowship at Cambridge University in England, and returned to get a master's degree in English literature from Columbia. I was very Jewish and perfectly American, having given up my religious observance at the age of sixteen after a summer spent in the mountains of Tennessee. In my last two years of high school, my best friend was the son of card-carrying Jewish Communists. In college and graduate school, many of my friends were not Jewish at all. We were a Keats and Donne, blues and bluegrass, one-wall-handball-and-two-hand-touch-football-playing crowd. By chance, a *Life* magazine photographer shot a bunch of us sitting with our bare toes in the Lincoln Memorial pool in Washington while listening to Martin Luther King's "I Have a Dream" speech in the summer of 1963. If you look carefully, you still won't see me, because I'm half an inch out of the picture.

So, like Yehuda Halevi, I grew up with *convivencia*. It was just that the *con* didn't go with the *vivencia*. Like wrong pieces of a puzzle, the two sides of me refused to fit together. The Jew and the American were barely on speaking terms.

The problem was that I had never been able to take American Jewish life seriously. There was romance for me in America—in the poetry of Whitman, and in country music, and in the streets of New York, and in coming out of the Rockies at dusk on my first cross-country car trip and suddenly seeing, beyond the dipping curve of the road, the endless prairie ahead of me, the twinkling lights of a continent. And there was romance in Jewish history, with its stretches of time as immense as America's spaces—a vast forest of it in which a people had gotten lost with its God, and wandered endlessly, and had great and terrible adventures, the greatest of which had now brought it home again. How anyone could care about being Jewish without wanting to be part of that was beyond me. Nothing seemed duller, thinner, more blandly institutionalized, more pitifully ersatz by comparison than American Jewry. Reading a history of it was like reading the minutes of a board meeting. I could imagine a life as an American in America and I could imagine a life as a Jew in Israel, but I couldn't imagine a life as an American Jew.

That winter in Israel, I led a vagrant existence. For a while I shared an apartment with someone in Haifa; for a while I lived in the empty house of an uncle of mine in the artist's village of Ein-Hod; for a while I stayed in Tel Aviv, where I translated a play for a Hebrew author in return for room and board. In the spring, I decided to look for a more long-term arrangement. There was a kibbutz I knew of high on the Lebanese border, with a bird's-nest view of Mount Hermon and the Hula Valley. It took several changes of buses to get there, and when I did, I declared my readiness to do any work that was outdoors and called for using my muscles. It was agreed that I would start at the end of June.

Meanwhile, I received a letter. Laura—I have neglected to say this was her name—had been offered a job for the coming year teaching English at Tuskegee Institute, a black college in Alabama. She was excited to be going down south at such a time. There was an opening for me in the English department, too. "Come!" she wrote.

I struggled to make up my mind. Alabama would be an experience and passing it up meant the end of our relationship. But I wasn't ready to leave Israel. Not now, when the country was perfumed with blossoming orange groves. Not yet, when the first thin layers of an Israeli self were being grafted onto me. I wanted to see if they would take, to watch them grow.

I wrote Laura that I was staying in Israel. Our correspondence stopped.

One June day I went to have lunch at a café in Haifa, on top of the Carmel. At a nearby kiosk, I bought a Hebrew newspaper to read while I ate. On the front page was a story about three American civil rights workers who had been lynched in Mississippi. One was black, two were Jewish. Suddenly, everything around me—the mothers with their baby carriages, the fiery flowers of the poinsettia tree across the street, the waiter bringing my hummus and malt beer— seemed beside the point.

I stared at the three photographs. "Come!" they said. "You're an American. We're your people. This is your battle."

I went to the post office and telegraphed Laura that I had changed my mind. In late August, we drove down to Alabama.

Today, when Israel has felt for so long like the only possible home for me, I could almost be writing about another person. Those years seem like a wild scribble on what would otherwise be a straight line running from my childhood.

Here is one of its memories. It is a Friday night. The Sabbath candles are lit. I am reading in the armchair in the living room, an eight-year-old. My father is in the corner, reciting the evening prayer. He is also listening to the radio, an old grille-cloth Philco. Suddenly he stops praying and comes over to hug me. "We've taken Ras-el-Eyn," he says. There are tears in his eyes. Although I know there is a war in Palestine, I don't know that Ras-el-Eyn is a village that controls the pumping station at the headwaters of the Yarkon River, from which a besieged Jerusalem will again get its drinking water. But we have taken it. I hug my father back.

Did I really sit in a café in Haifa and choose a different we?

I did. And spent a year in Alabama. And followed Laura to California, where she started law school. And broke up with her and moved with our two Irish setters to a house in a red-wood forest. And left the setters and took a Greyhound bus back to New York. And set out for New England in a bor-rowed car with $1,500 in cash and drove and drove until the price of land fell enough to buy 150 acres of woods with a brook in the middle of Maine. I was full of Thoreau and *The Whole Earth Catalog*, and I was going to build a log cabin and live in it.

I fell in love and married instead. My wife and I found a cheap rent-controlled apartment in one of the fanciest buildings on Central Park West. We were the first people to see it at six P.M. on the day it was advertised because it had been listed in the wrong column of the *New York Times* real estate section, and the agent, who doubted my sanity when I balked at living in a building where uniformed doormen rushed to take your shopping bags, had pity on my wife and let us think about it overnight. She agreed with him totally. She was teaching kindergarten in a rough neighbor-hood in Harlem and thought uniformed doormen were a fine idea. By morning, I gave in.

In June the Six Day War broke out. We spent that summer

living on our 150 acres in a tent, with a gas burner for a kitchen, a latrine for a bathroom, and mosquitoes for our house guests. The sun never shone and once a week we drove our old Chevrolet to a town on the Maine coast to do our laundry. There was a diner there that served wonderful blueberry muffins. I ate muffins and scanned the *Bangor Daily News* for news of Israel.

We returned to Manhattan. I had a job as an assistant editor at a Zionist magazine called *Midstream* and walked across the park to its office in good weather. It was the year of the Tet Offensive. Of love-ins and peace marches. Of the assassination of Martin Luther King. Of the New York teachers' strike, which my wife broke because she sided with the black community. Of the assassination of Bobby Kennedy. The cats wailed in the street all night, and when they stopped, she woke me and said, "He's dead," and he was. Another night we heard Shuli Natan singing "Jerusalem of Gold" on a 45 rpm record at someone's home and decided to visit Israel.

Leafing through *Letters to an American Jewish Friend* not long ago, I found an account of that visit. It was a heady time in Israel. The grimmer consequences of the 1967 victory had yet to sink in. Israelis, I wrote,

> still walked about as though in a dream, and there was truly something dreamlike about it. To suddenly pass through the gates of the Old City of Jerusalem, whose battlements until then had been as remote as the Great Wall of China . . . to be up on the Golan, looking down on the Sea of Galilee far below as the Syrians had done through their gun sights . . . to walk in the streets of

Hebron, Jericho, Bethlehem of Judea. . . . And yet for me, though I was dizzy with excitement, it was a time of almost unbearable sadness. Here I was, it was so much *mine*—I could no longer stand not belonging to it fully. What was I withholding myself for, from? I knew then that I had to decide. Either I would return to Israel to live or I would never return there again.

Less than two years later, we packed and moved.

And so when María Rosa Menocal writes in praise of "the accommodation of contradictions," I wonder what she is talking about. There are certainly contradictions that can be accommodated. I know a gourmet cook who is addicted to chocolate Oreo cookies and a clinical psychologist who believes in astrology. No one is obliged to be perfectly consistent in his or her tastes and opinions, even if inconsistency is at the root of nearly everything comic in this world.

But how do you accommodate what is tearing you apart? It is true that our selves are composites, not simple substances. We are coalitions of thoughts, inclinations, drives, fears, desires, imaginations, likes and dislikes; delicate balances of forces. But forging and maintaining a self means creating hierarchies and relationships among these forces, subordinating some to others, establishing a chain of command. There is a wholeness that is achieved not by "exclusivity," as Sidra Ezrahi would have it, but by order and integration. "If he were the prince of a country," the rabbi says to the Khazar king about the *ḥasid*, the harmonious man, "he would rule it as justly as he rules his body and soul."

Woe to the country whose prince cannot decide between its warring factions.

One can have multiple identities, multicultural affinities. One can be an American living in Paris with a Czech father and a Mexican mother and a Japanese wife and a second home in Tuscany and a command of six languages and friends from every country and passions for salsa and Chinese food and Russian literature: all this and much more can fit comfortably into a single person. Yet if this person is not to be a hodgepodge, there must be an organizing principle. Some things must matter more than others; most must be dispensable. And at least one, he must be willing to die for. It can be a friend, a love, a child, a value, a people, a country, a cause, a conception of honor or of dignity, but without it he is trivial.

When I was a boy in a Jewish day school in New York, we sometimes argued over the question: if Israel and America went to war, which would you fight for? As we grew older, this struck us as a foolishly theoretical conundrum and was put aside. I didn't think of it when, summoned for a physical after losing my student deferment by dropping out of graduate school during the Vietnam War, I had a psychiatrist write a letter that I was unfit for military service and was given a 4F. Nor did I think of it in 1974 when I did my basic training in the Israeli army, in which I went on to serve in an infantry battalion until I was wounded in Lebanon in 1982. By then, though, I had answered it.

Yehuda Halevi's friends missed the point when they urged him not to run the risk of travel to Palestine. The risk *was* the point. It was an expression of ultimate commitment, the putting in place of the final brick of the pyramid of self.

Was this commitment to God? To Judaism? To the Jewish people? To his own integrity? There is no way to separate what he labored so hard to unify. *The Kuzari* is the product of this labor. As its own end makes clear, though, it is not the end product. That, for Halevi, could only be a life.

The Kuzari is addressed to all Jews. It is a dialogue, not a meditation. To say, therefore, as does Raymond Scheindlin, that Yehuda Halevi's voyage was "no more a call for a mass movement to Zion than is the rabbi's solitary departure at *The Kuzari*'s end," is to show little of the discernment requested at *The Kuzari*'s beginning. Unless this departure is a demand made on all the book's readers, it reverts to the foolishness that Halevi feared it was. It is precisely a call for a mass movement to Zion, though not one he thought would be immediately responded to. He would have had to be a messianist to entertain such an illusion, and while messianic hopes figure in his earlier poetry, they play no role in *The Kuzari*. He was setting a bar; that was all he could do. What he was capable of, other Jews were also.

Does this make him the first Zionist? The question pertains less to Halevi than it does to the nature of Zionism. He was not a forerunner of Zionism in its Herzlian sense of a political struggle to gain Jewish independence in Palestine; no such goal was imaginable in his day, and there is little basis for Baer's portrait of him as a political thinker. Yet if one conceives of Zionism in its earlier form of a belief in the return of Jews to Palestine as an intrinsic good that the Jewish people must undertake for its own benefit, a strong case for Halevi's proto-Zionism can be made. The earliest collective return in post-exilic times was "the *aliyah* of the three hundred," and if Halevi had something to do with it, he was in fact the pivotal figure in Jewish history that Dinur made him out to be.

Of course, Dinur was himself a Zionist who had gone to live in Palestine and his Halevi, too, is a projection, just as is Heine's and Lebensohn's and Graetz's and my own. Were my personal history different, my Halevi would be different as well. But this is equally true of Raymond Scheindlin. Scheindlin and I were born in America at roughly the same time, educated in roughly the same circumstances, shaped by roughly the same environment. The Jewish Theological Seminary in New York, where he has taught since 1974, is the same institution at which my father taught for nearly four decades until 1970. Like nearly all American Jews, Scheindlin has remained in America; his Yehuda Halevi does not criticize him for that. I have settled in Israel and my Halevi thinks otherwise. This is as it should be. It is one of the measures of literary greatness that we see ourselves in it. The good reader reads with his whole mind; the best reader, with his whole life. Yehuda Halevi brings out the best in us.

María Rosa Menocal views the Spain of Halevi's day, with its "culture of tolerance," as a shining example of interfaith coexistence that Halevi repudiated. I have previously remarked on the idealized nature of this. Eleventh- and twelfth-century Spanish Jews, Muslims, and Christians did not experience their world in this way. They were more conscious of their differences than of their commonalities, and they did not confuse their ability to live side by side, or the cultural traits that they shared, with any deep sense of mutual acceptance. Although we cannot know what Muslims said in the privacy of their homes about Jews and Christians, or Jews and Christians about non-Jews and non-Christians, the literary evidence speaks of no little antagonism beneath the surface calm of everyday relations.

In the long run, the antagonism prevailed. Yehuda Halevi was born a few years after the terrible massacre of Jews by Muslims in Granada; was an adolescent at the time of the Almoravid invasion; was practicing medicine in Christian Toledo when severe anti-Jewish riots broke out there after the death of Alfonso VI; and left for Palestine on the eve of the Almohad conquest, from whose religious zealotry Andalusian Jewry never recovered. His Spain and Menocal's are hardly the same country. If his abandoning it was occasioned, as Menocal thinks it was, by his giving up on *convivencia*, the wisdom of his foresight was greater than that of her hindsight.

Rosy depictions of *convivencia* such as are common in popular histories of the period tell us more about our own times than they do about medieval Spain. They reflect the wish to believe that there are historical models for getting along with "the Other" that we can learn from, and that contemporary tensions between Islam and the West are at least as much the West's fault as Islam's. Long before 9/11 and the international emergence of radical political Islam, *convivencia* was mobilized by Arab and pro-Arab intellectuals as supposed proof of Muslim civilization's liberal attitude toward Otherness until driven to a defensive belligerence by Western colonialism and modern nationalism—especially, by Zionism, accused of introducing religious and ethnic animosities into a region that had not known them before. Prior to Zionism's appearance, the argument goes, Jews occupied an honored place in Muslim society, nowhere more than in pre-*reconquista* Andalusia.

Although she does not speak of Zionism, Menocal, one suspects, sees Halevi as a proto-Zionist, too; it is this that makes him the snake in her Eden of *convivencia*. Yet the real history of Andalusia is far from Edenic, certainly when seen through Jewish eyes. Contrary to Menocal's opinion, Halevi's attitude toward Christianity and Islam was typical of Jews of his age. Even her ecumenical hero Maimonides, in his *Epistle to Yemen*, referred to Muhammed as "the Madman," hoped the bones of Jesus would be "ground to dust," compared Christianity and Islam to "a monkey when it tries to imitate the actions of human beings," and wrote:

> Remember, my coreligionists, that on account of the vast number of our sins God has hurled us into the midst of this people, the Arabs, who have persecuted us severely, and passed baneful and discriminatory legislation against us. . . . Never did a nation molest, degrade, debase, and hate us as much as they.

Maimonides was thinking not only of the Jews of Yemen, ordered in 1165 by their ruler Abd-e-Nabi ibn Mahdi to convert to Islam under pain of death. He had his own life in mind, too. His epistle was written in Egypt, to which his family had fled from Almohad persecution in Morocco, where it had sought shelter from Islamic fanaticism in Spain. An unconfirmed tradition has it that, while in Morocco, he was forced to recite the Muslim profession of faith. Even if this is untrue, his identification with Yemen's Jews came from personal experience.

There was nothing unusual about Halevi's conviction of Jewish superiority. It was shared by nearly all Jews of his age, just as a similar conviction about themselves was held by Christians and Muslims. What was unique was his association of this with what today would be called genetic factors. Avraham Burg is right to point out the psychologically compensatory function of such a belief. I have called it a sign of historical desperation, an attempt to secure an embattled Judaism to some objective bulwark that the tides of events could not erode. Yet however helpful this may have been to Halevi and his readers in firming up their sense of Jewish self-worth, or consistent with the hierarchical structure of *The Kuzari*'s universe, one wishes it had been refrained from. It cannot but strike one as an anticipation of modern racist ideologies that *The Kuzari* would be better off without.

Nevertheless: having said as much, one must also insist that contemporary attacks on Halevi's "racism" are unjustified and perversely overlook the most important single feature of *The Kuzari*—namely, its telling the story of a gentile's conversion to Judaism. Had Halevi been the bigot that Yeshayahu Leibowitz accused him of being, he would not have plotted the book in this fashion. He could easily have chosen another character to be the rabbi's interlocutor—a philosophically inclined Jew, for example. Such a person is the addressee of Maimonides' *Guide for the Perplexed*, which was written, its author informs us, for the Jew who is "lost in perplexity and anxiety" because he has studied philosophy and "finds it difficult to accept as correct the teaching based on the literal interpretation of the Torah." Halevi could have adopted the same strategy.

He did not. He chose a king of the Khazars—and one reason for this was his desire to emphasize that Judaism is a religion for everyone and everyone is welcome to its fold. This was not self-evident to the Jews of Halevi's day. Rabbinic Judaism had stopped proselytizing many centuries previously, prevented from doing so by Christianity and Islam's ascendance to political power, and had turned increasingly inward in its grasp of its mission in the world. No longer did it aspire to compete for the minds and souls of all men. Although in theory it might still have a message for humanity, it had ceased to articulate or deliver it. Not even Maimonides' *Guide* evinces the slightest interest in presenting Judaism to the non-Jew.

Yehuda Halevi is the great exception. True, *The Kuzari*, too, is a book for Jews. It was not written for gentiles, who could not have read its Hebrew-lettered Arabic. Yet because it is about the conversion of a gentile, it is about what Judaism has to say to gentiles and the importance of a Jew's knowing what this is, since a religion that can speak only to its own adherents diminishes them as well. More than any other Jewish book of the Middle Ages, *The Kuzari* insists on Judaism as a universal faith. Nor is its gentile just a foil for its Jew. The Khazar king has a mind of his own; he asks the rabbi perceptive questions and more than once scores a point against him. He is the rabbi's equal in intelligence if not in knowledge, and his sincerity and determination to do the right thing are the cornerstone of the dialogue between them. Nowhere else in medieval Jewish literature is a non-Jew portrayed so sympathetically.

This is not the stuff of racism. It is so much its opposite that one wonders whether Halevi, afraid that his doctrine of inborn Jewishness might be abused, decided on a gentile as the rabbi's conversation partner in order to forestall this danger. If he did, however, he did not succeed past the first two-thirds of the twentieth century, when the Six Day War and its aftermath cast a new and harsh light on his thought.

It is far too harsh. Although it is legitimate to trace the history of specific ideas from Halevi to religious nationalism in post-1967 Israel, it is unfair to identify him with religious nationalist politics. Transporting historical figures to the present in order to ask their opinion (would Karl Marx have approved of the Soviet Union? What would the authors of *The Federalist Papers* say about contemporary America?) may have heuristic value in the case of men who lived close to our own times and thought about them. But Yehuda Halevi was born nearly a thousand years ago. To speculate on what might be his view of the settlement movement in the occupied territories, or what party he would have voted for in the last Israeli elections, is pointless. On the basis of *The Kuzari*, one could just as easily imagine him espousing the politics of a Yeshayahu Leibowitz as those that Leibowitz holds him responsible for. And while David Hartman is correct to observe that a man of Halevi's outlook would have asked himself, in 2010 no less than in 1140, what God expects politically from the Jews, there is no knowing the answer he would have given.

There is no knowing, either, what he thought or felt after disembarking in Acre in late May 1141. Sidra Ezrahi believes that only death could have kept him from disillusionment. The Jewish imagination, she writes, is inherently utopian; it is at home in exile, where it is free to dream of Zion, and in exile in Zion, where its dreams run aground on reality. Kneeling, as we might picture him, outside the gates of Jerusalem in the terrible heat of the Palestinian summer, his throat sore from the dry, dusty air, the rocks pinching his knees the same gray color as the stones of the city wall in front of him, her Yehuda Halevi is doomed to realize, as Azriel of Gerona would write a few generations later, that the Land of Israel is just a land like any other. Only the horseman galloping toward him can save him from that fate.

And if the horseman fails to arrive? Then Halevi will rise from his knees, brush off the dirt, enter Jerusalem, hand the coins in his pockets to the tattered beggar boys, their eyes sticky with flies, crowding around him, and make his way through the noisy market and down the descending steps of dirty streets to the Wailing Wall, where he will see more gray, grim stones. He will climb the Mount of Olives, from which there is a fine view of the city, rend his clothes in mourning in the manner of Jewish pilgrims, return to Acre, catch the first ship back to Alexandria, and reembark for Spain a wiser but sadder man, just as Israel Zinberg thought he did.

But can he? Alas, he is the author of *The Kuzari*. It is too late for it to be recalled; already scribes are copying the manuscripts given to Halfon ben Netanel and Shmuel ben Hananiah. Returning to Egypt or Spain will reduce the book to absurdity, make him absurd himself. The questioning looks, the barely hidden smiles of satisfaction! Even in the eyes of his closest friends he will forever see his failure reflected. Did he once remark that *The Kuzari* was foolishness? He did not know then how foolish it was. Now he is trapped by it, forced to live out his life in this place that is not what he imagined. . . .

I confess I might never have had such a reverie had I not been the author of *Letters to an American Jewish Friend*. And then, too, it was only prompted by a friend saying to me after reading the book, "Well, now you've done it! You couldn't go back to America any more even if you wanted to."

This gave me the idea of writing a story about Halevi.

In it, he cannot decide what to do. From the moment of stepping off the ship in Acre, he knows he has made a mistake. It isn't the crude, insulting officials in the port, bawling, ill-mannered Franks—they matter no more to him than do the screams of the gulls overhead. It's not the Jews, either, small, pettifogging traders who haven't a clue who he is. "Yehuda ben Shmuel Halevi?" repeats the sexton of the synagogue who has called him, a distinguished-looking visitor, to the Torah on the Sabbath after his arrival. The name occasions no recognition. "A merchant," he tells those who inquire about him when they approach him after the service, one of them to invite him for the Sabbath meal. What should he have replied? That he is the most famous living Hebrew poet and they are dunces for not knowing it? He prefers it this way. Better dull table talk about the price of silk in Acre than eager versifiers wanting to show him their rhymes at literary soirees in Alexandria.

No, it's the land itself. It hasn't spoken a word to him. The more intensely he scrutinizes it, the more it shrinks from him. He hadn't expected holiness to leap out at him. He knows it has no shape or color, that it is not like the glow around their god in the Christians' paintings in the churches of Toledo, or like the time he once saw on the road to Granada a cloud splay the light of the evening sun earthward in columned shafts of radiance such as must have fallen on Mount Sinai. Holiness isn't like that. It's like the spark in the flint that needs to be struck to be released. Over and over, on the way to Jerusalem, he has tried. All he needs is a single spark for the dry tinder of his soul to catch fire. But the gray rocks have yielded nothing. The sights along the way—nothing. Just stony hills and the withered grass of the Palestinian summer that not even God has had mercy on. The grass is dry, the stones are dry, his soul is dry.

And Jerusalem is no better. No, it is worse. In the market inside the gate, the fruit is stunted, the wares few and paltry. The steps leading down to the wall at the foot of the Temple Mount smell faintly of refuse. The houses are all of gray stone. He tries striking a spark from them. Nothing. The wall is gray stone. It turns away when he kisses it.

He ascends the Mount of Olives. The gray city below is the color of a wilderness. It is so small he could take it in his hand and crush it.

He finds an inn in the city. Some men are talking there. A caravan is leaving the next day for Damascus. In the morning he pays the price of a place in it and sets out.

Damascus is a large city. Its Jews are not like Acre's. Called up to the Torah this time, he does not give his real name. Afterwards, over the Sabbath meal, his hosts ask him about the Land of Israel. He tells them what he has seen there, careful to speak no ill of it. His visit was a short one. Just one thing worthy of mention occurred. There was a poet from Spain, a man named Yehuda Halevi—

"*The* Yehuda Halevi?" The Jews of Damascus are well bred and read poetry.

Yehuda Halevi. He can't say if it was *the*. He is a merchant and doesn't know about such things. A poet, anyway. Killed outside Jerusalem's gates. Trampled by a horseman as he was kneeling in prayer.

He spends several days in Damascus, looking for a caravan to take him further east. One is leaving for Baghdad; he joins it. But Baghdad, too, is not far enough. There is always a chance he will be recognized by someone arriving on business from Egypt. He needs to find a place with Jews in it where he can live out his life in peace. Perhaps Isfahan. Or Herat or Kabul. Or even—dark as his mood is, the thought makes him smile—the land of the Khazars. . . .

That was to be my story. I never wrote it, perhaps because it would not have expressed anything very true about myself. Never have I wanted to go back to America, and never have I felt disillusioned by Israel, having had no illusions to begin with. Nothing in the forty years I have lived there has made me say, "I didn't know Jews were capable of this" or "I wouldn't have thought such a thing could happen in a Jewish state," because I always thought Jews were capable of whatever anyone else was and would not have wanted to live among so many of them if I hadn't. I chose life in the Land of Israel because it was mine. Maybe Yehuda Halevi experienced its holiness similarly.

But there was another reason, too, why I never wrote my story about Halevi, which was that I came across a better one. It was written in 1935 by an undeservedly forgotten Hebrew author named Menashe Levin. Only a few pages long, it begins with Yehuda Halevi's ship docking not in Acre but in Jaffa and with his coming ashore. Then it continues:

The night descended, swooping from the hills with the lope of a thousand camels, blowing from the sea with a dusky flap of eagles' wings. The sand spread a black carpet before Jaffa, patterned in shadows by the moon.

Halevi entered Jaffa. Owls stared from the houses. There were gaps in the city wall. From one of them darted a bandit, a leprous beast.

He came to the mosque, its minaret a battered palm tree—not like the soaring mosque of Córdoba, adorned with legends and gem-studded lattices like a bejeweled pirate.

A woman passed, carrying a jug. A donkey came by, ridden by an old man. He spied Halevi, robe embroidered with silver, two eyes in the night.

"Stranger! My house is yours. My candlelight is yours. My bread is yours."

Halevi stepped into a vaulted room. A window in the wall faced the sea. He sat opposite the old man, his robe falling in folds, his hands cupping his beard.

The old man placed on the table a basket of fruit, a jug of water, and an earthenware mug. Halevi peeled a date. He rolled its pit in his mouth like a pebble.

"You're a seafarer?"

Halevi turned from the sea to the mountains. The moon walked on their bare humps, unburdened of the saddlebags of day.

"Old man, is it far to Jerusalem?"

"As far as night is from morning. . . ."

Oil lamps flickered in the crannies of Jaffa. The Mediterranean shone like an emerald, clasped between nocturnal Asia and Africa's half-rings.

Halevi chewed on a date, the mug in his hands.

"Old man, is there a camel in this town to take me to Jerusalem?"

The old man fluttered singed eyelashes. "There are robbers, like vipers, behind every rock in those mountains . . ."

Halevi put down the mug and turned to look at the sea.

The old man shuffled upstairs in his slippers. Halevi gathered his robe, wrapped himself in it, and left.

In Jaffa at night even the donkeys sleep like roosters. Cats scaled the balcony of the minaret.

Halevi emerged from the city wall and slipped out of town.

On one side was the sea, its gold and blue streaming through him like two decanted wines. On the other, the hills on the horizon, which he imagined as columns of words.

He was a horseman riding the moon. He breathed in the gardens of Castile and of the Song of Songs. How soft the night's breezes were!

Not a jackal wailed. It was the gazelles that ran after him, their velvet hoofs padding the rocks. The olive trees in the valleys combed their silver beards; they were the philosophers of Córdoba. The palm trees waved their fans; they were the ladies of Granada.

Halevi—all the shadows of night in his billowing

robe—strode toward the mountains that sprang away from him. Swift were the gazelles; his imagination overtook them. The mountains sprang away; it oversprang them, too. It was the night of the poet.

He made pictures of the stars, illustrations of the zodiac, turning the sky into a book. His book! He was still striding toward the mountains when it shut and he plunged into the dawn as though into a river.

O legend, spread your prayer shawl over him, silver-embroidered, as was that star-embroidered night!

During the months I lived with the Irish setters in the redwood forest, I was so cut off from the world that I didn't know that less than a mile away, Ken Kesey and his Merry Pranksters were throwing acid parties attended by an assortment of Hells Angels and such notables as Allen Ginsberg and Neal Cassady, the prototype of the hero of Jack Kerouac's *On the Road*. The sounds of their revels never reached me. All I heard at night was the creaking of the redwoods. From a clearing in the forest, there was a view of the Pacific and Half Moon Bay. Further down the coast was Monterey Bay.

I never drove as far as Monterey. It remained for me the town of John Steinbeck's *Cannery Row*, a novel best read, as it was by me, in adolescence. It, too, has a wild party, which ends with a poem that haunted me for years afterwards. I still remembered a few lines of it:

> Even now,
> If my girl with lotus eyes came to me again

Weary with the dear weight of young love,
Again would I give to her these starved twins of arms
And from her mouth drink down the heavy wine,
As a reeling pirate bee in fluttered ease
Steals up the honey from the nenuphar.

As a sixteen-year-old who didn't know what a nenuphar was, I thought this the world's most beautiful love poem. And when I first read Yehuda Halevi's "Why, My Darling, Have You Barred All News," I thought excitedly: *We* have one just as good!

At the time, they simply seemed to me two great poems. Today I realize they are more connected than that.

The author of the lines in *Cannery Row* was an eleventh-century Kashmiri poet named Bilharna Kavi. It is told that he had a love affair with the beautiful daughter of the king and was thrown into prison when it was discovered. He wrote his poem in his cell while awaiting a possible death sentence.

Bilharna's poem was composed over a hundred years before Yehuda Halevi's. Both belonged to a new kind of love poetry that, diffusing from its epicenter in Baghdad, spread like a contagion through the vast area between India and Spain; from Spain to southern France in the verse of the Troubadors; and thence to northern Europe in the medieval romance. Everywhere its themes were similar: the overwhelming impact of love's onset, the devotion of the lovers, their bliss at love's consummation, their grief at separation, their steadfastness in the face of it, their unshakable hope for reunion, their refusal to accept any consolation short of death. It marked a sea change in the culture of Europe: in art, in literature, in music, in religion, in taste, in values, in fashion, even in commerce and politics. It was as if a point had been reached in history at which the human self, more proudly aware than ever of its irreplicable uniqueness, had also grown so conscious of its insupportable aloneness that it desired only to lose itself in the beyond-itself: in the arms of the beloved, the embrace of God, the service of the nation or humanity.

This pride and desire are part of what we call romanticism, and Yehuda Halevi is the first great romantic figure in Jewish history. He is so in the quality of his longing; in his preference for immediate experience and intuition over cogitation and intellection; in his craving for wholeness. The romantic personality is averse to half-measures; while it may use irony as a tactic, it is unironic in its deepest grasp of things; it seeks unitary structures and resolutions and rejects partiality. All this is characteristic of Halevi.

But he was also a product of Jewish tradition, which was profoundly anti-romantic by nature. The Judaism he knew was a religion of law, not impulse; of communal discipline and solidarity rather than solo flights of the self; of a penchant for practicality and a distrust of all excess. Unlike Christianity, it did not emphasize the inward over the outward, faith over works. As opposed to Islam, it had no mystics who sought to blur the distinction between the finite and the infinite.

Halevi's romanticism comes to us filtered through the grid of Jewish attitudes and values. It is muted by them. There is a sobriety about him. He is the most meticulously musical of all medieval Hebrew poets. But he is also the most passionate. When he wrote,

Between us lies a sea of tears I cannot cross.
Yet should you but approach its moaning waves,
They'd part beneath your steps,
And if, though dead, I heard the golden bells
Make music on your skirt, or your voice asking how I
                                    was,
I'd send my love to you from the grave's depths,

there had been nothing like it in Hebrew literature since the Song of Songs, a poem traditionally ascribed to the young King Solomon—who, it was said, went on to compose the book of Proverbs in middle age and Ecclesiastes when he was old.

It is a neat way to divide a life: the exuberant, enamored youth, the self-satisfied paterfamilias, the cynical elder. Such stages exist, and if Solomon went through them, he was no different from many people.

How cunning life is! Time and again it convinces us that we are living our own lives when we are only living it. What, really, do the three Solomons have to do with one another? No more than do three boarders who occupy the same room in turn, each thinking it is his.

Yehuda Halevi's life was his own. Its romanticism was a disposition, not a phase. There is no middle-aged moralist in it, no jaundiced old man. There is the steady development of longing. For literary glory. For friendship. For a woman who left him. For Zion. Heine, with his usual acuity, saw at once that Halevi's songs of Zion were love poems. But though they use the language and imagery of sexual love, they are not its sublimation. Halevi's older self was not a convert from his younger one. The adolescent from Castile, "so young and still unsung" in the words of Moshe ibn Ezra, was still alive in the aging poet who wrote of standing near the Nile:

> And the foolish heart forgets how old it is,
> And remembers other boys and other girls,
> Here, in this paradise of Egypt,
> In these gardens, by the river, in these fields.

And added:

> The yellow stalks are a rich brocade,
> And when the sea breeze ripples through them,
> They bow and pray in gratitude to God.

Was it God he longed for most?

God was a living presence for Yehuda Halevi as He is not for most of us. Best, then, to let him speak for himself.

The poem that ends this book is the same poem that Avraham Yitzhak Hacohen Kook copied from memory into his notebook during a sleepless night in London. It was natural for him to think of it, for it, too, is about waking in the middle of the night. It has the form of a modified girdle song, with the single rhyme of its first four-line stanza serving as that of the fifth and last line of the following stanzas.

> יעירוני רעיוני וסוד לבי ומשאלו,
> הגות דברי תחנוני בזמרת אל ומהללו.
> ולא אתן שנת לעיני חצות לילה בגללו,
> לחזות בנועם אדוני ולבקר בהיכלו.

> הקיצותי ואחשוב: מי הוא אשר הקיצני?
> והנה קדוש יושב תהילותיו האזני,

וְנָתַן בְּאָזְנִי קֶשֶׁב וְחִזְּקַנִי וְאִמְּצַנִי,
וְכָל עוֹד רוּחִי הָשֵׁב אֲבָרֵךְ אֲשֶׁר יְעָצַנִי
צוּר, אֲשֶׁר הַנְּשָׁמָה לוֹ וְהַגְּוִיָּה מִפְעָלוֹ.

וְאֶתְפַּלֵּל לְפָנָיו — וּבַתְּפִלָּה אֶתְעַנָּג,
וּבָקְעוּ דִמְעֵי עֲנָנַי — וּמָתְקוּ מִצּוּף וּפְנָג,
וְגָבַהּ לִבִּי בְּעֵינַי, בְּעֵת נָמַס כַּדּוֹנַג,
כְּעֶבֶד לִפְנֵי אֲדוֹנָיו מִפַּחְדּוֹ יִתְמוֹגַג,
וְכִי יִזְכֹּר מַחְמַלּוֹ, יְנַסֶּה אֶת כָּל עֲמָלוֹ.

דּוֹם לֵיל וְהַכְבֵּד וְאַחַר שַׁחַר מָבוֹא,
עַד יִתְרַצֶּה עֶבֶד בְּתַחֲנוּנָיו אֶל רַבּוֹ,
וְיִשְׁפֹּךְ דַּם לֵב וְכָבֵד וְיַגִּיד נִגְעֵי לִבּוֹ,
וְיִתְיַחֵד הָעוֹבֵד עִם הַמֶּלֶךְ בִּמְסִבּוֹ,
וְיָשִׁיר וְיִשָּׂא מְשָׁלוֹ לְשֵׁם דִּגְלוֹ וּמִגְדָּלוֹ.

הִנֵּה עֶבֶד עֲבָדִים לִפְנֵי מֶלֶךְ מְלָכִים
עוֹמֵד, וְיָדָיו כְּבֵדִים וּדְמָעָיו נֶהְלָכִים —
לְךָ יְצוּרָיו נֶעֱבָדִים בְּעוֹד חַיָּיו נִמְשָׁכִים,
וְכָל אֲבָרָיו מוֹדִים וּמִתְוַדִּים וּמְבָרְכִים.
סְלַח לְרֹעַ מַעֲלָלָיו אֲשֶׁר כַּחוֹל מִשְׁקָלוֹ!

Waked by my thoughts and driven to profess
God's praise in song and plead my neediness,
I from my eyes brush midnight's sleepiness
To seek the pleasance of the Lord's palace.

Roused from drowsiness, I ask: Who stirred me?
The holy dweller in glory has spurred me.
He has taught me to listen; stood by me and beside
me;
To my last breath's thankfulness, advised me.
All souls are His, all forms bear His impress!

To Him I pray—and rapt is my prayer.
Its tears pierce His clouds and are sweeter than nectar.
If He finds me proud, my heart is like butter,
Melting with fear like a slave's of his master.
      May love make him forget his distress!

Stay, solemn night! Let dawn wait in the east
Till the vassal who offers his heart's blood has ceased
Pouring it out and his lord is appeased,
And the slave is alone with the king at his feast,
      Pledging his flag in his fortress!

A slave of slaves before the King of Kings!
With heavy hands and many tears he brings
His life and limbs as Your sworn underlings
To bless You and confess You in all things.
      Forgive like so much sand his sinfulness!

This is one of the most mystical of Halevi's poems. Comparing God to a king in a cloud-moated castle to which the poet, likened to a slave, tearfully but boldly seeks admission, it contrasts the human longing for God with the human incommensurability with Him. This tension reaches its height in the fourth stanza, which starts with an appeal, borrowed from the imagery of romantic love, for dawn, the enemy of trysting lovers, to be delayed so that the praying poet, or petitioning slave, can finish "pouring out" his "heart's blood," and ends with his gaining a seat at the king's nocturnal table. Even then, he remains aware of his lowliness, which allows him to pledge no more to the king's service than his own "life and limbs"—and even then he knows that this is the gift the king wants most.

The image of "the king at his feast" is taken from the Song of Songs. A second, more concealed biblical inset, however, is scarcely less important. This is the phrase "If He finds me proud"—literally, "If my heart is lifted up in His eyes" (*ve-gavah libi b'eynav*). The relevant passage is Ezekiel 28:2, which reads: "Son of man, say unto the prince of Tyre, Thus saith the Lord God, Because thine heart is lifted up, and thou hast said, I am a God, I sit in the seat of God, in the midst of the seas; yet thou art a man, and not God, though thou set thine heart as the heart of God."

Halevi was using this inset to disassociate himself from the radical Sufi goal of "becoming God" by mystical union with Him. Once again, the "softness" of his mysticism is in evidence. Although God is approachable when love overcomes fear, the nearer one draws to Him, the more conscious one is of how far away He remains. Yet mystical it still is in its belief that, just as a slave may be admitted to a palace, so a man may ascend to God's throne. This ascent is subtly traced in the poem, in whose first three stanzas the poet refers to himself as "I" and to God as "He." By stanza 4, however, the "I" has vanished, while in the poem's last stanza, God is addressed as "You." It is as though the poet, importunately seeking God from within the protective shell of his own self, suddenly finds himself outside it, standing before Him. There is perhaps a connection here to the Sufi doctrine of *fanaa*, the "passing away" of the mystic's ego that permits God to enter the space that has been cleared for Him.

On the whole, though, Halevi was more interested in the construction of the ego than in its dismantling. He would have said, I think, that one cannot make God the gift of oneself if there is no self to give. This, too, is woven into "Waked By My Thoughts." Look at its Hebrew text, in which the first letter of each stanza is printed in large typeface. Read from top to bottom, these letters form a signature. There is indeed a lifted-up heart in them—not of the man who would become God, but of the man who would become what he might be.

י

ה

ו

ד

ה

Yehuda. Son of Shmuel Halevi. His story is done.

APPENDIX A

Yehuda Halevi's place of birth was mentioned only once by a contemporary of his. This was by Moshe ibn Ezra in his *Book of Discussions and Remembrance* (see pp. 83). There we find an Arabic sentence that was long read as "Abu-el-Hassan ben Halevi, a man of rare wit who dived deep to retrieve the pearls [of poetry], and Abu-Is'hak ben Ezra, a master of pure and lofty language, are from Talitala and then Kurtaba [Córdoba]." The two poets in question are clearly Yehuda Halevi and his younger contemporary Avraham ibn Ezra, both referred to, as was Moshe ibn Ezra's practice, by their "paedonymic," or *kunya*, as it is known in Arabic— a language in which it is customary to this day to call married men by the names of their firstborn sons prefixed by *abu*, "father of" (see Appendix D).

Talitala was the Arabic name of Toledo, which was taken by nineteenth- and twentieth-century scholars to be Halevi and Avraham ibn Ezra's birthplace. In the 1970s, however, the Israeli literary historian Hayim Schirmann published an article arguing that the name of the city in the Bodleian Library's manuscript of *The Book of Discussions and Remembrance* should be read as Tatila, the Arabic name of Tudela. In support of this opinion, Schirmann cited a poem of Avraham ibn Ezra's that bears the acrostic signature "Avraham ben Ezra from [i.e., born in] the city of Tatila." Today this view is generally accepted. Since Tudela is in Navarre, and

Halevi was known as a Castilian, his family may have left Tudela for Castile, or sent him to study there, when he was young. It is also possible, however, that "Castile" was used by himself and others as a general term for the Christian north.

As for the date of Halevi's birth, it remains a matter of conjecture. We know only that he must have been in his teens when he set out for Andalusia and that he was in Granada with Moshe ibn Ezra, who left the city after it fell to the Almoravids in 1090 (see pp. 49–51). The question, then, is how old he was when invited to Granada by Ibn Ezra. The suggestion, made by scholars who have dated his birth to as late as 1075, that he was no more than fourteen or fifteen strikes me as unlikely. It is hard to believe that even a literary prodigy like Halevi could have replied to Ibn Ezra's friendship poem so skillfully and cleverly at such a young age. Most probably, he was at least a year or two older, which would put his birth in the early 1070s. This is also Schirmann's opinion.

It is true that since we do not know how soon after the Almoravid conquest of Granada Moshe ibn Ezra departed the city, he could theoretically have remained there for many more years and extended his invitation to Halevi in the course of them. This is the contention of Raymond Scheindlin in *The Song of the Distant Dove* (see pp. 278–81), in which he pushes the date of Halevi's birth back to circa 1085. Scheindlin's motive for doing so is that a younger Halevi suits his conception of the poet's later life better. Yet even if Moshe ibn Ezra remained in Granada throughout the 1090s, something for which there is no evidence, his loss of wealth and status following the Almoravids' arrival makes it improbable that he would then have offered to be Halevi's patron. Nor, even with such an invitation in hand, would Halevi have been likely to settle in Granada at a time when the city's educated Jewish elite, including Ibn Ezra's three brothers, had fled from it. Moreover, in none of the poems that he wrote while in Granada (see pp. 27–8) is there the slightest hint of the unhappy position and depressed state of mind that Ibn Ezra is known to have been in after 1090. All in all, placing Halevi in Granada in the late 1090s makes little sense.

APPENDIX B

The story of these two versions is a curious one that has never, as far as I know, been subject to a full investigation.

Although there are references to Hasdai ibn Shaprut's letter to the king of the Khazars in earlier Jewish sources, its purported text was not made public until the sixteenth century. This was done by an otherwise unknown Jew named Yitzhak Akrish, who lived in Constantinople and wrote a slim Hebrew book in 1577 entitled *Kol Mevaser*, "The Voice of the Herald." In this book, Akrish, after relating his lifelong interest in the legend of the Ten Lost Tribes and his desire to know if there was any truth in it, tells of a voyage he made in 1561–62 to Egypt, then under Ottoman control, in the course of which he was told of the existence of a powerful Jewish kingdom on the Arabian Sea "near Yemen." (Although Akrish does not refer to this kingdom by name, the independent Jewish warriors he heard about were undoubtedly the Falasha of Ethiopia, then at the height of their power.) While in Cairo, Akrish met a Jew, a court physician, who showed him a copy of a letter and poem, sent by Hasdai ibn Shaprut to the Jewish king of "Al-Kozar," which he, the physician, had been given by a high Ottoman official. Akrish recopied these and later printed them in *Kol Mevaser*. Having no idea of Al-Kozar's geographical location, he was apparently under the impression, like the official and the physician, that the addressee of Hasdai's letter was the ruler of the kingdom "near Yemen."

Are this letter and poem genuine? Although their authenticity has been challenged, the weight of scholarly opinion, for a number of historical and literary reasons, has come down in their favor. Their turning up among Ottoman officials in Cairo is not as improbable as it might seem. The Slavic diplomats to whom Hasdai entrusted his letter could well have sought to forward it to Khazaria via Constantinople, where a copy might have been filed away in the Ottoman archives and sent centuries later to Egypt in response to reports emanating from there of a Jewish kingdom in Ethiopia.

In writing Chapter 2 of this book, I had before me what is today the standard text of Menachem's poem, first published by Hayim Schirmann in his monumental two-volume anthology *Ha-shira ha-Ivrit b'S'farad u'v'Provans* ("The Hebrew Poetry of Spain and Provence," Tel Aviv, 1954). In Schirmann's version, the acrostic signature "I Hasdai bar Yitzhak bar Ezra bar Shaprut Menachem ben Saruk" appears in full. The poem's last ten lines (lines 28–37), the initial letters of which comprise all of the consonants and the final vowel of "Menachem ben Saruk," read:

28) *Me'od arkhu ha-itim ve-nimshekhu ha-yamim u'mofet lo nir'ah,*

29) *Neḥtam ḥazon ve-navi v'lo nifratz ru'aḥ v'lo mar'ah,*

30) *Ḥezyonei* ish ḥamudot lo niglu v'lo notar kol nevu'ah*

---

* The "ch" in "Menachem," a common English transliteration of the Hebrew letter *ḥet*, is represented here, as elsewhere in this book, by its international phonetic symbol of *ḥ*.

Yehuda Halevi

31) *Mi'el eyaluti—efros kapai b'nefesh ts'mei'ah,*

32) *B'zurei k'tsavot p'zurei afasim le'esof mei'eretz m'so'ah.*

33) *Nugei ha-mo'ed az l'el yabi'u: ha-et shekivinuha ve'hinei va'ah!*

34) *Sukat David kiryat melekh rav t'ki'em ka'asher ka'ah,*

35) *Romemut ma'oz tir'enah einai she'erit ha-nimtsa'ah*

36) *U'mamlekhet ben-Yishai b'sod hazut ha-nevu'ah:*

37) *"Karnekh asim barzel" lanetsah mei-ha-yom ha-hu vehal'ah.*

Yet after my book was completed, my suspicions having been aroused by a different wording of Menachem's poem that I came across in a nineteenth-century edition of Yehuda Halevi's *Kuzari*, I decided to compare Schirmann's version with Akrish's. Although the sole extant copies of the first edition of *Kol Mevaser* are in the Bodleian Library in Oxford, I found a later edition of the book, published in 1720 in Offenbach, in the National Library in Jerusalem, as well as a copy of *Liber Cosri*, a 1660 Latin translation of *The Kuzari* by the German Hebraist Johannes Buxtorf the Younger. Included in Buxtorf's introduction are the Hebrew texts of Hasdai's letter and Menachem's poem. These were copied by him, he writes, from Akrish's *Kol Mevaser*, which was lent him by a friend, the German theologian Philip Jacob Spener, who had acquired it from an Alsatian Jew.

With minor differences, Menachem's poem as it appears in the Offenbach edition of *Kol Mevaser* and in Buxtorf's *Liber Cosri* is the same. When one compares these two versions with Schirmann's, however, the differences are marked, especially in the first words of lines 28–37. Line 28 in the Offenbach edition and *Liber Cosri* begins with *Arkhu ha-itim* instead of *Me'od arkhu ha-itim*. Line 31 begins with *El el eyaluti* rather than *Mi-el eyaluti*. Line 34 begins with *Netsaḥ kiryat melekh rav* rather than *Sukat David kiryat melekh rav*. Line 32 in *Liber Cosri* begins with *P'zurei k'tsavot* rather than *B'zurei k'ts-avot;* here, the Offenbach edition agrees with Schirmann. Read acrostically, *Liber Cosri* has not "M-n-ch-m b-n S-ruk," but "A-n-ch-e p-n n-ruk." The Offenbach edition has "A-n-ch-e b-n n-ruk."

This raised two questions. The first was: if the version of Menachem's poem in the Offenbach edition and *Liber Cosri* was that of the first, Constantinople edition of *Kol Mevaser*—and there is no reason to doubt this*—where did Schirmann get his version from? And second, even if the full name "Menachem ben Saruk" is not spelled acrostically in lines 28–37 of Akrish's version, six or seven of its ten letters do occur in the right place and order. Can the fact that, on the one hand, Menachem was Hasdai ibn Shaprut's secretary, and that, on the other hand, over half of the letters of his name appear in acrostic form at the end of the poem that accompanied Hasdai's letter to the king of Khazaria, be a coincidence?

Clearly not. There must have been an original version of the poem in which "Menachem ben Saruk" was spelled fully and was changed by Hasdai, angry at his secretary for taking such a liberty. There is simply no other way of explaining lines 28–37 in *Kol Mevaser*.

---

* In his *History of the Jewish Khazars* (Princeton, 1954, p. 133), Columbia University professor D. M. Dunlop, who viewed the Bodleian's copies of *Kol Mevaser*, reported that Menachem ben Saruk's name appears in them "not quite perfectly. . . . but nearly enough [to make out]." Dunlop did not suspect, however, that the "imperfection" of Menachem's signature was Hasdai's doing.

But where is this original version and how did Schirmann get to see it?

The probable answer, I believe, is that it never survived Hasdai's editing and was not seen by Schirmann at all. What he almost certainly saw was an attempted reconstruction of it. If there was a deliberate fabrication, its perpetrator was not Yitzhak Akrish or his predecessors, but a fascinating nineteenth-century scholar, adventurer, collector, and swindler named Abraham Firkovitch.

Firkovitch was a well-known—notorious might be a better word—figure in the world of nineteenth-century Jewish scholarship. Born in Russia to an old Karaite family, he traveled widely in Europe, Central Asia, and the Middle East, acquiring many thousands of ancient manuscripts, one collection of which he sold to the Czarist State Library of St. Petersburg in 1856, while a second was purchased by it in 1876, two years after his death; he was also a vigorous defender of Karaism (by then, a nearly extinct sect) against rabbinic Judaism, claiming that the Karaites of Eastern Europe were descendants of the Ten Lost Tribes who, unlike the rabbis, had preserved the pristine Israelite religion of the Bible. Both as a Karaite polemicist and as an antiquities dealer, he was not above tampering with documents, or even forging them from scratch, when it suited him. To this day, it is not always clear what in the Firkovitch collections is entirely genuine, what partly so, and what not at all.

And indeed, the first cataloged item in the Second Firkovitch Collection is a version of Menachem ben Saruk's poem to the king of the Khazars that is substantially different from Yitzhak Akrish's! It or a copy of it was seen by the

Israeli historian Avraham Polak. "The rhymed prelude to Hasdai's letter," Polak wrote in his *Kazaria: Toldot Mam-lakhah Yehudit b'Iropa* ("Khazaria: The History of a Jewish Kingdom in Europe," Tel Aviv, 1943, p. 18), "with several variant readings, can be found in Document 1 of the Second Firkovitch Collection. . . . It dates to the nineteenth century and was probably transcribed from one of the printed editions of Akrish's book, the changes made in it being suggested corrections on the part of the transcriber." The "transcriber," no doubt, was Firkovitch himself.

Here, then, is the solution to the mystery. Schirmann, whose anthology appeared a decade after Polak's history, must have taken his version of Menachem's poem from the Second Firkovitch Collection, in Document 1 of which Firkovitch sought to restore Menachem's partially erased signature by inserting his own conjectural version of the words altered by Hasdai and passing the results off as an ancient manuscript. His motives might have been commercial, religious, or both. Menachem was suspected by Firkovitch's scholarly contemporary Shmuel David Luzzatto of having been a secret Karaite who was punished for his beliefs by Hasdai (see p. 43), a speculation that could have aroused Firkovitch's sympathy and inspired him to reassert Menachem's authorship of the poem with a bogus version of it. Taken in, unlike Polak, by the deception, Schirmann published it without comment as Menachem's original text.

Unfortunately, all this was discovered by me too late in the publication process to procure a copy of this document from the (subsequently renamed) Russian National Library in St. Petersburg. When it is consulted, however, I am confident that it will confirm my speculations. How accurate a restoration of Menachem's poem Firkovitch's forgery was, we of course have no way of knowing, but it no doubt brings us closer to the original than does the genuinely old version published by Akrish. The story is worthy of being one of Borges' *ficciones*!

APPENDIX C

The Arabic vowels *a*, *i*, and *u* can be either long or short, and the difference has phonemic value. Thus, for example, whereas *kataba* with a short first vowel means "he wrote," *kaataba* with a long "a" means "he corresponded." The regular alteration of long and short syllables in classical Arabic poetry is thus in harmony with the structure of the language.

In Hebrew, on the other hand, all vowels are of the same length except for the *shva na*, or short "uh" sound, which is often represented by an apostrophe and frequently elided in modern spoken Hebrew entirely. Dunash sought to take advantage of this by basing his system of Hebrew metrics on it. Since, however, he needed more than just one short vowel, he also did two other things. While in classical Hebrew grammar, the *shva na* turns into a *patah*, *segol*, or *kamatz* after the consonants *alif*, *ayin*, *het*, and *heh*, becoming an "ah," "eh," or "aw," its orthographic symbol continues to appear alongside the *patah*, *segol*, and *kamatz*'s in a vowel sign known as *hataf-patah*, *hataf-segol*, and *hataf-kamatz*. Although the latter's articulation is no different from that of an ordinary *patah*, *segol*, or *kamatz*, Dunash ruled that they, too, should be treated like short vowels. In addition, the *shva na* in the proclitic conjunction *v'*, "and," becomes a *shuruk* or "u" when attached to a word that begins with another *shva na* or with the consonants *bet*, *vav*, *mem*, or *peh*. (Thus, for instance, whereas the Hebrew word for boy is *yeled*, so that "and a boy" is *v'yeled*, the plural "boys," *y'ladim*, turns "and boys" into *uy'ladim*.) Though this *shuruk*, too, is no different in length from an ordinary *shuruk*, Dunash allowed it to be either long or short in accordance with the meter's requirements.

The results were artificial: a metrics that scanned on paper but not when read aloud. What saved it was the fact that the *shva na*, the three *hataf* vowels, and the *shuruk*-ized *vav* always occur in unstressed positions, so that while the supposed alternation of long and short syllables in Hispano-Hebrew verse is a fiction, a fairly regular sequence of stressed and unstressed syllables can nevertheless be heard. Ironically, therefore, syllabic stress, the organizing principle of pre-Hispano-Hebrew poetry that Dunash sought to get away from, ultimately determines the auditory flow of His-pano-Hebrew poetry as well.

Although my belief that Halevi mourned his own children in these poems is an intuitive one, there is some evidence in its favor. Of the dozens of elegies that Halevi wrote, six have an immediate family member as their speaker. (The sixth is for a dead brother.) This was a device rarely resorted to by Halevi, who cannot easily be imagined putting words of extreme grief in the mouth of someone other than himself. For what purpose? As an imaginative projection of himself into a mental and emotional state not his own? This was almost never done by Hispano-Hebrew poets. To be read aloud by the mourner at the funeral? It is hard to envision a distraught father reciting over a fresh grave "My Child! Had You Forgotten the Way," or "Snatched Was the Child from Its Father's Lap," from a text that Halevi had composed. Moreover, even had Halevi done this, he would have written only one poem for the occasion. Yet this does not appear to be the case with the poems before us.

Let us first consider the two poems about a boy. The second stanza of the fragmentary one reads:

> Woe is me in my depths!
> Bitter, they stir
> For the boy they brought forth,
> And wet are my tears

For the golden child seized,
My chief of delights.
Would, O my friends,
I had died in his place!
But the Prince of Death stole him
Away from my arms,
And the wound will only heal when
I lie me down again with my son.

A comparison of these lines with "Snatched Was the Child from Its Father's Lap" shows striking similarities. The two poems give the impression of having been written about the same event, the second perhaps at a slightly later point in time, when the poet could think of, and reject, the possibility of being reconciled to his loss.

The three poems on the death of an adolescent girl also have much in common. Each speaks of her dying after a sudden illness. Two depict her as being forced to marry, in place of the husband who should rightfully have been hers, "Death's firstborn son" (*bekhor mavet*, translated as "Death's minion" in "My Child! Had You Forgotten the Way"). Two compare her to an uprooted young grape vine; all three, to a heavenly star. Again we seem to be dealing with a single death, returned to several times.

Finally, there is the suggestive matter of Halevi's *kunya* in Moshe ibn Ezra's *Book of Discussions and Remembrance* (see Appendix A), which has gone curiously uncommented on. On the face of it, this *kunya* would appear to indicate that, just as Avraham ibn Ezra was called by the name of his son Yitzhak (Is'hak in Arabic), so Halevi bore the paedonymic of a son with the Arabic name of El-Hassan who died when young. (It was customary for a *kunya* to go on being used after a firstborn son's death. Muhammed, for example, is known in Muslim tradition as Abu-el-Qasim, even though his son Qasim died in infancy.) Since the name El-Hassan means "the beauty" in Arabic, there may even be a punning allusion to it in the middle stanza of "Snatched Was the Child from Its Father's Lap," with its Hebrew line *Ki mi-yif'ati ḥulalti*, "For of my beauty I have been despoiled."

This is not a far-fetched conjecture. As a rule, Jews in eleventh- and twelfth-century Muslim Spain gave their children Arabic names alongside Hebrew ones, whether for general use or to facilitate their contacts with Muslims. In many cases, these were simply the Arabic equivalents of Hebrew biblical names, such as Is'hak or Ibrahim. But purely Arabic names were not infrequently given, too. In the same passage in which he mentions Halevi and Avraham ibn Ezra, Moshe ibn Ezra refers to the noted Cordoban rabbi and poet Yosef ibn Sahl as Abu-Amru ibn Sahl and lists another Abu-el-Hassan, the poet Ezra ben Elazar.

And yet since having a *kunya* was de rigueur in Muslim society, so that one was given to a man on some other basis when he was childless or had only daughters, one cannot rule out this having happened with Halevi. Abu-el-Hassan, in any event, seems to have been an appellation used for him only by his Muslim acquaintances, as he is never called by it in any Jewish source or document apart from *The Book of Discussions and Remembrance*. If Moshe ibn Ezra made a point of referring to the noted Hispano-Hebrew poets of his age by their *kunya*s, this was probably because, writing in bitter exile in Christian Spain, he wished to emphasize the Islamo-Arabic environment in which the best Hebrew poetry of the age had been written.

The question of whether Avraham ibn Ezra's son Yitzhak was Yehuda Halevi's son-in-law has provoked such scholarly contention that when they come to it in their "Yehuda Halevi and His Circle: Documents from the Genizah," Ezra Fleischer and Moshe Gil break off their jointly written account to present different and opposing points of view. Fleischer argues for Yitzhak having been married to Halevi's daughter, Gil against it. I side with Fleischer (who is not responsible, however, for my account of the dilemmas that this relationship confronted Halevi with while in Egypt).

The belief in a marital connection between Halevi and the family of Avraham ibn Ezra is an old one, first attested to in the writings of the fifteenth-century Hispano-Jewish statesman and biblical commentator Don Yitzhak Abrabanel. According to Abrabanel, whose sources for the statement are unknown, it was Avraham ibn Ezra himself who married Halevi's daughter. This account was repeated by subsequent authors, most notably Gedalia ibn Yahya (see p. 237), who gave it a legendary embellishment. Halevi, Ibn Yahya wrote, was a wealthy man with a "single, beautiful daughter" whose mother so pestered him to find her a husband that he exasperatedly swore to marry her off to the first eligible bachelor to enter his home. This turned out to be Avraham ibn Ezra—who, however, appeared as a ragged beggar. Halevi, to his wife's dismay, insisted on keeping his vow and only afterwards discovered to his joy that his penniless son-in-law was a distinguished poet and scholar.

Modern Jewish historians dismissed this story out of hand. Yet in 1959, in an article entitled "The Biography of Rabbi Judah Ha-Levi in the Light of the Cairo Geniza Documents," Goitein proposed that Halevi's son-in-law had in fact been not Avraham ibn Ezra but his son Yitzhak. The attribution was made on the basis of a Judeo-Arabic letter sent to Yitzhak by Halfon ben Netanel in 1130, after Halfon's return to Egypt from Spain. In it, Halfon asked Yitzhak to convey his best wishes to "that most wondrous scholar and gentleman, Rabbi Avraham your father, and that noble mainstay [of Judaism] and model of erudition, our master Yehuda [*ravna* Yehuda] your *'am*." Certain that "*ravna* Yehuda" referred to Halevi, who is called this in many Geniza letters, Goitein debated how to translate the Arabic word *'am*. Although it generally means "paternal uncle" in medieval Arabic, such a reading would have made Avraham ibn Ezra and Yehuda Halevi brothers, which was clearly not the case. Opting, therefore, for a secondary meaning of the word that, although known in medieval Arabic, too, had never been encountered by him in a Geniza document, Goitein translated it as "father-in-law."

Yet Goitein was never entirely confident of this identification and was reported by his younger colleague Menahem Schmelzer to have retracted it in a conversation before his death. Apart from the fact that *'am* usually signifies an uncle, there were two main problems with it. The first was that in no other source is Yitzhak referred to as Halevi's son-in-law. The second was that while two documents do exist in which Yitzhak is called a relative of Halevi's, the term used in them is a general one. One of them, a letter written to Halfon by his Alexandrian cousin Amram ben Yitzhak in 1142 after Yehuda Halevi's death, when Yitzhak ibn Ezra was still in Fustat, ends with the request: "Do tell me what is doing with Rabbi Yitzhak, our master Yehuda Halevi's relative [*qarib*]." The other is the medieval *divan* of Yitzhak ibn Ezra's poems. Prefixed to an elegy of Yitzhak's for a man who was almost certainly Halevi (see below) appears the annotation: "And the author sent this to his father [Avraham ibn Ezra] upon the death of a relation [*qaraba*]."

Why "relative" and "relation" rather than "son-in-law" and "father-in-law"? Surely, if Yitzhak ibn Ezra was married to Yehuda Halevi's daughter, he would not have been designated in ways that could just as well pertain to a second cousin or a brother-in-law's nephew! It was this objection above all that convinced Gil and others (including, according to Schmelzer, Goitein himself in the end) that *'am* could not mean son-in-law in Halfon's letter.

Fleischer's arguments are more involved. Let us take them one by one.

1. If *'am* does not mean son-in-law in the letter, it must mean paternal uncle. Yet such a reading only makes what Halfon wrote even more puzzling and solves nothing.

2. In his poem "Driven by Longing for the Living God" (see pp. 187–9), in which he expresses his sorrow at leaving behind in Spain the trio of Yehuda, Azarel, and Yitzhak, Halevi calls the latter "so like a son, / my sun-blessed crop, / the years' rich yield." The only Yitzhak we know of from Halevi's world who might conceivably fit this description is Yitzhak ibn Ezra. Thirty or more years younger than Halevi and the son of a celebrated poet whom Halevi shared a birth-

place with and knew well, Yitzhak moved in Andalusian literary circles and was close to Halfon ben Netanel—for whom, several Geniza letters tell us, he managed various business transactions. A letter sent by him to Halfon in 1129, while the latter was in Spain, suggests that he may also have served as Yehuda Halevi's assistant or secretary. In it, he writes that he is returning to Halfon a single dinar received from him because it is "not good," i.e., worn or counterfeit. As Goitein observed, this was very likely the same dinar that Halfon contributed to Yehuda Halevi's campaign for the ransom of the captive girl in Toledo. If so, Yitzhak was helping Halevi to collect the ransom money and to conduct his correspondence regarding it.

3. In Yitzhak's elegy in his *divan*, composed in Fustat in 1141–42 before he left Egypt for Damascus, the mourned-for man is referred to in terms (e.g., "Without him all wisdom falls dumb and grows foolish / And all poems are vapid and blank") that could only, even allowing for the hyperbole of the times, apply to a prominent poet and intellectual. Yehuda Halevi is the sole Jewish figure known to have died in the eastern Mediterranean in that year of whom anything like this could be said. Moreover, Yitzhak's ties to the deceased are portrayed by the poem as having been intensely personal. He calls him "a father like none other" (this in a poem sent to his own father!) and continues:

> Like a father he raised me from ladhood,
> And pleasant his presence made all.
> Each day I learned something new from him,
> And never feared by his side.
> Filling my house with choice plenty,
> Each of its storerooms he blessed.

From his hands I ate yesterday's manna—
And today my bread tastes like charred wood.

Such a son-father relationship, which could easily be that of a young son-in-law living with or nearby his well-to-do father-in-law and being supported by him (Yitzhak's own father, as is reflected by Ibn Yahya's legendary account, led a penurious existence), corresponds closely to the father-son relationship described by Halevi in "Driven by Longing for the Living God." Nor is the elegy's having been written after Yitzhak's rupture with Halevi in Fustat any reason to doubt that Halevi is the subject of it. Nothing is more conducive to remorse over an estrangement than the death of the person one has loved and been estranged from.

4. We know that Yehuda Halevi had a young grandson named Yehuda whom he loved dearly and was pained deeply to part from. We also know that as he was waiting for his ship to sail from Alexandria, he received a letter from Spain in which a youngster named Yehuda ibn Ezra wrote that he was about to join him (see pp. 230–3). Can there be any doubt that the two Yehudas are the same? And if they are, and Yehuda Halevi's daughter was married to an Ibn Ezra, who but Yitzhak ibn Ezra could this have been? It would be a bizarre coincidence if Halevi had been extremely close to a Yitzhak who was "like a son" to him; had traveled to Egypt with Yitzhak ibn Ezra the son of Avraham ibn Ezra; had been mourned by the latter as having been "like a father"; and had had a daughter married to an entirely different Ibn Ezra who was not Yitzhak!

In addition, there is the matter, related by Abu Nasr ben Avraham in his letter to Halfon, of Halevi's forbidding

Yehuda to go to Fustat once he arrived in Egypt. Halevi had made wealthy and powerful friends in Fustat who would have lavished kindness on Yehuda before sending him on his way with warmest regards for his grandfather in Palestine. What reason could there have been to oppose this other than the fear that Yitzhak, then living in Fustat, might prevail upon his son to remain with him?

The weightiness of these considerations, in Fleischer's opinion, overrode the objections to Goitein's original conclusion. In agreeing, I would observe that these objections are less serious than they have appeared to be. *'Am* often means "father-in-law" in modern colloquial Arabic and may have been more common in the spoken Judeo-Arabic of the Middle Ages than in writing. Moreover, there is a simple explanation for the words *qarib* and *qaraba* as used by Amram ben Yitzhak and the editor of Yitzhak ibn Ezra's *divan*. Both men were writing after Halevi's death and knew that Yitzhak had abandoned Halevi's daughter. The question of how to refer to Yitzhak was therefore a delicate one. Calling him Halevi's son-in-law under such circumstances would have seemed wrong. Using a more general term like "relative" would have been a tactful way of getting around this.

To this, I would add one more point.

Although the story that Avraham ibn Ezra was Yehuda Halevi's son-in-law is obviously legendary, such a legend does not come from nowhere. There would have been no reason for Abrabanel, or anyone else, to invent it ex nihilo. In all likelihood, he and others were transmitting an account they had heard, the most probable explanation of which is that it was a garbling of an older and more accurate tradition that Halevi's son-in-law was Avraham's son Yitzhak. Yitzhak may have been replaced in this tradition by Avraham because his desertion of his family and conversion to Islam cast him in an unworthy light, or because, unlike his renowned father, he was forgotten by later generations. By the standards of Jewish folklore, it was Avraham who deserved to have married Halevi's daughter and who was ultimately credited with doing so.

The case for Yitzhak ibn Ezra's having been Halevi's son-in-law is a very strong one. If Goitein retracted his belief in it, he shouldn't have.

APPENDIX F

Translating Hispano-Hebrew poetry into English is in some respects a more difficult task than translating French, German, or Russian poetry. This is because, of its two main formal characteristics, mono-rhyme and Arabic-style meter, the first is rarely reproducible in English and the second never is.

Mono-rhyme is possible in Hebrew and Arabic, even in long poems, because both languages have numerous stressed grammatical suffixes that can be rhymed line after line. An example of this is the -ayikh ending used by Halevi in his "Why, My Darling, Have You Barred All News" (pp. 60–64). Another is in the long friendship poem to Moshe ibn Ezra, "Wander-life, You Are an Old Friend" (pp. 85–87), in which the last word of every one of the poem's thirty-four Hebrew lines has the masculine plural ending -im. In English, on the other hand, grammatical suffixes ("-s," "-ing," "-ed," etc.) are unstressed and do not rhyme. To be sure, Arabic-style mono-rhyming in Hebrew is not so easy, either, since the initial consonant of the rhyming syllable is expected to repeat itself, too; thus, in "Wander-life, You Are an Old Friend," each line ends in -mim and Halevi had to restrict his rhymes to plurals of nouns or verbs having the final Hebrew letter mem. Yet Hebrew has large inventories of such words, whereas a mono-rhymed thirty-four-line poem in English is all but unimaginable.

Nor, although English does have shorter and longer vowels (it takes fractionally less time to say "win" than "wean," "hop" than "harp"), are its speakers aware of the difference, no Dunash ben Labrat having arisen among them to codify it for poetic use. In theory, one could compose an English poem all of whose lines had the same pattern of long and short syllables. In practice, this would go unnoticed and be a sterile exercise.

But this is not to say that the English translator of Hispano-Hebrew verse can convey nothing of its formal qualities. As I point out in Appendix C, Arabic-style meter in Hebrew tends to result in regular patterns of stressed and unstressed syllables like those found in English poetry, so that a metrical line of John Donne's, say, is not very different in its effect from a metrical line of Yehuda Halevi's. In translating Halevi's poetry, therefore, I have generally fallen back on the common English meters. My translation of "Why, My Darling, Have You Barred All News" is mostly in iambic pentameter and sextameter; of "Wander-Life, You Are an Old Friend," in anapests shifting to iambs toward the end. These meters do not necessarily have the same stressed/ unstressed sequences that Halevi's Hebrew does, and I often chose them on the basis of the first line or two of a translation to come to mind, instinctively following my ear without noticing where it was leading me—but this, after all, is how a great deal of metrical poetry gets written. Because medieval Hebrew is a more highly inflected and compact language than English, I also usually turned the hemistiches of Halevi's Hebrew into separate lines of English. In some poems, such as "My Child! Had You Forgotten the Way" (pp. 78–81) or "Driven by Longing for the Living God" (pp. 187–90), I broke them up even more. In others, I created separate stanzas where none exist in the Hebrew, or, as in Halevi's verse letter written at sea (pp. 191–3), played with the arrangement of lines on the page.

When it comes to rhyme, the translator of Hispano-Hebrew poetry has recourses, too. In "Why, My Darling, Have You Barred All News" and "Zion! Do You Wonder?" (pp. 123–6), I ended each line with an "s" to create something of mono-rhyme's effects. In another poem, "Has a New Flood Drowned the Land?" (pp. 193–4), I did this with half-rhymes. Elsewhere, I used full and partial rhymes opportunistically, with no attempt at regularity, while in still other places, I rhymed little or not at all. In a poem like "Waked by My Thoughts" (pp. 310–11), which Halevi wrote not in mono-rhyme but in *muwashah* form, I was able to retain the original rhyme scheme in its entirety.

In short, in translating the poems in this book, I have not followed any one strategy. Each poem was a challenge in its own right and I sometimes responded to similar challenges in different ways. Like all Hispano-Hebrew poets, Halevi was extremely fond of puns, complicated wordplay, and alliteration, and I have sought to represent these aspects of his verse, too—although, again, not always on a direct basis: an alliterative cluster of words in one of his lines may have been transferred by me to another; a play on words that I could not capture where it occurred may have had a different one substituted for it further on. My only strict rule was to try to be as faithful to the lexical content of the poems as I was at times free with their form. I never knowingly bent or changed their meaning to accommodate my needs as a translator. This was one liberty I declined to take.

APPENDIX G

Halevi was answering a letter of Halfon's that had just been delivered and was, so he explained in his answer, dashing it off quickly so that it could be sent back with the same messenger. The messenger had probably arrived from Almería, the port on Andalusia's southeast coast from which most of the traffic with Egypt was conducted and from which Halfon in all likelihood sailed.

Two things this letter makes clear are: Halevi and Halfon had met in company not very long beforehand; and Halevi next expected to see Halfon in Egypt. Although it is not definite that Halfon was in Spain only once, Fleischer and Gil argue convincingly that it was at the end of his first, 1127–29, visit that Halevi's letter was written. Such a date matches the information provided by Yosef ibn el-Lakhtush (see pp. 133–4 and Appendix H) that Halevi set out, or almost set out, for Egypt in the spring of 1130.

APPENDIX H

Goitein, loath to revise Halevi's biography so radically, sought to minimize the importance of Ibn el-Lakhtush's letter by interpreting it as referring to a trip that Halevi took to visit Halfon somewhere in Spain. Yet as Fleischer and Gil observe, Ibn el-Lakhtush's language implies a far more momentous parting than this would have entailed, and by the spring of 1130, Halfon, from whom Ibn el-Lakhtush regretfully states in his letter that he is now separated by "a great distance," was almost certainly back in Egypt.

On the other hand, Fleischer and Gil's hypothesis of a journey aborted in North Africa, which leans partly on a statement by Shlomo ibn Parhon (see p. 239) that Halevi and Avraham ibn Ezra once traveled together to "Afriki" (a medieval Hebrew term for Tunis), is unconfirmable. It rests heavily on two poems of Halevi's, "Driven by Longing for the Living God" (see pp. 187–9), and "Can Bodies Be Rooms for an Eagle-Winged Heart," in which the poet describes himself as a man who

> fought with his friends
> and left his lodgements
> and roamed to the ends
> of lands habitable,
>
> riding the sea
> to a blistered country,

to the lion-laired scree
and the pard-haunted hill,

until the wolves were
in his sight lovelier
than the maidens that stir
youthful hearts, and until

the ostriches' shrieks
were like music at feasts,
and the howl of beasts
like the shepherd's whistle.

This certainly could be a description of someone who
sailed from Spain to Tunis and then struck out eastward over
rough terrain. Suggestively, too, "Can Bodies Be Rooms"
switches to the future tense when speaking of the traveler
continuing to "the land of Canaan," leaving one with the
impression that it was written in midcourse. Yet ultimately,
the evidence is inconclusive. Halevi may have traveled with
Avraham ibn Ezra to Tunis on some other occasion and may
have written, while in Spain, imaginary accounts of a trip
that never took place. All we know for certain is that in the
spring of 1130, Yosef ibn el-Lakhtush had it on good
authority that Halevi would soon be in Egypt. It is odd that
nowhere in Halevi's poetry is there any explicit reference to
such a failed journey, which one would think would have left
its mark. Perhaps this is reason to believe that he never left
Spain.

As for what made Halevi change his mind, Fleischer and
Gil speculate that Halfon's psychological incapacitation by

the death of his brother, which is attested to in a letter of his to Yitzhak ibn Ezra, made Halevi realize it was an inadvisable time to arrive in Egypt. But even if Halevi had had a way of finding out about this while in North Africa, he would not have been so dependent on Halfon that he could not have arranged for a stay in Egypt and transportation from there to Palestine with the help of others; aborting his journey would hardly have been necessary. Nor does this explain why, having returned to Spain, he waited ten more years before setting out again. The entire episode remains shrouded in mystery.

CHRONOLOGY

586 B.C.E. The Kingdom of Judah is conquered by the Babylonians and much of its population exiled to Babylon.

539 B.C.E. Persian emperor Cyrus the Great, having overrun the Babylonian Empire, allows exiled Jews to return to the land of Israel and to rebuild the Temple. Many remain in Babylon, thus beginning the Jewish Diaspora.

70 C.E. The Roman emperor Titus finishes crushing the Jewish revolt in Palestine, destroying the Temple in Jerusalem. In the following centuries, Jewish communities spread throughout the Mediterranean world. Rabbinic Judaism takes shape and becomes dominant in Jewish life.

c. 200 The Mishnah, the first body of rabbinic law expounding the commandments of the Torah, is codified.

early C.E. centuries Jews settle in Spain as part of their Mediterranean dispersal. With the establishment in the early fifth century of the staunchly Catholic kingdom of the Visigoths, Spain enacts a series of anti-Jewish measures, including forced baptism, that are alternately promulgated and rescinded by a series of kings. At the 17th Council of Toledo in 693, all Spanish Jews, under suspicion of supporting a threatened Muslim invasion from North Africa, are declared slaves; their possessions are confiscated and their children are ordered raised as Christians.

6th century   The Jerusalem and Babylonian Talmuds, voluminous rabbinic commentaries on the Mishnah, are redacted.

622   Muhammed and his followers arrive in the city of Medina in northern Arabia. Islam begins its period of rapid expansion.

623   Fustat founded as the administrative capital after the Muslim conquest of Egypt.

711   Arab and Berber warriors from North Africa conquer most of Spain and make their capital in Córdoba. The country's Jews welcome them.

928   Sa'adia ben Yosef, an Egyptian-born scholar living in Babylonia, is appointed head, or *ga'on*, of the important Talmudic academy in Sura. A prolific author of rabbinic and halakhic literature, Sa'adia Gaon is also one

of the first medieval Jewish philosophers and a
pioneer figure in the integration of Judaism with
Arabic culture and thought.

c. 960 Menachem ben Saruk publishes in Córdoba a
grammar and lexicon of biblical Hebrew titled
Sefer ha-Pitronot.

Dunash ben Labrat, a student of Sa'adia's who has
imported Arabic rules of composition into Hebrew
poetry, is embroiled in a linguistic controversy with
Menachem.

969 The future city of el-Kahira, or Cairo, is founded
by the first Fatimid Caliph as a royal district
adjacent to Fustat.

c. 970 Death of Hasdai ibn Shaprut, the personal
physician in Córdoba of Caliph Abd-el-Rahman III
and a supporter of the new style of Hebrew poetry
introduced by Dunash.

c. 993 Birth of Shmuel Hanagid, the first of the great
Hispano-Hebrew poets.

c. 1021 Birth of Shlomo ibn Gabirol, another leading
Hispano-Hebrew poet and philosopher.

1038 Hanagid becomes vizier of Granada and
henceforward helps lead its armies into battle.

c. 1055 Birth in Granada of Moshe ibn Ezra, a leading
Hebrew poet and the young Yehuda Halevi's future
patron.

1066 In the first persecution of Jews in Muslim Spain, three thousand of them are massacred in Granada.

c. 1070–1075 Yehuda Halevi is born in Christian Spain, probably in Tudela.

1085 Toledo is conquered by Christians under the leadership of Alfonso VI as the slow Christian reconquest of the Iberian peninsula begins.

c. 1080 Birth in Tudela of Avraham ibn Ezra, the last of the great Hispano-Hebrew poets and a noted biblical commentator.

late 1080s Yehuda Halevi sets out for Andalusia to seek his literary fortune and settles in Granada at the invitation of Moshe ibn Ezra.

1090 The Almoravids, fervent Muslims from Morocco, invade southern Spain, drive the Christians back to the gates of Toledo, and conquer Granada, exiling the city's Jewish elite. Halevi commences a period of wandering.

1093 Pope Urban II preaches that Christians should retake Jerusalem from the Muslims, initiating the First Crusade. Christian soldiers set out for the Holy Land, massacring Jews in France, the Rhineland, and Bohemia along the way.

1099 Crusader Godfrey of Boullion conquers Jerusalem, killing its Jewish and Muslim inhabitants.

1103 Halevi's friend Yosef ibn Megas becomes headmaster of the renowned Lucena yeshiva.

c. 1108 Yehuda Halevi moves to Toledo in Christian Spain, where he spends the next two decades.

1109 Alfonso VI dies and is succeeded by his son-in-law, Alfonso I of Aragon. Riots break out in Toledo during the succession and Jews are killed.

1115 Tudela falls to Christians.

1119 An anti-Almoravid revolt in Córdoba shows the growing influence and power of the fervently Muslim Almohads, then gaining strength in Morocco.

1129 Yehuda Halevi completes an early version of *The Kuzari*, a defense of Judaism written in the form of a dialogue between a Khazar king and the rabbi who converts him.

1130 Halevi plans and perhaps embarks on an aborted trip to Palestine. At about this time, he moves from Toledo back to Córdoba, in Muslim territory.

c. 1138 Moshe ibn Ezra dies in northern Spain.

1138 Birth of the great Jewish philosopher and halakhist Moshe ben Maimon, or Maimonides.

1140 Halevi completes *The Kuzari* and sets out for the land of Israel via Egypt; he arrives in Egypt in early fall.

May 1141 Halevi sails from Alexandria for Acre.

summer 1141 Halevi dies somewhere in Palestine. Until the
discovery in the Cairo Geniza in the 1950s of
an 1141 letter testifying to this, nothing
certain is known about his fate.

1146 Almohads conquer southern Spain,
persecuting Jews throughout their territory.
The center of gravity of Jewish life shifts to
northern Spain.

1167 Yehuda ibn Tibbon translates *The Kuzari* into
Hebrew.

1169 Benjamin of Tudela, a Spanish Jewish
traveler, visits Palestine, where he claims to
have seen Yehuda Halevi's grave in Tiberias.

1190 Maimonides completes his *Guide to the
Perplexed*, an attempted reconciliation of
religion and philosophy with which *The
Kuzari* has often been contrasted.

1209–1211 "The Aliyah of the Three Hundred," in
which Jews from England and France, possibly
influenced by Halevi, settle in the land of
Israel, the first mass immigration to Palestine
in the history of the Diaspora.

13th century *The Kuzari*, in Ibn Tibbon's translation,
becomes an influential text in northern
Spain and Provence, read by the philosopher
and biblical commentator Nachmanides and

his circle and by some of the early
kabbalists.

1267 Nachmanides settles in Palestine, the first major
medieval Jewish figure to follow Halevi in
stating explicitly that living in the land of Israel
is a commandment incumbent on every Jew.

c. 1270–80 The seminal kabbalistic text the *Zohar* is
composed in northern Spain.

1391 Jews are massacred throughout Christian
Castile and Aragon. The Jewish community of
Barcelona is destroyed and many of its members
convert to Christianity.

1492 The armies of Ferdinand and Isabella complete
the Christian reconquest of Spain. Jews are
forced to convert or leave the country. Those
who continue to practice Judaism secretly are
hounded by the Inquisition.

1570s The Italian rabbi Yehuda Moscato writes his *Kol
Yehuda*, the first complete commentary on *The
Kuzari*.

1586 Gedalia ibn Yahya, a Venetian Jew, publishes his
Shalshelet ha-Kabbalah, in which the legend of
Yehuda Halevi's death at the gates of Jerusalem
appears in print for the first time.

1790s Two additional commentaries on *The Kuzari* are
published by the early *maskilim* Yisra'el of
Zamosc and Yitzhak Satanow.

1838 A *divan* or medieval collection of Yehuda Halevi's poems, most of them previously unknown, is discovered in Tunis.

1840 The Italian Jewish scholar Shmuel David Luzzatto publishes an annotated volume of sixty-six of Halevi's poems from the recently discovered *divan*.

1851 Heinrich Heine publishes his collection of poems *Romanzero*, which includes his long ballad "Jehuda ben Halevi."

1882 Members of the Hibbat Tsiyyon, or "Lovers of Zion" organization, commence Zionist immigration to Palestine by founding five agricultural settlements, launching the "First Aliyah."

1896 Discovery of the Cairo Geniza, a repository of a thousand years' worth of documents from the Jewish community of Egypt, including letters to, from, and about Yehuda Halevi.

1897 Theodor Herzl convenes the first Zionist Congress in Basel, marking the beginnings of political Zionism.

1904 Rabbi Avraham Yitzhak Hacohen Kook immigrates to Palestine, where his writings on Zionism and Judaism, in which Yehuda Halevi's influence can be detected, form part of the discourse of religious Zionism.

1948 The founding of the State of Israel.

1950s The German-born Israeli-American scholar S. D. Goitein unearths and publishes Geniza material, shedding new light on Halevi's life.

1967 Israel conquers and occupies the Jordanian part of Jerusalem and the West Bank, the biblical territories of Judea and Samaria.

1974 The founding of Gush Emunim, the religious settlers' movement, that calls for Jewish sovereignty over all of the occupied territories. Its spiritual mentor is Avraham Yitzhak Hacohen Kook's son Tsvi Yehuda Kook.

1977 Israeli religious thinker Yeshayahu Leibowitz attacks Halevi for his "nationalist chauvinism," between which and Gush Emunim he sees an intellectual link, thus inaugurating the "anti-Halevian" discourse of recent decades.

A NOTE ABOUT THE AUTHOR

Hillel Halkin's work includes *Across the Sabbath River: In Search of a Lost Tribe of Israel*, *Letters to an American Jewish Friend*, *A Strange Death*, and a translation of Sholem Aleichem's *Tevye the Dairyman and The Railroad Stories*. His essays and columns have appeared regularly in *Commentary* as well as in *The New Republic*, *The Jerusalem Post*, *The New York Sun*, and other publications. He lives in Israel.